W9-ARB-823

The Commonwealth Series

Winfred E. A. Bernhard, General Editor

University of Massachusetts Press

Amherst 1976

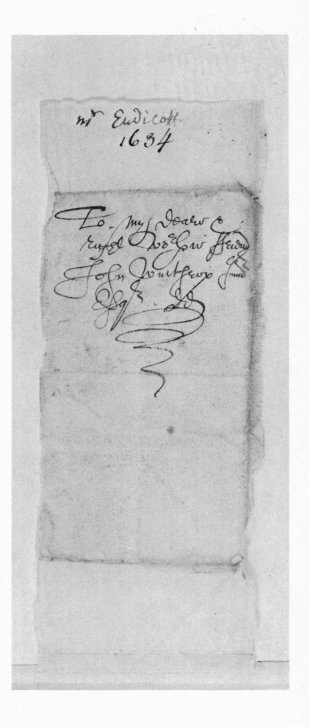

Letters from New England

The Massachusetts Bay Colony, 1629-1638

Edited by Everett Emerson

Copyright © 1976 by
The University of Massachusetts Press
Library of Congress Catalog Card Number 75—32484
ISBN 0-87023-209-6
Printed in the United States of America
Designed by Mary Mendell
Frontispiece: part of a letter from John Endecott
to John Winthrop, Jr., December 8, 1634
Library of Congress Cataloging in Publication Data
Main entry under title:
Letters from New England.

    (The Commonwealth series ; [v. 2])
    Bibliography: p.
    Includes index.
    1. Massachusetts—History—Colonial period, ca. 1600-
1775—Sources. I. Emerson, Everett, 1925–
II. Series: The Commonwealth series (Amherst, Mass.) ;
v. 2.
F67.L663   974.4'02   75-32484
ISBN 0-87023-209-6

For Elliot L. Richardson and Louis B. Wright

That is the best history which is collected out of letters.
Baronius

Letters of affairs, from such as manage them or are privy to
them, are of all others the best instructions for history, and
to a diligent reader the best histories in themselves.
Bacon

Letters are by some wise men counted the best parts of histories.
Bradford

ACKNOWLEDGMENTS

The letters of John Masters, Thomas Welde, John Eliot, William Hammond, John Winthrop (September 26, 1633; July 21, 1634; July 20, 1635; June 24, 1636), and Anthony Thacher are published from manuscripts in the British Library with the permission of the British Library Board. The facsimile of John Masters's letter is published with the permission of the British Library Board.

The letters of John Winthrop (July 4, 1632; May 22, 1634), John Winthrop and John Wilson, the planters of New England, James Cudworth, Israel Stoughton, George Burdett, and Henry Vane [?] are published from manuscripts in the Public Record Office. Transcripts of Crown-copyright records in the Public Record Office appear by permission of the Controller of H. M. Stationery Office, London.

The letter of John Wiswall is published from the manuscript in the possession of Lord Kenyon, Gredington, Whitchurch, Shropshire, with his permission.

The letter of Richard Saltonstall is published from the manuscript in the possession of Lord Lothian, Melbourne Hall, Derbyshire, with his permission.

The letter of John Endecott (December 8, 1634) is published from the manuscript in the collection of the James Duncan Phillips Library, Essex Institute, Salem, Massachusetts, with the permission of the librarian. The facsimile of John Endecott's letter is published by permission of the librarian.

The letters of Edward Trelawny are published from the manuscripts in the collection of the Maine Historical Society, Portland, by permission of the Standing Committee.

The letter of John Endecott (December 25, 1634) is published from the manuscript in the Harvard College Library by permission of the Harvard College Library.

The letter of John Cotton (December 19, 1637) is published from the manuscript in the Department of Rare Books and Manuscripts of the Boston Public Library by courtesy of the Trustees of the Boston Public Library.

The letters of John Cotton (December 3, 1634) and John Winthrop (September 6, 1638) are published from manuscripts in the Massachusetts Archives, with the permission of John F. X. Davoren, Secretary of State of the Commonwealth.

The letters of John Winthrop (March 1631; April 6, 1638) are published from the Early Court Records on file in the Clerk's Office of the Supreme Judicial Court for the County of Suffolk, Massachusetts.

The letters of Francis Higginson (July 24, 1629), John Winthrop (July 14, 1630; July 16, 1630; July 23, 1630 [two letters]; August 14, 1630; September 9, 1630 [two letters]; November 29, 1630; March 28, 1630/1 [two letters]; November 6, 1634; December 12, 1634), John [?] Pond, Richard Mather, Mary Downing, and Bartholomew Greene are published from manuscripts in the Massachusetts Historical Society, with its permission. The letter of John Winthrop (June 5, 1634) is published from a photocopy in the Massachusetts Historical Society, with its permission. The portrait of John Winthrop the Younger and the facsimiles of the letters of Richard Mather and John Winthrop (March 28, 1631) are published from the Massachusetts Historical Society's collection, with its permission.

The portrait of John Cotton is reproduced from the original in the Connecticut Historical Society, with its permission.

The portrait of John Winthrop is reproduced from the collection of the American Antiquarian Society, with its permission.

The portrait of Sir Henry Vane the Younger is reproduced from the collection of the National Portrait Gallery, London.

CONTENTS

SERIES EDITOR'S PREFACE

This second volume in the Commonwealth Series has been
edited by Everett Emerson, professor of American literature at the University of Massachusetts, Amherst. To recapture
the experiences of the first puritans in New England for the
contemporary reader, he has carefully gathered, transcribed and
edited all known letters sent to friends, business acquaintances,
and family in England by these early settlers. Here in brief compass is a full collection of unique documents which illumine
many aspects of the social growth of Massachusetts Bay Colony
during the first decade of its existence. As the colonists recount-
ed their experiences in lively detail or voiced their concerns,
they revealed for future generations much of the quality of
their lives as well as their response to the arduous task of settlement. Sometimes consciously striving to create a favorable
image for their English correspondents, at other times starkly
candid, the writers of these letters are an unusual cross-section
of the puritan community. The thorough editorial commentary
accompanying the letters enhances their value, placing them in
their proper historical light.

The fifty-six letters, some previously published, others newly
transcribed from manuscript, readily fit into the parameters of
the Commonwealth Series. This series is posited on the assump-
tion that the specialist and the general reader interested in delv-
ing into the New England past will find an ongoing need to
consult modern, scholarly editions of manuscripts and classic
works elucidating the history of the region. From the innumerable source materials reflecting New England's intricate
development, representative and outstanding works have been
selected for the Commonwealth Series. Initially concentrating
on the formative years, the Series will also give attention to
distinctive aspects of the society, polity, economy, and intellect
in later periods. These literary and historical sources are brought
before the public and the scholarly community in newly cast
editions, avoiding the obvious shortcomings of mere reprinting.
Prepared for publication in accord with modern canons of ed-
iting, the volumes necessarily include the whole text of the

original. Particularly with reference to seventeenth-century items, facsimile reproduction of the text has been avoided in preference to limited modernization of orthography for the sake of utility and readability.

The initial volume of the series, *God's Plot: The Paradoxes of Puritan Piety*, ably edited by Professor Michael McGiffert, ideally fits the concept of the series. McGiffert's edition of the highly introspective and emotional journal and autobiography of the Reverend Thomas Shepard, minister of the Cambridge Church, affords an exceptionally close view of the puritan as theologian in the New England milieu. Emerson's fascinating collection of letters concerns a different puritan. Here is the alien in a wilderness, haltingly groping to establish himself with other men in a new environment. This view of the New England puritan, revealed by the words of such men as the prominent John Winthrop or the obscure William Pond, contrasts strongly with that of the self-absorbed, pious individual in McGiffert's book. Instead, Emerson's puritans struggle for survival in diverse ways in the physical world—at the mercy of oceanic storms, contending with shortages of supplies as much as with loneliness, yet remaining conscious of the bountifulness of the New World.

The sequence of letters makes clear the rapid expansion of Massachusetts Bay within a few years of its founding. At first the puritan found no secure haven in the environs of a nascent Boston. John Winthrop's poignant reference to "this strange land, where we have met many troubles and adversities" expressed an early reaction to the taxing experience of the move to New England. Yet by 1638 attitudes and outlook had a more positive cast. Then John Wiswall stated with certitude, "It is a pleasant country to look upon. Truly, sir, I like it very well, and so I think any godly man God calls over will. . . ."

More than a little human drama pervades these letters despite their often stilted seventeenth-century prose. In Professor Emerson's deft arrangement, the ideas and interests of a rugged generation are vividly delineated.

Winfred E. A. Bernhard

Amherst, Massachusetts
November 1975

FOREWORD

Letters from New England tells the story of the founding of the
Massachusetts Bay Colony in the words of the founders. It is
addressed to all who are interested in the beginnings of the
United States, whether they are professional historians, students, or general readers. Like William Bradford's history of
Plymouth, it is meant for those who would know the "very root
and rise" of the colony that made an enormous contribution
to American culture. In the pages that follow are collected all
fifty-six of the letters known to exist of the many sent to England during the first decade of the Massachusetts Bay Colony.
Here these letters, some hitherto unpublished, are placed in
their historical context with an interweaving narrative and ex-
planatory notes.

Some twenty thousand English men, women, and children
immigrated to New England during the years from 1629 to
1642. A few returned immediately to England, and others
found their way home after having settled, perhaps, for many
years. "Planting" in America did not, at least for a time, involve
a permanent commitment, and the New Englanders, especially
those of the first generation in America, were first of all Englishmen. But since the Atlantic crossing was far from easy, it was
not undertaken casually. How did Englishmen know about this
remote new land to which they might travel? Doubtless some
learned by word of mouth from those who had seen New England, but most learned from the letters that came back from
friends who had just arrived. One who styled himself an "old
planter," writing in 1694 of the events of sixty years earlier,
describes, echoing the Book of Proverbs, how "The good news
from this far country, and from these men of desires, being
carried into England was as cold waters to a thirsty soul." "A
letter then from New-England was venerated as a sacred script,
or as the writings of some holy prophet, 'twas carried many
miles, where divers came to hear it. . . ."

Though chance was a large factor in the survival of many of
the letters gathered here, they provide a remarkably full picture
of the land, the Indians, the structures of church and state that

were created, the growth and development of the colony, and the important events that occurred. From these assembled letters one senses in a way not previously available the rapidity of the colony's transformation from a struggling infant into a mature adult with highly distinctive characteristics. Because the Jamestown colony has pride of place as the first permanent English colony in America and because the Plymouth colony was the first permanent colony in New England, the beginnings of Massachusetts Bay have been somewhat neglected by history. But the fruits of the labors in the Massachusetts wilderness during the short space of ten years constitute one of humanity's greatest achievements. Within that time nearly twenty towns were settled, a college was educating young men close to the frontier, and a new kind of commonwealth had been established. The letters tell of adventures, such as Anthony Thacher's shipwreck off Cape Anne after a hurricane; of historical moments, such as the beginning of classes at Harvard; of the new forms of church and town government; of the movement of the colonists to Connecticut, Plymouth, and Rhode Island; of the character of the governor, John Winthrop; of the difficulties of surviving in a new land. From these letters can be constructed a vivid picture of early Massachusetts, and since the letters were all written to England, they were the basis for the Englishman's conception of New England. William Hubbard writes of these years as "the golden age of New England," and many later puritans, notably Cotton Mather, looked back perhaps unrealistically to this time as the holy days of New England's patriarchs. The letters show the peculiar mixture of economic motives behind the migration to the colony. Unlike the beginnings of Jamestown and Plymouth, the first decade of Massachusetts Bay is a story not merely of survival but of triumph. If in time the colony proved rigid and intolerant, nevertheless its phenomenal achievements in its earliest years provoke only admiration.

One of the reasons for this volume is its assemblage of letters that have until now been scattered. Isolated letters that can be found only in nineteenth-century historical collections, in genealogical magazines, and in similar remote locations are gathered together for the first time. Another group of letters, those in the *Winthrop Papers* being published by the Massachusetts Historical Society, have a limited audience in that form, for they appear without historical context and with limited notes: the *Papers* are specifically addressed not to the general reading public but to advanced scholars. A third group consists of previously unpublished letters, notably by John Cotton and Richard Mather. The publication of these letters needs no justification, but in the context provided by this collection publication is especially useful. Possibly other letters not yet published will appear, though the editor has scoured the resources of all likely collections, including the uncatalogued one of an important repository where 140 boxes of manuscripts yielded nothing at all. The editor would welcome word of other extant letters written from Massachusetts Bay in its first ten years.

Another feature of the collection is its provision of fresh and often more complete readings of all of the manuscripts. For example, Anthony Thacher's letter telling of his adventure with a New England hurricane has been famous since Increase Mather published a version of it in his *Essay for the Recording of Illustrious Providences* (1684). But Mather abridged the work substantially. A fuller version, not in Thacher's handwriting but made within twenty years of the original, has survived at the British Museum and is here transcribed. While nine letters are based on printed originals, most of the extant letters are in manuscript, forty of which appear to be holographs, while six are seventeenth-century copies. Reading them is a task that requires training, because they are written in the now obsolete secretary hand, widely used in England from about 1500 till about 1650. Transcripts of manuscripts written in that hand were made with the benefit of expert instruction from Laetitia Kennedy-Skipton Yeandle of the Folger Shakespeare Library, who also provided readings of individual words that are all but illegible.

Because a verbatim transcript of many of the letters would produce a text unreadable without serious effort, the texts here are modernized. Following the recommendations set forth in the *Harvard Guide to American History* and exemplified in Samuel Eliot Morison's edition of Bradford's history of Plymouth, I have used modern spelling throughout except for proper names and a few words with no modern equivalent. In addition, I have followed modern practice in capitalization, italicization, and punctuation, since some of the letters lack all three. Proper names have not, however, been regularized, because the original form is frequently revealing and interesting. Thus one will find here, as in the originals, both "new england" and "New England." Generally the paragraphing of the original has been followed, but in letters with few or no paragraph divisions, they have been supplied. The difference between the modernized versions provided in this collection and literal versions may be suggested by the following parallel texts of William Hammond's September 26, 1633, letter.

literal version	*modernized version*
I am sumthinge bould to wreight	I am something bold to write
unto youer worshipe deseyreing	unto your worship, desiring
youer woorshipe to pardon me my	your worship to pardon me my
wreighteinge vnto yoer worshipe is	writing unto your worship is
to sarteyfeye youer worshipe in	to certify your worship in
sume thinge consarninge new Eing-	something concerning new Eing-
land in amereyca my son tellethe	land in amereyca. My son telleth
me that youer worshipe ded giue	me that your worship did give
him xx£ to bey you a	him twenty pounds to buy you a
cuppele of bullockes her to bred a	couple of bullocks here to breed a
stock	stock.

Hammond was one of the least literate writers in this collection, but his letter is so revealing that it deserves to be read without the hindrance of the writer's exotic spelling.

What is frequently called the first American book, Captain John Smith's *True Relation of . . . occurrences . . . in Virginia* (1608), was a letter written to Smith's friends back in England. It has sufficient literary merit to have been anthologized in collections of American literature. Similarly, *Letters from New England* includes some letters that can be called literary, for while some writers merely jotted down notes in haste and some were scarcely literate, others composed with careful attention to style. Thomas Dudley's letter is a good example, as are the letters of Thomas Welde (who addressed his letter to his former congregation in England), John Cotton and Richard Mather (both of whom wrote letters that serve almost as public policy statements), and Edmund Browne (who called part of his letter a report). Each of these writers seems to have recognized that his letter would be read by many readers and therefore to have taken special care in composition. That the letters have survived is some evidence that they were considered to have special value. The John Winthrops, father and son, used one of Francis Higginson's letters to prepare would-be migrants for this transition to America. A reliable indication that letters from New England were widely read is the fact that the colony's religious innovations were widely known to English puritans. One who was interested in Massachusetts Bay's religious practices wrote to Winthrop in 1637, "I have read and heard of sundry letters written from some with you unto others with us," and then proceeded to summarize several letters. At least one letter, Higginson's report printed as *New Englands Plantation* (1630), was written for a large readership, and the extant version of Richard Mather's letter appears in a manuscript prepared for publication. Hence, although the letters as a group are important primarily for the information they convey and the attitudes they reveal, they can also be said to constitute the earliest body of literature produced in the Massachusetts Bay Colony.

This collection is restricted to letters written to England. Other early letters survive, addressed to people within the Bay Colony or to colonists in Rhode Island, Connecticut, or Plymouth. Though many of these letters have value, they assume a familiarity with the New England scene that considerably reduces the value for twentieth-century readers. I have, however, included letters that were written to a New Englander temporarily in England, such as John Winthrop the younger. One letter here was written from the Plymouth Colony, but its author, James Cudworth, had originally come to Massachusetts Bay, and he wrote from the perspective of a Bay colonist. Limiting the collection to letters from the first decade is less arbitrary than it seems, for by the early fall of 1638 the fundamental religious, political, and social patterns of the Massachusetts Bay Colony had been firmly established, though codification was to follow. All dates are new style, except for letters dated between January and March 24, for which both old and new style dates are given (that is, 1630/1).

This collection is entitled *Letters from New England* because New England is what the founders of the Bay Colony called their new home. Higginson, Winthrop, Dudley, and their followers found the Indian name *Massachusetts* uncomfortable on their tongues. Higginson refers to "Masathulets Bay" and William Hammond later referred to the body of water as

"Marthateutyeis Bay." Calling their dwelling place "New England" permitted these Englishmen to domesticate their wilderness, and I have followed their practice.

In addition to improved and more complete versions of several of the manuscripts, this collection also provides the first publication—as far as I can determine—of John Cotton's letter to John Dod and Richard Mather's letter to William Rathband. The letter of George Burdett and the one ascribed to Henry Vane have only been summarized and quoted in the *Calendar of State Papers*, Colonial Series. Thacher's letter is ten percent longer here than in Increase Mather's version, and the letter from the Planters of New England includes a document omitted in the previous publication of that letter in Charles E. Banks's *Planters of the Commonwealth* (Boston, 1930).

My dedication of this collection to Louis B. Wright and Elliot Richardson suggests my hope that the book will be read by more than specialists. Specifically, I own through the dedication to Dr. Wright a debt to a devoted humanist who has provided me and many others with personal encouragement and a model of the kinds of research a person interested in human concerns might usefully undertake. Through the dedication to Mr. Richardson I own a debt to a public servant whose courage and devotion to the common weal is in the best Massachusetts tradition.

Obviously this collection could not have been made without the help of a great many people. The work was begun at the Folger Shakespeare Library in Washington, where I enjoyed a senior fellowship while on sabbatical leave from the University of Massachusetts. At the Folger many people were helpful, especially Dorothy Mason, Megan Lloyd, Richard Schoeck, Laetitia Yeandle, and Virginia Callahan. Many other Folger friends were encouraging. Others who have helped include David Berkowitz of Brandeis University, David D. Hall of Boston University, John J. McCusker of the University of Maryland, and Winfred Bernhard and Mason Lowance, my colleagues at the University of Massachusetts. I am grateful to the officials of the Library of Congress, the John Carter Brown Library, the Boston Public Library, the Massachusetts Archives, the libraries of Amherst College and the University of Massachusetts, the British Museum, the Public Record Office, the Institute for Historical Research, London, and more particularly the American Antiquarian Society and the Massachusetts Historical Society, especially the latter's Marjorie F. Gutheim and Winifred Collins. A grant from the American Philosophical Society's Penrose Fund permitted me to work at the Public Record Office and the British Museum. I owe a special debt to my wife, Katherine, for help with the transcriptions and for many other kinds of help.

INTRODUCTION

I As early as 1623 the Dorchester Company of Adventurers, a group of merchants who lived in the west of England, established a small settlement on the Massachusetts coast, at Cape Ann, just south of what is now Gloucester Harbor. The settlers there were to work with the fishermen from vessels that came each summer to fish off Cape Ann, and also to build houses, make salt, plant corn, and hunt game. They could thereby supply fresh provisions for the fishermen, and since it was planned that their group would in time include a minister, they would also serve the religious needs of the fishermen. The clergyman might also seek to christianize the Indians. But the venture was not a financial success and was therefore dissolved in 1626. John White, a minister of Dorchester, England, who was active in the enterprise though he never came to America, explained that ". . . no sure fishing place in the land is fit for planting, nor any good place for planting found fit for fishing, at least near the shore, and, secondly, rarely any fishermen will work at land, neither are husbandmen fit for fishermen but with long use and experience." Roger Conant, the ablest man in the Cape Ann group, chose to stay on, as did a few others. He selected a new location sixteen miles to the southwest at Naumkeag, where later the towns of Salem and Beverly came to be built. Meanwhile in England the Dorchester Company's property was transferred, largely through the efforts of White, to the newly formed New England Company. Acting from motives both commercial and religious, and with stronger financial resources than the earlier company had possessed, the New England Company in the spring of 1628 sent some fifty planters to Naumkeag under the leadership of Captain John Endecott. They were a kind of advance party for a larger group that was to leave the following year.

A few other settlers besides the Naumkeag group were in the Massachusetts Bay area at this time. Some twenty miles to the south, Thomas Walford had a dwelling at what was to become Charlestown; just to the north of him at Winnisimmet, Samuel

Maverick had built a fortified house as early as 1625; the Reverend William Blackstone lived on the peninsula of Shawmut, later Boston. A few miles to the south at Wessagusset, later Weymouth, were William Jeffrey and John Burslem. Most of these men probably had come over with Captain Robert Gorges in 1623 to found a colony, one that failed to thrive. None of them was a puritan or in any way sympathetic to puritanism.

There was uncertainty about who had rights to the land in Massachusetts. Presumably it was available to the New England Company by virtue of a patent from the Council for New England, a group that included Sir Ferdinando Gorges. But in 1623 the council had granted Robert Gorges, son of Ferdinando, some of this land. He had tried to colonize it and had conveyed his rights to others when he died. A large group from eastern England, clearly identified with puritanism, wished to join the company, but they believed that a dependable legal basis for land ownership in Massachusetts was required. As a remedy, White, his westerners, and the eastern contingent sought and obtained a royal charter in March 1629. It granted all the land between the Merrimack River and the Charles River, and three miles beyond in each direction, to the renamed company. The Governor and Company of the Massachusetts-Bay in New England had a charter, or patent as the colonists often called it, that specified how the company was to be governed. In time it was of crucial importance, since it served as a constitution for the colony. The charter granted the status of freemen to the petitioners and their associates (including at this time Endecott, Isaac Johnson, Increase Nowell, and others later to migrate to Massachusetts, but not John Winthrop, who had not yet affiliated with the group) and to "all such others as shall hereafter be admitted" by the governor and his assistants. That is, the freemen or stockholders of the group constituted "one body politic and corporate in deed, fact, and name." They were to elect a governor, a deputy governor, and eighteen assistants for one-year terms (the first twenty officers were named in the charter). The governmental functions were divided: the governor or deputy and at least seven assistants were to meet at least monthly to deal with the business of the company; the freemen, including the officers, were to meet four times a year as the "great and general court" to make laws.

By this time there had grown up within the Church of England a strong party of clergy and laymen devoted to preaching and to the virtues associated with the rising middle class, "the industrious sort of people," as they have been called. These churchmen of the Reformed tradition had inherited the values of the Elizabethan nonconformists and advocated living by high standards of morality. For them the proper functions of the church were preaching and discipline, and they rejected much of the Church of England's ceremonial. Having failed in their efforts to purify the church of what they considered the relics of popery, the puritan ministers tried to ignore those ecclesiastical requirements that they considered offensive. In 1628, William Laud, who valued highly the authority of the episcopal hierarchy and the church's ceremonial requirements, was made Bishop of London; later he became Archbishop of Canterbury. He zealously enforced the church's laws and prevented offending ministers from preaching. As a result the idea of emigration to avoid episcopal authority was attractive to many. Holland had long been a shelter both for separatists, who had left the Church of England completely, and for puritans, who remained within the church but were dissatisfied with its policies and emphases. But Holland was not satisfactory as a permanent home, for its ways were not English ways. So had found the separatists, and some of them had gone to America in 1620 and the years immediately following: these were the "pilgrims" of Plymouth. Now the creation of the strongly backed Massachusetts Bay Company offered the less radical puritans a means of mass migration to America, to the area already named New England by Captain John Smith.

The puritans who were to come to Massachusetts Bay were mostly solid yeomen and middle-class folk. Not a thoroughly homogeneous group, they had a good deal in common. They were mostly people who took religion seriously. They embraced the Bible; they embraced the predestinarian theology of Calvinism, which stressed God's sovereignty and the experience of religious conversion. They conceived of religion in the context of the church, a gathering of committed Christians. They believed in education, and they looked upon the learned ministers who guided them as men of religious authority. These ministers were nearly all members of the "spiritual brotherhood" of like-minded men who were related by common educational experience at Cambridge University, by marriage, by association. The puritans were tough-minded, hard-working people, strong-willed enough to risk their lives in the wilderness of America. If their hearts were fixed on heaven, their minds were still able to focus intently on their worldly chores and responsibilities.

Within the leadership of the Massachusetts Bay Company, one group of puritans, men from East Anglia and London, identified themselves with a special variety of puritanism, the sort advocated by such ministers as William Ames and Thomas Hooker. They emphasized the role of the congregation; Hooker declared that "A particular congregation hath complete power by Christ his institution to give a complete call to a minister." This elemental form of Congregationalism had attracted enough ministers to enable the Massachusetts Bay Company, which was dominated by the easterners, to send to America mostly ministers of their own persuasion. Thus the colony was to be puritan, Congregational puritan.

Although economic conditions have been considered at least as important a motive for migration as Laud's pressure on the puritans, the separation of economics from religion is false to the radical this-worldliness of puritanism, which emphasized the value of laboring in one's calling. The early years of the seventeenth century saw the disintegration of the old agrarian society, and when the birthpangs of the new capitalism proved painful to many, puritan ideals became the midwife's manual. Life was made insecure by depressions in the years 1619 to 1624, 1629 to 1631, and 1637 to 1640; by plague years; and by bad harvests. The year 1629 was particularly bad in East Anglia, where economic conditions reached crisis levels. These were years when many observers commented on the striking decline in morality: drunkenness, sexual promiscuity, and robbery were all on the increase, or were reported to be. To escape, Englishmen fled not only to New England but to the Caribbean and to the Chesapeake, though those who went south were mostly individuals rather than groups and mostly poor. Few families migrated to the warmer colonies. Those who went to New England sought an opportunity to make a fresh start: to create a new life and to practice their Bible-centered religion in pristine purity.

II It is one of the characteristics of human nature that man should find the idea of a fresh start especially attractive. Caught in the complexity of forces of our own or other men's making,

we would eagerly begin again, however much we may know that
we cannot slough off the burdens that at times seem to constitute our inheritance. The founding of the Massachusetts Bay
Colony provides an unusually attractive example of the possibil-
ities and the limitations of such an enterprise. The colony's intellectual leaders demonstrated from an early date that they
sought to create something new and different. John Winthrop,
much the most influential leader for the first twenty years, set
forth in a shipboard sermon on the way to America what the
new colony should strive to be.

Winthrop first sought to establish the need for a proper relationship between men. He argued as the right one "that every
man afford his help to another in every want or distress . . . out
of the same affection which makes him careful of his own
good. . . ." He then set out some general rules for the exercise of
charity. In a "community of peril" in a new and unknown land,
he noted, men must exercise greater charity and be less concerned
for their own welfare. Especial charity is due to fellow Christians—and here Winthrop clearly assumed that his fellow migrants
were Christians: since "each discerns by the work of the spirit
his own image and resemblance in another, and therefore cannot
but love him as he loves himself," they should undertake "by a
mutual consent through a special overruling providence, and a
more than ordinary approbation of the churches of Christ, to
seek out a place of cohabitation and consortship under a due
form of government both civil and ecclesiastical." Having committed themselves to this goal, they must reach it, since God
"will expect a strict performance." This commitment consti-
tutes a covenant between God and man. Keeping this covenant
will bring blessing on "the land we go to possess." Failure will
mean that "we shall perish out of the land."

Winthrop did not specify in his sermon the exact form that
the ecclesiastical and civil governments were to take, though the
shape of the civil government had been partly determined by
those who drew up the charter. It gave absolute authority to the
governor and a few other stockholders. Thus the company declared in 1629 that it was "incorporated into a body politic
with ample power to govern and rule all his majesty's subjects
that reside within the limits of our plantation." The anticipated
integrity of the new colony as a community was not realized,
since circumstances forced the colonists of the Winthrop fleet to

disperse. But once the colonists had arrived, Winthrop's first decision as governor was to share with the many (all the adult males except servants) the authority given by the charter to the few. He sought to build the new commonwealth on a covenant basis. He believed that "it is of the nature and essence of every society to be knit together by some covenant, either expressed or implied." Though later migrants were not permitted to share in the political power unless they were church members, Winthrop truly created a new kind of state. As the letters below demonstrate, it was experience, need, and the familiar struggle for power that were to determine the allotment of responsibility in the representative government, which, if not fully democratic, was a major step in that direction.

Though legally wholly subject to English law and English jurisdiction, this new state was independent of England in principle and in practice. Nothing makes clearer the sense of independence of the new commonwealth (as it called itself) than the freeman's and inhabitant's oaths adopted in 1634. The former reads as follows:

I (A.B.) being by God's providence, an inhabitant, and freeman, within the jurisdiction of this Commonwealth; do freely acknowledge myself to be the subject to the government thereof: And therefore do here swear by the great and dreadful name of the ever-living God, that *I* will be true and faithful to the same, and will accordingly yield assistance and support thereunto, with my person and estate, as in equity *I* am bound; and will also truly endeavor to maintain and preserve all the liberties and privileges thereof, submitting myself to the wholesome laws and orders made and established by the same. And further, that *I* will not plot or practice any evil against it, or consent to any that shall so do; but will timely discover and reveal the same to lawful authority here now established, for the speedy preventing thereof.

Moreover, *I* do solemnly bind myself in the sight of God, that when *I* shall be called to give my voice touching any such matter of the state, in which freemen are to deal, *I* will give my vote and suffrage as I shall judge in mine own conscience may best conduce and tend to the public weal of the body, without respect of persons, or favor of any man. .

So help me God in the Lord Jesus.

It is difficult to imagine anyone's taking this oath lightly, and by it one swears allegiance to a commonwealth, without reference to the King of England or his government.

If the government of the colony was a dramatic departure from tradition, even more radically new was the system of local government. In the last few years several New England towns have been closely studied, and only now has it become clear how extraordinary was the process of innovation. The historian of Sudbury, Massachusetts, Sumner C. Powell, describes the number of changes from the English norm as "staggering." For him the explanation is that the men of Sudbury were creating "a community of free townsmen." The beginnings of the town of Dedham were even more utopian.

The famous New England town meetings began as early as 1632 in Newtown (later Cambridge), where monthly meetings were held. In the Dorchester town records one finds the following "agreement made by the whole consent and vote of the plantation, made Monday, eighth October, 1633":

Imprimis: it is ordered that for the general good and well ordering of the affairs of the plantation there shall be every Monday before the court by eight of the clock in the morning, and presently upon the beating of a drum, a general meeting of the inhabitants of the plantation at the meeting house, there to settle and set down such orders as may tend to the general good as aforesaid, and every man to be bound thereby without gainsaying or resistance.

By 1635 Boston's system of town meetings was well established. From an early date town meetings and worship services were held in the same building, the meetinghouse, with town meetings sometimes directly following religious assemblies. In 1636 the General Court delegated authority to town meetings for the disposition of land, making local laws, and electing town officers. At least in Boston any inhabitant could participate in town meetings.

The creation of a new kind of church paralleled the creation of a new political system. Like the state, the church rested on a covenant. But whereas the commonwealth of Massachusetts Bay was made up wholly from new cloth, the theoretical basis of the church had already been formulated in Europe, if only in a general way. The ecclesiastical system that was to become Congregationalism supposed that the essential body was the "particular church." Such a church was created by the covenanting of a body of people who promised (as the Boston-Charlestown church covenant put it) "to walk in all our ways according to the rule of the gospel." This body then had the power to perform various functions, notably "to choose and call her own officers and members." These were the rudiments of the system, and they can be observed in the founding of the first Massachusetts Bay church, at Salem, in 1629. Like the state, the church evolved the ramifications of its system slowly, over a long period of time. The new power that communicants or church members enjoyed probably had much to do with the strong political role they took in town meetings, since the two gatherings had much in common. The Congregational system was so shockingly novel that its early dominance in Massachusetts is hard to account for. John Cotton, who in time became its chief spokesman, was originally so disturbed by it that he protested vigorously. He knew, he told the Salemites in a letter written from England on October 2, 1630, that they "went hence of another judgment." If the theory was not new, the practice surely was.

Closely related to both church and state was the new legal system created in Massachusetts. Though it drew on the Bible as the law of God and on the precedent of English law, Massachusetts law was not simply a combining of the two, for the leaders of the commonwealth saw that they had the opportunity to create a new and improved legal system. Accordingly they simplified and ordered the laws that they borrowed, sought to be far less severe than was traditional, and attempted to establish new laws for new circumstances. They gave to the state powers that had formerly belonged to the church (recording of births, marriages, deaths; jurisdiction over marriage and divorce), and they made laws that offered guidance instead of mere prohibition and punishment. Like the ordering of church and state, the new legal system was not created wholly in the first ten years of the colony. It grew "pro re nata [out of existing circumstances]," as Winthrop put it, and codification was avoided since it would have revealed, Winthrop feared, how much the new system of laws was "repugnant to the laws of England." But by the end of the first decade, it is clear, a new direction was being taken in the making of laws. Later Cromwell's regime in England looked to the Massachusetts legal system as a model for reforming English law.

If the new land provided an opportunity for a new kind of

state and a new kind of church and even a new legal system, it was because these institutions were susceptible of radical reformation. But in many areas of life, changes could not have been made so easily, even if they had been considered desirable. Patterns of culture in Massachusetts Bay were particularly conservative. Settlements were not permitted except where there was a church or a prospect of one, and settlers were required to build their houses in compact villages (for purposes of defense) within a half mile of the meetinghouse, the political and religious center of the town. In each community the intellectual leaders were clergymen who were products of the English university system. Some had spent many years at the university, where tradition was very strong: John Cotton was ten years at Cambridge and Thomas Hooker fourteen. And most of the ministers were mature men: John Maverick was fifty-five when he came to America, Peter Bulkeley was fifty-two, Nathaniel Ward was in his mid-fifties, and Cotton was nearly fifty. What these men taught and the example they set were naturally much of a piece with their English experience. Moreover, the Massachusetts villages in which the preachers held forth were physically modelled after English villages, and agricultural practices were modelled after English practices. New Englanders had migrated in families, and the family structure was perpetuated in the New World. In some places its strength was so great that children were kept dependent on their parents even after marrying and establishing separate households.

Early Massachusetts literature and the educational system at Harvard suggest the force that traditional culture had. *New Englands First Fruits* (London, 1643) explains how Harvard used what was essentially the Oxford and Cambridge curriculum with public declamations in Latin and Greek, disputations in logic and philosophy. The earliest imaginative literature, the *Quaternions* of Anne Bradstreet and the consolatory verses attempted by John Wilson and other clergymen, is highly derivative. The circumstances of a frontier society, albeit an unusually intellectual one, were unsuitable for the creation of a literature that broke new ground.

Change, or at least development, was of course inevitable in Massachusetts Bay, but the process was slowed by banishing those whose ideas conflicted sharply with the standing order and by restricting immigration to those approved by the magistrates. When a split occurred between groups within the power structure, the side favoring order always dominated. Thus tradition was preserved. For many years after 1640 very few migrants from England joined the colony. What had begun as a colony radically new in significant ways became within a generation thoroughly conservative of its initial pattern. The most important internal developments were probably the growth of commercialism and the increasing interest of the individual in his own welfare as distinct from the community's; a resulting unequal distribution of wealth, which led to a redistribution of power into the hands of the wealthy; a decline in the percentage of the population who were church members as a result of the restriction of membership to those who could give evidence of salvation; the fragmentation of the sense of community as population growth required new settlements and new churches; the diverging of interests as some towns became trading centers while others remained agricultural. The central town, Boston, was also the place where change was most rapid.

"In the beginning" is an appealing phrase. One finds William Bradford's opening sentence gratifying: "Of Plimouth Plantation and first of the occasion and inducements there unto; the which that I may truly unfold, I must begin at the very root and rise of the same." No such systematic history of Massachusetts Bay was written by a contemporary. We can find one, however, by piecing together the vivid letters of the period. The accomplishments of the Massachusetts Bay colony in its first decade make its chronicles of lasting interest. It is thoroughly fitting that its chronicle be told not by a single historian but by many participants.

1629

The first colonizing activity of the Massachusetts Bay Company
after it received its charter in March of 1629 was to send a fleet
of ships and colonists to Naumkeag in New England. Among
those who left in late April under the new auspices was the Reverend Francis Higginson. Then about forty-two, Higginson was
a graduate of Cambridge University. Some time after being ordained to the priesthood he had fallen under the influence of
puritan preachers, one of whom was Thomas Hooker; as a result
he became a nonconformist. When in the 1620s Anglican authorities became increasingly determined to establish conformity,
Higginson, now a leader of the puritan party, fell into disfavor
and found it difficult to keep a preaching post. He therefore vol-
unteered his services to the group planning settlement in New
England and was accepted, for the company was looking for just
such a man, a "Congregationalist." Soon Higginson was appointed to the eight-man governing council for Naumkeag, along with
Samuel Skelton, another congregational-minded clergyman.
(Skelton may have served as chaplain to the Earl of Lincoln,
whose household was a center for planning the Massachusetts
Bay commonwealth.) The terms of Higginson's contract were
generous, including provisions for a manservant and two maid-
servants besides a good salary. (Higginson had a wife and eight
children.) His duties and Skelton's were to teach and preach to
the immigrants and to the Indians. The instructions of the company to John Endecott in 1628 state emphatically that "the
propagating the gospel is the thing we do profess above all to be
our aim in settling this plantation." The ministers, according to
this letter, have "declared themselves to be of one judgment and
to be fully agreed on the manner how to exercise their ministry." This comment has been interpreted to mean that they had
agreed to establish a Congregational church at Naumkeag.

Some two hundred planters and servants on several ships made
the voyage to Naumkeag. Just as Endecott's party was to have
prepared the way for the next group of settlers, so Higginson's
company in turn was to prepare the way for the 1630 planters,
now rapidly growing in numbers. Most of the 1629 group were

laborers hired to prepare dwellings and plant crops for those to
come. Their crossing is described in the journal Higginson kept
and sent back as a letter. He seems to have agreed to keep a record and to supply information about his experiences to those
who were to come. Three separate letters have survived: the record of his crossing, advice to would-be migrants, and a report on
what he found in America. The first two of these appear to have
been sent home on one of the ships that left Naumkeag in July;
it arrived in September. The original manuscript of the first of
these has not survived, but a contemporary copy of much of it
is in a manuscript at the Massachusetts Historical Society. This
manuscript was used by its first editor, Thomas Hutchinson, in
the eighteenth century, and is the basis of the present text.
(Hutchinson chose to trim a passage of two sentences on five
boys who committed sodomy. The manuscript is marked, "omit
this.") At the point where the manuscript copy breaks off,
Thomas Hutchinson's version, presumably prepared from this
same manuscript when it was complete, is the basis of the present text, from *A Collection of Original Papers Relative to the
History of the Colony of Massachusetts-Bay* (Boston,1769; reprinted by The Prince Society, 1865).

Francis Higginson to His Friends in England
July 24, 1629

A true relation of the last voyage to new England declaring all
circumstances with the manner of the passage we had by sea
and what manner of country and inhabitants we found when we
came to land, and what is the present state and condition of the
English people that are there already, faithfully recorded according to the very truth for the satisfacton of very many of my loving friends who have earnestly requested to be truly certified in
these things. Written from new England, July 24, 1629.

If any curious critic that looks for exactness of phrases or expert seaman that regard propriety of sea terms, etc.

A true relation of the last voyage to new England made the
last summer, begun the twenty-fifth of April, being Saturday,
Anno Domini 1629.

The company of new England, consisting of many worthy
gentlemen in the city of London, dorchester, and other places,
aiming at the glory of God, the propagation of the Gospel of

Christ, the conversion of the Indians, and the enlargement of
the King's majesty's dominions in America, and being authorized by his royal letters patents for that end, at their very great
costs and charge furnished five ships to go to new England, for
the further settling of the English plantation that they had already begun there.

The names of the five ships were as followeth. The first is
called the *Talbot*, a good and strong ship of three hundred tons
and nineteen pieces of ordnance, and served with thirty mariners. This ship carried above one hundred planters, six goats, five
great pieces of ordnance, with meal, oatmeal, peas, and all manner of munition and provision for the plantation for a twelve
month. The second, the *George*, another strong ship also, about
three hundred tons, twenty pieces of ordnance, served with
about thirty mariners; her chief carriage were cattle, twelve
mares, thirty kine, and some goats. Also she had in her fifty-two
planters and other provisions. The third is called the *lyons whelpe*,
a neat and nimble ship of 120 tons, eight pieces of ordnance, carrying in her many mariners and above forty planters, specially
from Dorchester and other places thereabouts, with provision
and four goats. The fourth is called the *4 Sisters*, as I hear of
about three hundred tons, which fair ship carried many cattle
with passengers and provision. The fifth is called the *Mayflower*,[1]
carrying passengers and provision.

Now amongst these five ships, the *George* having some special
and urgent cause of hastening her passage, set sail before the
rest, about the midst of April.[2] And the *4 Sisters* and the *Mayflower*, being not thoroughly furnished, intended as we heard to
set forth about three weeks after us. But we that were in the
Talbot and *Lions whelpe*, being ready for our voyage by the
good hand of God's providence, hoisted up sail from graues end[3]
[April 25[4]] on Saturday the 25th of April about seven o'clock
in the morning. Having but a faint wind, we could not go far
that day, but at night we anchored against Lee, which is twelve
miles from Graves end, and there we rested that night and [26]
kept Sabbath the next day.

[27] On Monday we set forward and came to the flats, a passage somewhat difficult by reason of the narrowness of the channel and shallowness of the water, and going over this we were in
some danger, for our ship, being heavy laden and drawing deep
water, was sensibly felt of us all to strike three or four times on
the ground, but the wind blowing somewhat strong, we were

1. This was not the same
ship that carried the Pilgrims to Plymouth.
This second *Mayflower*
and the *Talbot* carried
thirty-five members of the
Leyden (Holland) congre-
gation to Plymouth.
2. The ship carried Samuel
Sharpe, who was acting as
agent of the company; he
carried a duplicate of the
recently granted royal
charter and instructions to
prevent any other claim-
ants to the land from oc-
cupying the company's
territory. See Nathaniel B.
Shurtleff, ed., *The Rec-
ords of the Governor and
Company of the Massachu-
setts Bay in New England*,
5 vols. in 6 (Boston, 1853-
54), 1:386-87, 396-97
(hereafter cited as *Mas-
sachusetts Records*).
3. Just outside London.
4. The bracketed dates
appear in the manuscript
margin.

carried swiftly on and at last by God's blessing came safe to anchor at Gorin roade.[5] [28] Tuesday we went a little further and anchored over against margret Towne, staying for a wind for the Downs. [29] Wednesday we came safely though with much turning and tacking, through the gulles into the downs[6] and stayed that night. [30, May 1, 2] Thursday, Friday, and Saturday the wind blew hard from southwest and caused our ship to dance, and divers of our passengers and my wife specially were seasick. Here the king's ship called the *Assurance* pressed two of our mariners. Here we saw many porpoises playing in the sea, which they say is a sign of foul weather. [3] Sabbath day a windy day and cold we kept Sabbath, staying still at the downs.

[4] Monday God sent us a fair gale of wind north-north-east, whereby we came merrily from the downs, and passing Dover we saw six or seven sail of dunkirks [pirate ships] wafting after us, but it seemed they saw our company was too strong for them, for then we had with us three or four ships that went for the straits,[7] so they returned back from pursuing us any longer. But sailing with a good wind we went speedily and at night came near the Isle of Wight, but being dark we durst not put into the channel but put back for sea room four hours and then other four hours sailed back again the same way.

[5] Tuesday early in the morning we entered the channel, the wind being weak and calm, and passed by Portsmouth very slowly, but in the afternoon the wind quickened, and we were forced to anchor a little on this side Cowcastle,[8] but the wind growing more favorable, we weighed and came to anchor again right against Cowcastle, thinking to stay that night, the wind being very calm. Here I and my wife and my daughter Mary and two maids and some others with us obtained of the master of the ship to go ashore to refresh us and to wash our linens, and so we lay at Cowes that night. But the wind turning when we were absent, they hoisted sail and left us there, and anchored eight miles further over against Yarmouth about eight of the clock at night. [May 6] Wednesday betime in the morning the shallop was sent from the ship to fetch us to Yarmouth, but the water proved rough and our women desired to be set on shore three miles short of Yarmouth, and so went on foot by land and lodged in Yarmouth that night.

[7, 8] On Thursday and Friday there master Beecher,[9] allowed by the Company, gave me forty shillings to make our provision of what things we would for the voyage. [9] Saturday we went

5. The Gore, an anchorage below Margate.
6. An anchorage off Deal.
7. Straits of Gilbraltar.
8. A small castle at West Cowes.
9. Captain of the *Talbot;* he commanded the same vessel the next year when it was part of the Winthrop fleet.

to board again, and this day we had two other men pressed to serve the king's ship, but we got one again by entreaty. [10] The Sabbath next day we kept the ship, where I preached in the morning and in the afternoon was entreated to preach at Yarmouth, where mr meare and captayne Borley entertained us very kindly and earnestly desired to be certified of our safe arrival in new England and of the state of the country.

[11] Monday morning blew a fair wind from east-southeast, and the *lions whelpe* having taken in all her provision for passengers, about three of the clock in the afternoon we hoisted sail for the Needles[10] and by God's guidance safely passed that narrow passage a little after four o'clock in the afternoon. And being entered into the sea, from the top of the mast we discerned four sail of ships lying southward from us. But night coming on we took in our longboat and shallop. [12] And the next day we had a fair gale of easterly wind that brought us towards night as far as the Lizzard.[11] [13] Wednesday the wind still holding easterly, we came as far as the land's end, in the utmost part of Cornwall and so left our dear native soil of England behind us, and sailing about ten leagues further, we passed the Iles of Sillie and launched the same day a great way into the main ocean. And now my wife and other passengers began to feel the tossing waves of the western sea and so were very seasick. And this is to be noted, that all this while our passage hath been upon the coast of England and so ought truly [this day] to be accounted the first day of our parting with old England.

[14] Thursday the same easterly wind blew all day and night, and the next day, so that some of the seamen thought we were come by this time one hundred leagues from England, but toward night the wind was calm. [May 16] Saturday we were becalmed all day. This day met us a little ship of Bristoll that came from Christopher Islande.[12] [17] Sabbath, being the first Lord's Day we held at sea, was very calm, especially in the morning, but we were disturbed in our morning service by the approach of a Biskainers [Spanish] ship, a man-of-war that made towards us and manned out his boat to view us, but finding us too strong for him, he durst not venture to assault us but made off. This day my two children Samuel and Mary began to be sick of the smallpox and purples [purpura] together, which was brought into the ship by one mister Browne, which was sick of the same at graues end, whom it pleased God to make the first occasion of bringing that contagious

10. Sharp rocks at the western end of the Isle of Wight.
11. A promontory in Cornwall.
12. Saint Christopher or Saint Kitts, in the West Indies.

sickness among us, wherewith many were after afflicted.

[18] Monday [was] calm still, the wind being northwest blowing a little towards evening but contrary to our course. [19] Tuesday wind [was] southwest, as little helpful as the former and blowing very weak. This day the master of our ship, myself, and another went aboard the *Lions whelp* where mister Gibs made us welcome with bountiful entertainment. And this day towards night my daughter grew sicker, and many blue spots were seen upon her breast, which affrighted us. At the first we thought they had been the plague tokens, but we found afterwards that it was only an high measure of the infection of the pox, which were struck again into the child, and so it was God's will the child died about six of the clock at night, being the first in our ship that was buried in the bowels of the great Atlanticke Sea, which as it was a grief to us her parents and a terror to all the rest as being the beginning of a contagious disease and mortality. So in the same judgment it pleased God to remember mercy in that child, in freeing it from a world of misery wherein otherwise she had lived all her days. For being about four years old a year since, we know not by what means [she] swayed in the back, so that it was broken and grew crooked, and the joints of her hips were loosed and her knees went crooked, pitiful to see, since which time she hath had a most lamentable pain in her belly and would ofttimes cry out in the day and in her sleep also, "My belly!" which declared some extraordinary distemper, so that in respect of her we had cause to take her death as a blessing from the Lord to shorten her misery.

[May 20] Wednesday, a wet morning, the wind was west-southwest and in the afternoon northwest and by west, both being contrary to our course which was to sail west and by south. Thus it pleased God to lay his hand upon us by sickness and death, and contrary winds and stirred up some of us to make the motion of humbling ourselves under the hand of God by keeping a solemn day of fasting and prayer unto God, to beseech him to remove the continuance and further increase of these evils from us, which was willingly condescended unto as a duty very fitting and needful for our present state and condition.

[21] Thursday, there being two ministers in the ship, mister Smith and myself, we endeavored together with others to consecrate the day as a solemn fasting and humiliation to Almighty God as a furtherance of our present work. And it pleased God the ship was becalmed all day, so that we were freed from any

encumbrance, and as soon as we had done prayers, see and behold the goodness of God, about seven o'clock at night the wind
turned to the northeast, and we had a fair gale that night as a
manifest evidence of the Lord's hearing our prayers. I heard
some of the mariners say they thought this was the first sea-fast
that ever was kept and that they never heard of the like performed at sea before.

[22] Friday the wind [was] fair and east-northerly and for
our purpose for new England. It did blow strongly and carried
us on amain with tossing waves, which did afright them that
were not wonted to such sights. [23] Saturday the same wind
[was] blowing but more gently. Now we were comforted with the
hope of my son Samuel's recovery of the pox. [24] The second
Lord's Day [was] a fair day, an orderly wind and prosperous.
[25] On Monday [was] a fair frum [rising] gale, the wind
south south-west. [26] Tuesday about ten of the clock in the
morning whilst we were at prayers a strong and sudden blast
came from the north that hoisted up the waves and tossed us
more than ever before and hold us all that day till towards night
and then abated by little and little till it was calm. This day
mister Goffe's[13] great dog fell overboard and could not be
recovered.

[27] Wednesday the wind [was] still north and calm in the
morning, but about noon there arose a south wind which increased more and more so that it seemed to us that are land men
a sore and terrible storm, for the wind blew mightily, the rain
fell vehemently, the sea roared and the waves tossed us horribly.
Besides, it was fearful dark and the mariners' maid was afraid,
and noise on the other side with their running here and there,
loud crying one to another to pull at this and that rope. The
waves poured themselves over the ship [so] that the two boats
were filled with water, that they were fain to strike holes in the
midst of them to let the water out. Yea, by the violence of the
waves the longboat cord which held it was broken, and it had
like to have been washed overboard, had not the mariners with
much pain and danger recovered the same. But this lasted not
many hours, after which it became a calmish day. All which
[was] while I lay close and warm in my cabin, but far from having list to sleep with Jonah, my thoughts were otherwise employed as the time and place required. Then I saw the truth of
the Scripture, Psalm 107 from the 23 to the 32. And my fear at
this time was the less when I remembered what a loving friend of

13. Thomas Goffe was a
member of the company.

mine, a minister accustomed to sea storms, said to me, that I
might not be dismayed at such storms, for they were ordinary at
seas, and it seldom falls out that a ship perisheth at storm if it
have sea room, which I the rather wait that others as well as myself by the knowledge hereof may be encouraged and prepared
against those ordinary sea storms.

[28] Thursday [there was a] south wind, calm at night.
[29] On Friday [there was] a boisterous wind blowing cross,
but [it] was allayed towards night with a shower of rain.
[30] Saturday [there was a] southwest wind but fair and quiet.
[31] Sabbath Day, being the third Lord's Day, [was] fair and
calm. We saw abundance of grampus fishes, two or three yards
long and a body as big as an ox. [June 1] Monday the wind
[was] westerly and calm, but besides our being stayed by contrary winds we began to find the temperature of the air to alter
and to become more sultry and subject to unwholesome fogs.
For coming now to the height of the western islands, some of
our men fell sick of the scurvy and others of the smallpox, which
more and more increased, yet thanks be to God none died of it
but my own child mentioned. And therefore according to our
great need we appointed another fast for the next day.

[2] Tuesday we solemnly celebrate[d] another fast. The Lord
that day heard us before we prayed and gave us an answer before we called, for early in the morning the wind turned full
east, being as fit a wind as could blow. And sitting at my study
on the ship['s] poop, I saw many bouny fishes [bonitos] and
porpoises pursuing one another and leaping some of them a yard
above the water. Also as we were at prayer under the hatch some
that were above saw a whale puffing up water not far from the
ship. Now my wife was prettily well recovered of her seasickness.

[3] Wednesday [was] a fair day, and [there was a] fine gale
of full east wind. This day myself and others saw a large round
fish sailing by the ship's side, about a yard in length and round-
ness every way. The mariners call it a sunfish; it spreadeth out
the fins like beams on every side, four or five. [June 4,5] Thursday and Friday the wind [was] full east; we were carried with
admiration on our journey. By this we were more than half way
to new England. This day I saw a fish very strange to me; they
call it a carvel, which came by the ship side, wafting along the
top of the water, it appeared at the first like a bubble, above the
water . . . as big as a man's fist, but the fish itself is about the

bigness of a man's thumb, so that the fish itself and the bubble
resembleth a ship with sails, which therefore is called a carvel.

[6] Saturday wind [was] direct east still. [7] The fourth
Sabbath we kept at sea the wind [was] full easterly till noon,
and then it came full southeast, a strong gale that night and [8]
the next day till night. [9] Tuesday the same wind held till nine
o'clock in the morning, and then a great shower which lasted till
about seven at night, and then it was a very calm. Here we
sounded with a dipled [deep lead] line above one hundred fathom and found no bottom. This day we saw a fish called a tuckle
[turtle], a great and large shellfish, swimming above the water
near the ship. [10] Wednesday wind [was] northerly, a fine
gale but calmish in the afternoon.

[11] Thursday the wind [was] at north, an easy gale and fair
morning. We saw a mountain of ice, shining as white as snow,
like to a great rock or cliff on the shore. It stood still and therefore we thought it to be on ground and to reach the bottom of
the sea, for though there came a mighty stream from the north,
yet it moved not, which made us sound, and we found a bank of
forty fathom deep whereupon we judged it to rest, and the
height above was as much. We also saw six or seven pieces of ice,
floating on the sea, which was broken off from the former
mountain. We also saw great store of waterfowl swimming by
the ship within musket shot, of a pied color and about the bigness of a wild duck, about forty in a company. The mariners
call them hagbirds [mergansers?]. Toward night came a fog that
the *lions whelp* was lost till morning. And now we saw many
bonitos, porpoises, and grampuses, every day more and more.

[12] Friday [was] foggy and calmish, the wind northerly in
the morning, but about noon it came southeast, a dainty loom
[moderate] gale which carried us six leagues a watch. [13] Saturday the same wind [blew] till night, and we saw great store of
porpoises and grampuses. [14] The fifth Sabbath the same wind
[blew]; towards noon it began to be foggy, and then it rained
till night. We went four or five leagues a watch. [June 15] Monday [was] a fair day but foggy, the same wind blowing but with
fresh gale carried us seven leagues a watch. In the afternoon it
blew harder, so the sea was rough, and we lost the sight of the
lions whelpe. It being foggy, we drummed for them and they shot
off a great piece of ordnance, but we heard not one another.

[16] Tuesday wind [was] south and by east, foggy till about

ten o'clock. While we were at prayers it cleared up about an hour, and then we saw the *lions whelpe* distant about two leagues southward. We presently tacked about to meet her, and she did the same to meet us, but before we could get together a thick fog came, that we were long in finding each other. This day we sounded divers times and found ourselves on another bank, at first forty fathom, after thirty-six, after thirty-three, after twenty-four. We thought it to have been the bank over against chap [Cape] Sable, but we were deceived, for we knew not certainly where we were because of the fog. After three or four hours' company we lost the *lions whelpe* again and beat our drum and shot off a great piece of ordnance and yet heard not of of them. But perceiving the bank to grow still the shallower we found it twenty-seven and twenty-four fathoms. Therefore being a fog and fearing we were too near land, we tacked about for sea room for two or three watches and steered south east.

[17] Wednesday [was] very foggy still, and wind south and by west, and sounding found no bottom that we could reach. [18] Thursday wind [was] full west and contrary to us. This day a notorious wicked fellow that was given to swearing and boasting of his former wickedness bragged that he had got a wench with child before he came this voyage and mocked at our days of fast, railing and jesting against puritans, this fellow fell sick of the pox and died. We sounded and found thirty-eight fathom and stayed for a little to take codfish and feasted ourselves merrily.

[19] Friday [the] wind [was] west still, a very fair, clear day. About four o'clock in the afternoon some went up to the top of the mast and affirmed to our great comfort they saw land to the north-eastward. [20] Saturday [the] wind [was] southwest, a fair gale. We sounded and found forty, thirty, twenty-two, and a little after no ground. [21] Sabbath, being the sixth Lord's Day, [the] wind [was] westerly but fair and calm. [22] Monday [the] wind [was] easterly, a fair gale. This day we saw a great deal of froth not far from us; we feared it might be some breach of water against some weed grails [shoals]. Therefore the master of our ship hoisted out the shallop and went with some of the men to see what it was but found it only to be a froth carried by the stream. [June 23] Tuesday the wind [was] northeast, a fair gale. This day we examined five beastly sodomitical boys, which confessed their wickedness not to be named. The fact was so

foul we reserved them to be punished by the governor when we came to new England, who afterward sent them back to the company to be punished in old England, as the crime deserved.

[24] Wednesday [the] wind [was] north-east, a fair day and clear. About nine o'clock in the morning we espied a ship about four leagues behind us, which proved the *lions whelpe*, which had been a week separated from us. We stayed for company. This day a child of Goodman Black's, which had a consumption before it came to ship, died. This day we had all a clear and comfortable sight of America and of the Chap Sable that was over against us seven or eight leagues northward. Here we saw yellow gillyflowers on the sea.

[25] Thursday [the] wind [was] still north-east, a full and fresh gale. In the afternoon we had a clear sight of many islands and hills by the seashore. Now we saw abundance of mackerel, a great store of great whales huffing up water as they go. Some of them came near our ship. Their greatness did astonish us that saw them not before. Their backs appeared like a little island. At five o'clock at[14] night the wind turned southeast a fair gale. This day we caught mackerel. [26] Friday [was] a foggy morning but after, clear and [the] wind calm. We saw many schools of mackerel, infinite multitudes on every side our ship. The sea was abundantly stored with rockweed and yellow flowers like gillyflowers. By noon we were within three leagues of Capan [Cape Ann], and as we sailed along the coasts we saw every hill and dale and every island full of gay woods and high trees. The nearer we came to the shore the more flowers [were] in abundance, sometimes scattered abroad, sometimes joined in sheets nine or ten yards long, which we supposed to be brought from the low meadows by the tide. Now what with fine woods and green trees by land and these yellow flowers painting the sea, [it] made us all desirous to see our new paradise of New England, whence we saw such fore-running signals of fertility afar off. Coming near the harbor towards night we tacked about for sea room.

[27] Saturday [was] a foggy morning but after eight o'clock in the morning very clear, the wind being somewhat contrary at south and by west. We tacked to and again with getting little, but with much ado about four o'clock in the afternoon, having with much pain compassed the harbor and being ready to enter the same, see how things may suddenly change! There came a

14.Here the manuscript ends; Hutchinson's text is followed hereafter.

fearful gust of wind and rain and thunder and lightning, whereby we were borne with no little terror and trouble to our mariners, having very much ado to loose down the sails when the fury of the storm held up. But, God be praised, it lasted but a while and soon abated again. And hereby the Lord showed us what He could have done with us if it had pleased Him. But blessed be God, He soon removed this storm, and it was a fair and sweet evening.

We had a westerly wind which brought us between five and six o'clock to a fine and sweet harbor, seven miles from the head point of Capan.[15] This harbor twenty ships may easily ride therein, where there was an island whither four of our men with a boat went and brought back again ripe strawberries and gooseberries and sweet single roses. Thus God was merciful to us in giving us a taste and smell of the sweet fruit as an earnest of his bountiful goodness to welcome us at our first arrival. This harbor was two leagues and something more from the harbor at Naimkecke,[16] where our ships were to rest, and the plantation is already begun. But because the passage is difficult and night drew on, we put into Capan harbor. [28] [The next day was] the Sabbath, being the first we kept in America and the seventh Lord's Day after we parted with England.

[29] Monday we came from Capan to go to Naimkecke, the wind northerly. I should have told you before that the planters spying our English colors, the governor sent a shallop with two men on Saturday to pilot us. These rested the Sabbath with us at Capan, and this day, by God's blessing and their directions, we passed the curious and difficult entrance into the large, spacious harbor of Naimkecke. And as we passed along it was wonderful to behold so many islands replenished with thick wood and high trees and many fair green pastures. And being come into the harbor, we saw the *George* to our great comfort there, being come on Tuesday, which was seven days before us. We rested that night with glad and thankful hearts that God had put an end to our long and tedious journey through the greatest sea in the world.

[30] The next morning the governor came aboard to our ship and bade us kindly welcome and invited me and my wife to come on shore and take our lodging in his house, which we did accordingly.

Thus you have a faithful report collected from day to day of

15. Gloucester Harbor.
16. The Indian name for what became Salem.

all the particulars that were worth noting in our passage. Now in our passage divers things are remarkable. First, through God's blessing our passage was short and speedy, for whereas we had one thousand leagues, that is, three thousand miles English, to sail from Ould to New England, we performed the same in six weeks and three days. Secondly, our passage was comfortable and easy for the most part, having ordinarily fair and moderate wind and being freed for the most part from stormy and rough seas, saving one night only, which we that were not used thought to be more terrible than indeed it was, and this was Wednesday at night, May 27th.

Thirdly, our passage was also healthful to our passengers, being freed from the great contagion of the scurvy and other maledictions, which in other passages to other places had taken away the lives of many. And yet we were in all reason in wonderful danger all the way, our ship being greatly crowded with passengers, but through God's great goodness we had none that died of the pox but that wicked fellow that scorned at fasting and prayer. There were indeed two little children, one of my own and another besides, but I do not impute it merely to the passage, for they were both very sickly children and not likely to have lived long if they had not gone to sea. And take this for a rule, if children be healthful when they come to sea, the younger they are, the better they will endure the sea and are not troubled with seasickness as older people are, as we had experience in many children that went this voyage. My wife, indeed, in tossing weather was something ill by vomiting, but in calm weather she recovered again and is now much better for the seasickness. And for my own part, whereas I have for divers years past been very sickly and ready to cast up whatsoever I have eaten and was very sick at London and Gravesend, yet from the time I came on shipboard to this day I have been strangely healthful. And now I can digest our ship diet very well, which I could not when I was at land. And indeed in this regard I have great cause to give God praise that he hath made my coming to be a method to cure me of a wonderful weak stomach and continual pain of melancholy wind from the spleen. Also divers children were sick of the smallpox but are safely recovered again, and two or three passengers towards the latter end of the voyage fell sick of the scurvy but coming to land recovered in a short time.

Fourthly, our passage was both pleasurable and profitable, for we received instruction and delight in beholding the wonders of the Lord in the deep waters and sometimes seeing the sea round us appearing with a terrible countenance and as it were full of high hills and deep valleys, and sometimes it appeared as a most plain and even meadow. And ever and anon we saw divers kinds of fishes sporting in the great waters, great grampuses and huge whales going by companies and puffing up water-streams. Those that love their own chimney corner and dare not go far beyond their own town's end shall never have the honor to see these wonderful works of Almighty God.

Fifthly, we had a pious and Christian-like passage, for I suppose passengers shall seldom find a company of more religious, honest, and kind seamen than we had. We constantly served God morning and evening by reading and expounding a chapter, singing, and prayer. And the Sabbath was solemnly kept by adding to the former preaching twice and catechizing. And in our great need we kept two solemn fasts and found a gracious effect. Let all that love and use fasting and praying take notice that it is as prevailable by sea as by land, wheresoever it is faithfully performed. Besides the ship-master and his company used every night to set their eight- and twelve-o'clock watches with singing a psalm and prayer that was not read out of a book. This I write, not for boasting and flattery, but for the benefit of those that have a mind to come to New England hereafter, that if they look for and desire to have as prosperous a voyage as we had, they may use the same means to attain the same. So letting pass our passage by sea, we will now bring our discourse to land on the shore of New England, and I shall by God's assistance endeavor to speak nothing but the naked truth and both acquaint you with the commodities and discommodities of the country.

By October at the latest, John Winthrop appears to have received the continuation of Higginson's letter, which contained advice. By that time Winthrop was committed to going to America the following year, and he naturally found what Higginson had to say valuable. On October 9 Winthrop wrote to his son to ask him to copy a portion of a letter containing all the latest news from New England and to show it to those planning to undertake the next voyage. The copied portion seems to be all that has survived: it was published by Thomas Hutchinson in his *Collection of Original Papers* (1769). Hutchinson, whose edition alone is extant, calls it "Some brief Collections out of a Letter that Mr. Higginson sent to his friends at Leicester," where Higginson had formerly lived. He refers to two groups planning to come to New England: a Dorsetshire group who later founded Dorchester, Massachusetts, and a Lincolnshire group who settled Boston.

The Rev. Francis Higginson to His Friends at Leicester
July 1629

Some brief collections out of a letter that Mr. Higginson sent to his friends at Leicester.

There are certainly expected here the next spring the coming of sixty families out of Dorcettershire, who have by letters signified so much to the governor to desire him to appoint them places of habitation, they bringing their ministers with them. Also many families are expected out of Lincolnshire and a minister with them, and a great company of godly Christians out of London. Such of you as come from Leister, I would counsel you to come quickly and that for two reasons. First, if you linger too long, the passage of Jordan through the malice of Sathan may be stopped that you cannot come if you would. Secondly, those that come first speed best here and have the privilege of choosing choice places of habitations. Little children of five years old may by setting corn one month be able to get their own maintenance abundantly. Oh what a good work might you that are rich do for your poor brethren, to help them with your purses only to convey them hither with their children and families, where they may live as well both for soul and body as anywhere in the world. Besides they will recompense the cost by helping to build houses and plant your ground for a time, which shall be difficult work at the first except you have the help of many hands. Mr. Johnson[1] out of Lincolnshire and many others have helped our godly Christians hither to be employed in their work for a while and then to live of themselves.

 We have here about forty goats that give milk and as many milch kine. We have six or seven mares and an horse and do eve-

1. Isaac Johnson, whose wife was Lady Arbella, for whom Winthrop's flagship was named. A wealthy backer of the company, Johnson arrived with his wife in the spring of 1630.

ry day expect the coming of half a score mares more, and thirty kine by two ships that are to follow us. They that come, let them bring mares, kine, and sheep as many as they can. Ireland is the best place to provide sheep, and lies in the way. Bring none that are in lamb, nor mares in foal, for they are in more danger to perish at sea. Of all trades carpenters are most needful; therefore bring as many as you can. It were a wise course for those of abilities to join together and buy a ship for the voyage and other merchandise. For the governor would that any man may employ his stock in what merchandises he please, excepting only beaver skins, which the company of merchants reserve to themselves, and the managing of the public stock. If any be of the mind to buy a ship, my cousin Nowell's counsel would be good.[2] Also one Mr. ___,[3] a very godly man and the master of the ship we went in, and likewise one Mr. Graves,[4] the master's mate dwelling in Wapping, may herein stand you in stead. The payment of the transportation of things is wondrous dear, as 5 pounds a man and 10 pounds a horse and commonly 3 pounds for every ton of goods, so that a little more than will pay for the passage will purchase the possession of a ship for all together.

No man hath or can have a house built for him here unless he comes himself, or else send servants before to do it for him. It was an error that I now perceive both in myself, and others did conceive by not rightly understanding the merchant's meaning. For we thought that all that put in their money into the common stock should have a house built for them, besides such a portion of the land; but it was not so. They shall indeed have so much land allotted to them when they come to take possession of it, and make use of it but if they will have houses they must build them. Indeed we that are ministers and all the rest that were entertained and sent over and maintained by the rest of the company as their servants, for such a time in such employments, all such are to have houses built them of the Company's charge, and no others nor otherwise. They that put money into the stock, as they do a good work to help forwards so worthy a plantation, so all the gain they are likely to have is according to the increase of the stock at three years' end,[5] by the trade of beaver, besides the lands which they shall enjoy when they will.

All that come must have victuals with them for a twelve-month; I mean they must have meal, oatmeal, and suchlike sustenance of food till they can get increase of corn by their own labor. For otherwise so many may come without provision at the first as that

2. Increase Nowell, who came to Massachusetts in 1630; he was the first ruling elder of the Boston-Charlestown church.
3. Thomas Beecher, captain of the *Talbot* in Winthrop's fleet, settled at Charlestown.
4. A seaman who made yearly voyages to New England.
5. Probably a mistake for seven.

our small beginnings may not be sufficient to maintain them.

Before you come be careful to be strongly instructed what things are fittest to bring with you for your more comfortable passage at sea, as also for your husbandry occasions when you come to the land. For when you are once parted with England you shall meet neither with taverns nor alehouse, nor butchers, nor grocers, nor apothecaries' shops to help what things you need in the midst of the great ocean, nor when you are come to land here are yet neither markets nor fairs to buy what you want. Therefore be sure to furnish yourselves with things fitting to be had before you come, as meal for bread, malt for drink, woolen and linen cloth, and leather for shoes, and all manner of carpenter's tools, and a good deal of iron and steel to make nails and locks for houses, and furniture for plows and carts, and glass for windows, and many other things which were better for you to think of them than to want them here.

Whilst I was writing this letter my wife brought me word that the fishers had caught sixteen hundred bass at one draught, which if they were in England were worth many a pound.

In September, Higginson sent back a fuller letter, based on his experiences during the first three months in Massachusetts. (His references to winter are misleading; he writes as if he had been at Naumkeag longer than he had.) The letter arrived by late November and was published soon after, before Winthrop's fleet left in April 1630. Though it is fuller than might be expected under the circumstances, one very important subject is only touched on: the organization of the church established at Naumkeag. A contemporary account sent by Charles Gott to Governor William Bradford of Plymouth, dated Salem, July 30, 1629, reports:

The twentieth of July it pleased God to move the heart of our governor to set it apart for a solemn day of humiliation for the choice of a pastor and teacher. The former part of the day being spent in praise and teaching, the latter part was spent about the election, which was after this manner. The persons thought on (who had been ministers in England) were demanded concerning their callings. They acknowledged there was a two-fold calling, the one an inward calling, when the Lord moved the heart of a man to take that calling upon him and fitted him with gifts for the same. The second, the outward calling, was from the people, when a company of believers are joined together in covenant to walk together in all the ways of God. Every member, being men, are to have a free voice in the choice of their officers, etc. Now we being persuaded that these two were so qualified as the Apostle speaks to Timothy, where he saith, "A bishop must be blameless, sober, apt to teach," etc., I think I may say as the eunuch said unto Philip, "What should let him from being baptized, seeing there was water, and he believed." So these two servants of God, clearing all things by their answers and being thus fitted, we saw no reason but that we might freely give our voices for their election after this trial. Their choice was after this manner: every fit member wrote in a note his name whom the Lord moved him to think was fit for a pastor, and so likewise whom they would have for a teacher. So the most voice was for Mr. Skelton to be pastor and Mr. Higginson to be teacher, and they accepting the choice, Mr. Higginson, with three or four more of the gravest members of the church, laid their hands on Mr. Skelton, using prayers therewith. This being done, then there was imposition of hands on Mr. Higginson. Then there was proceeding in elections of elders and deacons.

This letter implies that at some earlier time "a company of believers" had covenanted together, and that each of these "fit members" voted.

The creation of a church by covenant and the election and ordination of ministers by the church members, not by bishops, were innovations for these colonists, who had not, at least technically, separated themselves from the Church of England. Higginson himself had proclaimed on leaving England, according to Cotton Mather's report, that his group were not separatists. Later Massachusetts church leaders followed suit. A year later William Ames, who set forth the theoretical bases of the Bay colonists' Congregationalism, devoted two chapters of his *De Conscientia* to a justification of the seeming contradiction embodied in the Massachusetts policy, beginning new churches but contending that no separation from the Church of England was intended. (In the debates about the polity of the Church of England in the 1640s, the Bay colonists found that they were still in a position to advocate its adoption of Congregationalism, since they had not technically abandoned the church they wished to transform.)

The novelty of the Salem arrangement is and was striking. By October 1630 word had gotten back to England of what had

happened, and John Cotton, who had preached the farewell
sermon to John Winthrop's party, promptly protested to
Skelton. He found erroneous Salem's emphasis on the importance of the particular congregation, the concept that grew into
Congregationalism. Whether Salem's ways were influenced by
the separatist Congregationalism of Plymouth is a much disputed point. Discussions between Deacon Samuel Fuller of Plymouth and the Salem leaders did take place. In any case, Salem's
example was immensely influential in the founding of the
churches of the Bay Colony, though clearly many of the ministers were predisposed to accept a Congregational pattern when
they arrived.

One suspects that Higginson was aware of the controversial
nature of the church arrangement and so avoided discussing it.
As it was, his letter was widely read; three editions of the printed version appeared before the year was over. The published letter is called *New-Englands Plantation. Or, A Short and True Description of the Commodities and Discommodities of that Countrey.* The text below is from the third edition, 1630. It is a careful work of art, and it is also propaganda. While Higginson mentions New England's discommodities, he is clearly enthusiastic.
It was some time before realistic reports were sent back to England, though Thomas Dudley, in the letter on pages 66-83
below, was at least cautious.

Though Higginson celebrated the health that New England
had brought him, he himself soon became ill; he died in August
1630.

The Rev. Francis Higginson to His Friends at Leicester
September 1629

*New-Englands Plantation. Or, A Short and True Description of
the Commodities and Discommodities of that Countrey.*

Letting pass our voyage by sea, we will now begin our discourse
on the shore of New England. And because the life and welfare
of every creature here below and the commodiousness of the
country whereas such creatures live doth by the most wise ordering of God's providence depend next unto himself upon the
temperature and disposition of the four elements, earth, water,

air, and fire (for as of the mixture of all these, all sublunary things are composed, so by the more or less enjoyment of the wholesome temper and convenient use of these consisteth the only well-being both of man and beast in a more or less comfortable measure in all countries under the heavens), therefore I will endeavor to show you what New England is by the consid - eration of each of these apart, and truly endeavor by God's help to report nothing but the naked truth, and that both to tell you of the discommodities as well as of the commodities, though as the idle proverb is, "Travellers may lie by authority," and so may take too much sinful liberty that way. Yet I may say of myself as once Nehemiah did in another case: "Shall such a man as I lie?" No, verily. It becometh not a preacher of truth to be a writer of falsehood in any degree, and therefore I have been careful to report nothing of New England but what I have partly seen with my own eyes and partly heard and inquired from the mouths of very honest and religious person[s], who by living in the country a good space of time have had experience and knowledge of the state thereof and whose testimonies I do believe as myself.

First, therefore, of the earth of New England and all the appurtenances thereof. It is a land of divers and sundry sorts all about Masathulets Bay,[1] and at Charles River is as fat black earth as can be seen anywhere, and in other places you have a clay soil, in other gravel, in other sandy, as it is all about our plantation at Salem, for so our town is now named (Psalm 76.2).[2]

The form of the earth here in the superficies of it is neither too flat in the plainness, nor too high in hills, but partakes of both in a mediocrity, and fit for pasture or for plow or meadow ground, as men please to employ it. Though all the country be as it were a thick wood for the general, yet in divers places there is much ground cleared by the Indians, and especially about the plantation, and I am told that about three miles from us a man may stand on a little hilly place and see divers thousands of acres of ground as good as need to be, and not a tree in the same. It is thought here is good clay to make brick and tiles and earthen pots as needs to be. At this instant we are setting a brick kiln on work to make bricks and tiles for the building of our houses. For stone, here is plenty of slates at the Isle of Slate in Masathulets Bay, and limestone, freestone, and smoothstone, and ironstone, and marblestone also in such store that we have

1. The name, derived from the name of the Indian tribe, was variously spelled. For an especially odd spelling, see Hammond's letter, below.
2. "His [God's] abode has been established in Salem, his dwelling place in Zion." *Salem* is the ancient form of the name *Jerusalem*; it is related to the Hebrew word for *peace*.

great rocks of it and a harbor hard by.[3] Our plantation is from thence called Marble-harbor.[4]

Of minerals there hath yet been but little trial made, yet we are not without great hope of being furnished in that soil.

The fertility of the soil is to be admired at, as appeareth in the abundance of grass that groweth everywhere both very thick, very long, and very high in divers places, but it groweth very wildly with a great stalk and a broad and ranker blade, because it never had been eaten with cattle, nor mowed with a scythe, and seldom trampled on by foot. It is scarce to be believed how our kine and goats, horses, and hogs do thrive and prosper here and like well of this country.

In our plantation we have already a quart of milk for a penny, but the abundant increase of corn proves this country to be a wonderment. Thirty, forty, fifty, sixty [fold] are ordinary here. Yea, Joseph's increase in Egypt is outstripped here with us. Our planters hope to have more than a hundredfold this year, and all this while I am within compass, what will you say of two hundredfold and upwards? It is almost incredible what great gain some of our English planters have had by our Indian corn. Credible persons have assured me, and the party himself avouched the truth of it to me, that of the setting of thirteen gallons of corn he hath had increase of it fifty-two hogsheads, every hogshead holding seven bushels of London measure, and every bushel was by him sold and trusted to the Indians for so much beaver as was worth eighteen shillings, and so of this thirteen gallons of corn which was worth six shillings eight pence, he made about 327 pounds of it the year following as by reckoning will appear, where you may see how God blesseth husbandry in this land. There is not such great and beautiful ears of corn I suppose anywhere else to be found but in this country, being also of variety of colors, as red, blue, and yellow, etc., and of one corn there springeth four or five hundred. I have sent you many ears of divers colors that you might see the truth of it.

Little children here by setting of corn may earn much more than their own maintenance. They have tried our English corn at New Plymouth Plantation, so that all our several grains will grow here very well, and have a fitting soil for their nature. Our governor hath store of green peas growing in his garden as good as ever I eat in England.

This country aboundeth naturally with store of roots of great

3. Higginson's Isle of Slates is otherwise unknown; marble is likewise unknown in this area.
4. Presumably Salem Harbor is meant; the present Marblehead is four miles away.

variety and good to eat. Our turnips, parsnips, and carrots are here both bigger and sweeter than is ordinarily to be found in England. Here are also store of pumpions, cowcumbers, and other things of that nature which I know not. Also, divers excellent potherbs grow abundantly among the grass, as strawberry leaves in all places of the country, and plenty of strawberries in their time, and pennyroyal, winter savory, sorrel, brooklime, liverwort, carvel and watercresses, also leeks and onions are ordinary, and divers physical herbs. Here are also abundance of other sweet herbs delightful to the smell, whose names we know not, etc., and plenty of single damask roses very sweet, and two kinds of herbs that bear two kind of flowers very sweet, which they say are as good to make cordage or cloth as any hemp or flax we have.

Excellent vines are here up and down in the woods. Our governor hath already planted a vineyard with great hope of increase. Also mulberries, plums, raspberries, currants, chestnuts, filberts, walnuts, small nuts, hurtleberries, and haws of whitethorn near as good as our cherries in England, they grow in plenty here.

For wood there is no better in the world, I think, here being four sorts of oak differing both in the leaf, timber, and color, all excellent good. There is also good ash, elm, willow, birch, beach, sassafras, juniper, cypress, cedar, spruce, pines, and fir that will yield abundance of turpentine, pitch, tar, masts and other materials for building both of ships and houses. Also here are store of sumac trees; they are good for dying and tanning of leather. Likewise such trees yield a precious gum called wine benjamin [benzoin] that they say is excellent for perfumes. Also here be divers roots and berries wherewith the Indians dye excellent holiday colors that no rain nor washing can alter. Also we have materials to make soap ashes and saltpeter in abundance.

For beasts there are some bears, and they say some lions also, for they have been seen at Cape Ann. Also here are several sorts of deer, some whereof bring three or four young ones at once, which is not ordinary in England. Also wolves, foxes, beavers, otters, martens, great wildcats, and a great beast called a molke [moose?] as big as an ox. I have seen the skins of all these beasts since I came to this plantation excepting lions. Also here are great store of squirrels, some greater and some smaller and lesser. There are some of the lesser sort, they tell me, that by a certain skin will fly from tree to tree though they stand far distant.

New England hath water enough both salt and fresh. The greatest sea in the world, the Atlanticke Sea, runs all along the coast thereof. There are abundance of islands along the shore, some full of wood and mast to feed swine, and others clear of wood and fruitful to bear corn. Also we have store of excellent harbors for ships, as at Cape Anne and at Masathulets Bay and at Salem, and at many other places, and they are the better because for strangers there is a very difficult and dangerous passage into them, but unto such as are well acquainted with them, they are easy and safe enough. The abundance of sea fish are almost beyond believing, and sure I should scarce have believed it except I had seen it with mine own eyes. I saw great store of whales and grampus and such abundance of mackerels that it would astonish one to behold, likewise codfish abundance on the coast and in their season are plentifully taken. There is a fish called a bass, a most sweet and wholesome fish as ever I did eat. It is altogether as good as our fresh salmon, and the season of their coming was begun when we came first to New-England in June, and so continued about three months' space. Of this fish our fishers take many hundred together, which I have seen lying on the shore to my admiration. Yea, their nets ordinarily take more than they are able to haul to land, and for want of boats and men they are constrained to let a many go after they have taken them, and yet sometimes they fill two boats at a time with them. And besides bass we take plenty of skate and thornback and abundance of lobsters, that the least boy in the plantation may both catch and eat what he will of them. For my own part I was soon cloyed with them, they were so great and fat and lucious. I have seen some myself that have weighed sixteen pound, but others have had divers time so great lobsters as have weighed twenty-five pound, as they assured me. Also here is abundance of herring, turbot, sturgeon, cusks, haddocks, mullets, eels, crabs, mussels, and oysters. Besides there is probability that the country is of an excellent temper for the making of salt, for since our coming our fisherman have brought home very good salt which they found candied by the standing of the sea water and the heat of the sun upon a rock by the seashore, and in divers salt marshes that some have gone through they have found some salt in some places crushing under their feet and cleaving to their shoes.

And as for fresh water the country is full of dainty springs and some great rivers and some lesser brooks, and at Masathulets Bay [at Charlestown] they digged wells and found water at three foot deep in most places, and near Salem they have as fine, clear water as we can desire, and we may dig wells and find water where we list.

Thus we see both land and sea abound with store of blessings for the comfortable sustenance of man's life in New England.

Of the Air of New-England with the Temper and Creatures in it.

The temper of the air of New-England is one special thing that commends this place. Experience doth manifest that there is hardly a more heathful place to be found in the world that agreeth better with our English bodies. Many that have been weak and sickly in old England by coming hither have been thoroughly healed and grown healthful and strong. For here is an extraordinary clear and dry air that is of a most healing nature to all such as are of a cold, melancholy, phlegmatic, rheumatic temper of body. None can more truly speak hereof by their own experience than myself. My friends that knew me can well tell how very sickly I have been and continually in physic, being much troubled with a tormenting pain through an extraordinary weakness of my stomach and abundance of melancholic humors, but since I came hither on this voyage, I thank God I have had perfect health and [am] freed from pain and vomitings, having a stomach to digest the hardest and coarsest fare who before could not eat finest meat; and whereas my stomach could only digest and did require such drink as was both strong and stale, now I can and do oftentimes drink New-England water very well, and I that have not gone without a cap for many years together, neither durst leave off the same, have now cast away my cap and do wear none at all in the daytime, and whereas beforetime I clothed myself with double clothes and thick waistcoats to keep me warm, even in the summertime, I do now go as thin clad as any, only wearing a light stuff cassock upon my shirt and stuff breeches of one thickness without lining. Besides, I have one of my children that was formerly most lamentably handled with sore breaking out of both his hands and feet of the king's evil,[5] but since he came hither he is very well over he was, and there is hope of perfect recovery shortly, even by the very wholesomeness of the air, altering, digesting, and drying up the

5. Scrofula, which was thought to be cured by the king's touch. The belief persisted through the early eighteenth century.

cold and crude humors of the body, and therefore I think it is a wise course for all cold complexions to come to take physic in New-England, for a sup of New-England's air is better than a whole draft of old England's ale.

In the summertime in the midst of July and August, it is a good deal hotter than in old England, and in winter, January and February are much colder as they say, but the spring and autumn are of a middle temper.

Fowls of the air are plentiful here and of all sorts as we have in England, as far as I can learn, and a great many of strange fowls which we know not. Whilst I was writing these things, one of our men brought home an eagle which he had killed in the wood; they say they are good meat. Also here are many kinds of excellent hawks, both sea hawks and land hawks, and myself walking in the woods with another in company sprung a partridge so big that through the heaviness of his body could fly but a little way. They that have killed them say they are as big as our hens. Here are likewise abundance of turkeys often killed in the woods, far greater than our English turkeys, and exceeding fat, sweet, and fleshy, for here they have abundance of feeding all the year long, as strawberries; in summer all places are full of them and all manner of berries and fruits. In the wintertime I have seen flocks of pigeons and have eaten of them.[6] They do fly from tree to tree as other birds do, which our pigeons will not do in England. They are of all colors as ours are, but their wings and tails are far longer, and therefore it is likely they fly swifter to escape the terrible hawks in this country. In wintertime this country doth abound with wild geese, wild ducks, and other sea fowl, that a great part of winter the planters have eaten nothing but roast meat of divers fowls which they have killed.

Thus you have heard of the earth, water, and air of New England. Now it may be you expect something to be said of the fire proportionable to the rest of the elements.

Indeed, I think New-England may boast of this element more than of all the rest, for though it be here something cold in the winter, yet here we have plenty of fire to warm us, and that a great deal cheaper than they sell billets and faggots in London. Nay, all Europe is not able to afford to make so great fires as New-England. A poor servant here that is to possess but fifty acres of land may afford to give more wood for timber and fire

6. Presumably the passenger pigeon, described below by Dudley and by Hammond. See pp. 81, 111.

as good as the world yields than many noblemen in England can afford to do. Here is good living for those that love good fires. And although New-England have no tallow to make candles of, yet by the abundance of the fish thereof it can afford oil for lamps. Yea, our pine trees that are the most plentiful of all wood doth allow us plenty of candles, which are very useful in a house, and they are such candles as the Indians commonly use, having no other, and they are nothing else but the wood of the pine tree cloven in two little slices something thin, which are so full of the moisture of turpentine and pitch that they burn as clear as a torch. I have sent you some of them that you may see the experience of them.

Thus of New-England's commodities; now I will tell you of some discommodities that are here to be found.

First, in the summer season for these three months, June, July, and August, we are troubled much with little flies called mosquitoes, being the same they are troubled with in Lincolnshire and the Fens, and they are nothing but gnats, which except they be smoked out of their houses are troublesome in the night season.

Secondly, in the winter season for two months space the earth is commonly covered with snow, which is accompanied with sharp, biting frosts, something more sharp than is in old England, and therefore [we] are forced to make great fires.

Thirdly, this country, being very full of woods and wildernesses, doth also much abound with snakes and serpents of strange colors and huge greatness. Yea, there are some serpents called rattlesnakes that have rattles in their tails that will not fly from a man as others will but will fly upon him and sting him so mortally that he will die within a quarter of an hour after, except the party stinged have about him some of the root of an herb called snakeweed to bite on, and then he shall receive no harm, but yet seldom falls it out that any hurt is done by these. About three years since an Indian was stung to death by one of them, but we heard of none since that time.

Fourthly and lastly, here wants as yet the good company of honest Christians to bring with them horses, kine, and sheep to make use of this fruitful land. Great pity it is to see so much good ground for corn and for grass as any is under the heavens, to lie altogether unoccupied, when so many honest men and their families in old England through the populousness thereof do make very hard shift to live one by the other.

Now, thus you know what New-England is, as also with the commodities and discommodities thereof. Now I will show you a little of the inhabitants thereof and their government.

For their governors they have kings which they call *sagamores*, some greater and some lesser, according to the number of their subjects. The greatest sagamores about us cannot make above three hundred men, and other less sagamores have not above fifteen subjects and others near about us but two. Their subjects about twelve years since were swept away by a great and grievous plague that was amongst them so that there are very few left to inhabit the country.[7] The Indians are not able to make use of the one-fourth part of the land, neither have they any settled places, as towns to dwell in, nor any ground as they challenge for their own possession but change their habitation from place to place.

For their statures, they are a tall and strong-limbed people. Their colors are tawny. They go naked save only they are in part covered with beasts' skins on one of their shoulders and wear something before their privities. Their hair is generally black and cut before like our gentlewomen, and one lock longer than the rest, much like to our gentlemen, which fashion I think came from hence into England.

For their weapons, they have bows and arrows, some of them headed with bone and some with brass. I have sent you some of them for an example.

The men for the most part live idly. They do nothing but hunt and fish. Their wives set their corn and do all their other work.[8] They have little household stuff, as a kettle, and some other vessels like trays, spoons, dishes, and baskets. Their houses are very little and homely, being made with small poles pricked into the ground and so bended and fastened at the tops, and on the sides they are matted with boughs, and covered on the roof with sedge and old mats,[9] and for their beds that they take their rest on, they have a mat.

They do generally profess to like well of our coming and planting here, partly because there is abundance of ground that they cannot possess nor make use of, and partly because our being here will be a means both of relief to them when they want and also a defense from their enemies,[10] wherewith (I say) before this plantation begun they were often endangered.

7. The plague of 1616-17 killed at least a third of the Indian population of eastern New England.

8. This quality was frequently noted and condemned by early European observers. See Alden Vaughan, *New England Frontier: Puritans and Indians, 1620-1675* (Boston, 1965), p. 45.

9. Many of the early settlers built "English wigwams" after the Indian model. See George F. Dow, *Domestic Life in New England in the Seventeenth Century* (Topsfield, Mass., 1925), pp. 3-5.

10. The Abnaki or Tarrantines of Maine.

For their religion, they do worship two gods, a good god and an evil god. The good god they call *Tantum*, and their evil god, whom they fear will do them hurt, they call *Squantum*. For their dealing with us, we neither fear them nor trust them, for forty of our musketeers will drive five hundred of them out of the field. We use them kindly. They will come into our houses sometimes by half a dozen or half a score at a time when we are at victuals, but will ask or take nothing but what we give them. We purpose to learn their language as soon as we can, which will be a means to do them good.

Of the Present Condition of the Plantation, and what it is.

When we came first to Neihum-kek, we found about half a score houses and a fair house newly built for the governor. We found also abundance of corn planted by them, very good and well liking. And we brought with us about two hundred passengers and planters more, which by common consent of the old planters were all combined together into one body politic, under the same governor. There are in all of us both old and new planters about three hundred, whereof two hundred of them are settled at Nehum-kek, now called Salem, and the rest have planted themselves at Masathulets Bay, beginning to build a town there which we do call Cherton, or Charles Town. We that are settled at Salem make what haste we can to build houses, so that within a short time we shall have a fair town.

We have great ordnance, wherewith we doubt not but we shall fortify ourselves in a short time to keep out a potent adversary. But that which is our greatest comfort and means of defense above all other is that we have here the true religion and holy ordinances of Almighty God taught amongst us. Thanks be to God, we have here plenty of preaching and diligent catechizing, with strict and careful exercise and good and commendable orders to bring our people into a Christian conversation with whom we have to do withal. And thus we doubt not but God will be with us, and "if God be with us, who can be against us?"

Included with Higginson's report in its third edition was a brief letter from Thomas Graves. Unfortunately, a longer report by Graves, extant as late as 1713, has since been lost. Appointed engineer because of his experience and skill in locating minerals, working iron, making salt works, planning fortifications, and surveying, Graves was well paid: his salary was five pounds a month at a time when a master artisan made only a pound and a half, and Graves was promised other benefits if he stayed three years or longer. Soon after he arrived in America, John Endecott sent him twelve miles south, to a place just north of the Charles River soon to be called Charlestown (Thomas Walford lived there). Graves laid out a town plan and supervised the building of a large house for those who were to come over the next year. This second settlement became headquarters for Winthrop and his 1630 group. Graves seems to have returned to England after a short while, no longer than the year or two required by his contract. The edition below is based on the version in Higginson, *New Englands Plantation* (third edition, 1630).

Thomas Graves to ?
September 1629

Thus much I can affirm in general, that I never came in a more goodly country in all my life, all things considered. If it hath not at any time been manured and husbanded, yet it is very beautiful in open lands, mixed with goodly woods and again open plains, in some places five hundred acres, some places more, some less, not much troublesome for to clear for the plough to go in, no place barren but on the tops of the hills. The grass and weeds grow up to a man's face; in the lowlands and by fresh rivers abundance of grass and large meadows without any tree or shrub to hinder the scythe. I never saw [the like] except in Hungaria, unto which I always paralled this country, in all or most respects, for everything that is here either sown or planted prospereth far better than in Old-England. The increase of corn is here far beyond expectation, as I have seen here by experience in barley, the which because it is so much above your conception I will not mention. And cattle do prosper very well, and those that are bred here far greater than those with you in England. Vines do grow here, plentifully laden with the biggest grapes that ever I saw, some I have seen four inches about, so that I am bold to say of this country, as it is commonly said in Germany of Hungaria, that for cattle, corn, and wine, it excelleth. We have many more hopeful commodities here in this country, the which time will teach to make good use of. In the meantime we abound with such things which next under God do make us subsist, as fish, fowl, deer, and sundry sorts of fruits as muskmelons, watermelons, Indian pompions, Indian peas, beans, and many other odd fruits that I cannot name, all which are made good and pleasant through this main blessing of God, the healthfulness of the country which far exceedeth all parts that ever I have been in. It is observed that few or none do here fall sick, unless of the scurvy, that they bring from aboard the ship with them, whereof I have cured some of my company only by labor. Thus making an end of an imperfect description, and committing you to God, etc.

1630

Having sent the Higginson-Skelton party off, the Massachusetts Bay Company now needed a leader for the larger group that was to migrate in 1630. One of those beginning to have an interest in New England was John Winthrop. In 1629 he was at a crucial point in his life. Then forty-one, he could look back upon studies at Cambridge University and legal studies in London. He divided his time between a fairly important legal position that required extended stays in London, and his position as lord of the family manor at Groton in Suffolk. He was a serious-minded man, much devoted to the religious preoccupations identified with puritanism, especially self-examination. Looking without, he found both his personal circumstances and the world he lived in unsatisfactory. In May 1629 he wrote to his wife, "The Lord hath admonished, threatened, corrected, and astonished us, yet we grow worse and worse, so as his spirit will not always strive with us, he must give way to his fury at last. . . . I am verily persuaded, God will bring some heavy affliction upon this land, and that speedily. . . ." But he found comfort in the thought that "If the Lord seeth it will be good for us, he will provide a shelter and hiding place for us and ours. . . . "

Gradually Winthrop became involved in the plans of the Massachusetts Bay Company. He drew up a list of reasons for considering a plantation in New England, and he listed for himself "Particular considerations in the Case of J. W. ":

1. It is come to that issue as (in all probability) the welfare of the plantation depends upon his going, for divers of the chief undertakers (upon whom the rest depend) will not go without him.

2. He acknowledge[s] a satisfactory calling, outward from those of the plantation, inwardly by the inclination of his own heart to the work. . . .

3. Though his means be sufficient for a comfortable subsistence in a private condition here, yet the one half of them being disposed to his three elder sons, who are now of age, he cannot live in the same place and calling with that which remains. . . .

4. His wife and such of his children as are come to years of discretion are voluntarily disposed to the same course.

5. Most of his friends (upon the former considerations) do consent to his change.

Finally Winthrop became one of the dozen men who on August 26, 1629, committed themselves to go to New England, provided that the company authorized the transfer of the government and the charter permanently to Massachusetts. Presumably they did not wish to be governed by men unfamiliar with local conditions, a problem that had beset the Jamestown colony in its early years. This important provision was accepted by the company a few days later, and in two months Winthrop was elected governor. By March 1630, the company had issued a broadside list of "Provisions Needful for Such as Intend to Plant themselves in New England." Other publications followed the departure of the Winthrop party: *The Humble Request of his Maiesties loyall Subjects*, asking for prayers and other help; John Cotton's sermon *Gods Promise to His Plantation*; John White's *Planters Plea*, which provides a religious argument for colonization; Captain John Smith's *Advertisements for the unexperienced Planters of New England, or any where*.

In the spring some one thousand people were ready to depart for New England. Four hundred left with the so-called Winthrop fleet in early April; the entire group under Winthrop included some seven hundred. (A smaller group planned to live together in a separate location; they subsequently founded Dorchester.) Something of the steps leading to the exodus of 1630 is contained in the classic account of Thomas Dudley in his letter to the Countess of Lincoln, below.

Winthrop particularized the religious and economic considerations already cited in noting eight reasons why men might choose to leave England for New England: (1) transporting the Gospel "into those parts of the world"; (2) creation of "a refuge for many, whom he [God] means to save out of the general destruction"; (3) overpopulation in England; (4) the difficulty in making an adequate living in England; (5) the corruption of learning and religion in England; (6) the ready availability of land in America; (7) the opportunity to help "raise and support a particular church while it is in the infancy"; and (8), a more personal reason, providing an example for others who may pray for or join the plantation.

Winthrop's first communication back to England was a note

to his close friend and brother-in-law, Emmanuel Downing. Strictly a business matter, it reminds us that in addition to the letters that were sent back to England, those returning brought news as well. The bearer of the letter was a servant of the wealthy backer of the company, Thomas Goffe. The man for whom Winthrop was acting as agent, John Johnson, had come over with Winthrop.

The original letter is Massachusetts Historical Society manuscript W. I. 81.

John Winthrop to Emmanuel Downing
July 14, 1630

Brother Downing:

I pray pay to this bearer Mr. Edward Hopwood or his assignee the sum of four pounds, which is to be paid on the part of John Johnson for the passage of Wm. Timewell into England. I pray let it be paid upon sight hereof or within six days after.

So I rest.

Your loving brother,
Jo: Winthrop

Charlton[1] in N:[ew] Eng:[land]
July 14, 1630
[Endorsed] Willm Timewell bill

John Winthrop had married his third wife, Margaret Tyndale, daughter of Sir John Tyndale of Essex, in 1616. Three weeks after his arrival in New England, he wrote to her. By his first wife Winthrop had four children who were still alive when he left for America, but two sons died before the year 1630 was over, as we learn in the letter below. In addition, Margaret and John had four surviving children when he left for the new world: Stephen (1619-58) and Adam (1620-52), who came to America with their father; Deane (1623-1704), who came to America in 1635; and Samuel (1627-74), who crossed the Atlantic with his mother in 1631. Margaret was with child when Winthrop left, but Anne, born in April, died on her way to

1. A common abbreviation for Charlestown.

America with her mother. This letter, along with the earlier note to Downing, was presumably carried on the *Lyon*, the first ship to return to England in 1630. It lacks details about the new land because Winthrop assumed its bearer would provide a report. Winthrop wrote from Charlestown, where he lived in the large house that had been built in 1629 to serve as a kind of headquarters, and was later to become the town meetinghouse.

Winthrop's five letters to Margaret from Massachusetts, as well as the whole of their exchange both before and after his coming to America, are among the most appealing in all literature. Margaret Winthrop seems to have been a completely suitable partner for the great leader of the Bay Colony, who appears at his very best in his letters to her.

The original letter is Massachusetts Historical Society manuscript W. 7A. 44.

John Winthrop to Margaret Winthrop
July 16, 1630

Charleton in N[ew] England, July 16, 1630

My dear wife:

Blessed be the Lord our good God and merciful Father that yet hath preserved me in life and health to salute thee and to comfort thy long longing heart with the joyful news of my welfare and the welfare of thy beloved children.

We had a long and troublesome passage,[1] but the Lord made it safe and easy to us, and though we have met with many and great troubles (as this bearer[2] can certify thee), yet He hath pleased to uphold us and to give us hope of a happy issue.

I am so overpressed with business as I have no time for these or other mine own private occasions. I only write now that thou mayest know that yet I live and am mindful of thee in all my affairs: the larger discourse of all things thou shalt receive from my brother [Emmanuel] Downinge, which I must send by some of the last ships.[3] We have met with many sad and discomfortable things as thou shalt hear after, and the Lord's hand hath been heavy upon myself in some very near to me: my son Henry, my son Henry, ah poor child![4] Yet it grieves me much

1. About two months, the length of Higginson's voyage.
2. Arthur Tyndal, Margaret's brother.
3. The last ships of the Winthrop fleet to return to England; the discourse is not extant.
4. Henry Winthrop, aged twenty-two, had come to America with his father; he was drowned near Salem on July 2.

more for my dear daughter.[5] The Lord strengthen and comfort her heart to bear this cross patiently. I know thou wilt not be wanting to her in this distress. Yet for all these things, I praise my God I am not discouraged, nor do I see cause to repent or despair of those good days here which will make amends for all.

I shall expect thee next summer (if the Lord please), and by that time I hope to be provided for thy comfortable entertainment. My most sweet wife, be not disheartened. Trust in the Lord and thou shalt see his faithfulness. Commend me heartily to all our kind friends at Castleins, Groton hall, Mr. Leigh and his wife, my neighbor Cole and all the rest of my neighbors and their wives, both rich and poor.[6]

Remember me to them at Assington Hall and Codenham Hall, Mr. Brande, Mr. Alston, Mr. Mott, and their wives, goodman Ponde, Charles Newton, etc.[7] The good Lord be with thee and bless thee and all our children and servants.[8] Commend my love to them all. I kiss and embrace thee, my dear wife and all my children and leave thee in His arms who is able to preserve you all and to fulfill our joy in our happy meeting in His good time, Amen.

> Thy faithful husband,
> Jo: Winthrop

I shall write to my son John by London.[9]
To my very loving wife Mrs. Winthrop the elder at Groton in Suffolk near Sudburye. From N:[ew] England.

Because the ships delivering Massachusetts Bay colonists arrived almost daily and soon returned, Winthrop had another opportunity to write to his wife just a week later. Winthrop was now acutely aware of the risky position of the colonists. His letter combines instructions concerning what she must prepare for the voyage to America and the importance of every colonist's having provisions to last a full eighteen months with testimonials of his affection and lack of discouragement. The original letter is Massachusetts Historical Society manuscript W. I. 81.

5. Elizabeth (Fones) Winthrop, Henry's widow.
6. Castlins Hall was the home of the Cloptons, who were related to Winthrop through his first wife; Groton Manor was Winthrop's own estate, soon to be sold.
7. More friends and neighbors of Winthrop's. A letter to William Pond from his son is given below.
8. Unbeknownst to Winthrop, his son Forth, age twenty, had died in late November.
9. Presumably the letter below, written a week later.

John Winthrop to Margaret Winthrop
July 23, 1630

My dear wife:

I wrote to thee by my brother Arthur, but I durst write no more. Then I need not care though it miscarried, for I found him the old man still.[1] Yet I would have kept him to ease my brother but that his own desire to return and the scarcity of provisions here yielded the stronger reason to let him go. Now (my good wife) let us join in praising our merciful God, that (howsoever he hath afflicted us, both generally and particularly mine own family in His stroke upon my son Henry), yet myself and the rest of our children and family are safe and in health and that He upholds our hearts that we faint not in all our troubles but can yet wait for a good issue. And howsoever our fare be but coarse in respect of what we formerly had (peas, puddings, and fish being our ordinary diet), yet He makes it sweet and wholesome to us, that I may truly say I desire no better. Besides in this, that He begins with us thus in affliction, it is the greater argument to us of His love and of the goodness of the work which we are about, for Sathan bends his forces against us and stirs up his instruments to all kind of mischief, so that I think here are some persons who never showed so much wickedness in England as they have done here. Therefore be not discouraged (my dear wife) by anything thou shalt hear from hence, for I see no cause to repent of our coming hither, and thou seest (by our experience) that God can bring safe hither even the tenderest women and the youngest children, as He did many in divers ships, though the voyage were more tedious than formerly hath been known in this season.

Be sure to be warm clothed and to have store of fresh provisions: meal, eggs put up in salt or ground malt, butter, oatmeal, peas, and fruits, and a large, strong chest or two, well locked, to keep these provisions in, and be sure they be bestowed in the ship where they may be readily come by, which the boatswain will see to and the quartermasters, if they be rewarded beforehand. But for these things my son will take care. Be sure to have ready at sea two or three skillets of several sizes,

1. Margaret's brother was still, in Winthrop's view, untrustworthy because unregenerate. In a letter written in April from aboard ship, Winthrop comments with surprise and pleasure, "My brother Arth[ur] hath carried himself very soberly since he came on shipboard." Allyn B. Forbes et al., eds., *Winthrop Papers*, 5 vols. to date (Boston, 1929-), 2:229.

a large frying pan, a small stewing pan, and a case to boil a pudding in, store of linen for use at sea, and sack to bestow among the sailors, some drinking vessels, and pewter and other vessels, and for physic you shall need no other but a pound of Doctor Wrighte's *Electarium lenitium*,[2] and his direction to use it, a gallon of juice of scurvy grass to drink a little [of], five or six mornings, together with some saltpeter dissolved in it, and a little grated or sliced nutmeg.

Thou must be sure to bring no more company than so many as shall have full provision for a year and a half, for though the earth here be very fertile, yet there must be time and means to raise it. If we have corn enough we may live plentifully. Yet all these are but the means which God hath ordained to do us good by. Our eyes must be towards Him, who as He can withhold blessing from the strongest means, so He can give sufficient virtue to the weakest.

I am so straightened with much business as can no way satisfy myself in writing to thee. The Lord will in due time let us see the faces of each other again to our great comfort. Now the Lord in mercy bless, guide, and support thee. I kiss and embrace thee, my dear wife. I kiss and bless you all, my dear children, Forth, Mary, Dean, Sam, and the other.[3] The Lord keep you all and work His true fear in your hearts. The blessing of the Lord be upon all my servants, whom salute from me: Jo[hn] Sanford, Amy, etc., Goldston, Pease, Chote, etc., my good friends at Castlins, and all my good neighbors, Goodman Cole and his good wife, and all the rest.

Remember to come well furnished with linen, woolen, some more bedding, brass, pewter, leather bottles, drinking horns, etc. Let my son provide twelve axes of several sorts of the Braintree smith or some other prime workman, whatever they cost, and some augers great and small, and many other necessaries which I can't now think of, as candle, soap, and store of beef suet, etc. Once again, farewell, my dear wife.

> Thy faithful husband,
> Jo: Winthrop.

Charlton in N:[ew] England
July 23, 1630

2. Apparently a panacea prepared by Dr. Lawrence Wright, who had helped Winthrop during an illness in 1628.
3. The other is presumably Anne, whose name and sex her father could not yet know.

The first of several letters that Winthrop sent to his son John was written on the same day as the above letter. The younger John, who makes frequent appearances in the letters below, was born in 1606, when his father was only eighteen. In 1622 he enrolled at Trinity College, Dublin, where he studied for two years. After a period studying law, he took part in an unsuccessful effort to relieve the French Protestants who were besieged at La Rochelle. Though he had considered joining Captain John Endecott's group headed for Salem, instead he made an extended tour of the Mediterranean. On his return to London, he decided to join the Massachusetts Bay Company but agreed to act first as his father's agent by arranging the sale of Groton Manor, so that his father could be on his way to America without delay. The younger Winthrop was an able businessman and an effective leader; in time he became the governor of the Connecticut colony. The original letter is Massachusetts Historical Society manuscript W. 7A. 45.

John Winthrop to John Winthrop, Jr.
July 23, 1630

My good son:

The blessing of God All sufficient be upon thee ever. Amen.

It hath pleased the Lord to bring us hither in peace. (Blessed be His name.) For the course of our voyage and other occurants you shall understand them by a journal which I send with my letters to your uncle D[owning].[1] We had a comfortable passage, and I found that love and respect from Capt. Milburne, our master, as I may not forget. I pray (if he be returned before you come hither), take occasion to see him and remember my kind salutations to him and his wife.

It is like you shall hear (before this come to you) how the Lord hath disposed of your brother Hen[ry]. The Lord teach you and the rest by it to remember your creator in the days of your youth and to improve your time to His service, while it lasts.

The unexpected troubles and necessities which are fallen upon us will bring a great deal of business and care upon thee, but be not discouraged. It is the Lord who hath cast it upon thee, and he will uphold and deliver thee.

1. Probably a missing journal, perhaps the same as the "relation" mentioned later in this letter.

We are forced to send to Bristowe for supply of provisions by Mr. Peirce and Mr. Allerton,[2] for which I have given them a bill of exchange. You must needs take order the money may be provided presently for them, for they can't stay. If all means fail, Mr. Revell hath promised to help me with one hundred pounds.[3] He hath a bill also for money for provisions, which I took up of him here. So have divers others, which you must take care to see paid.

For the freight for the ships, you shall receive some bills from Sir Rich[ard], Mr. Johnson, and Mr. Dudlye,[4] but it is doubtful whether their monies will be ready. What you can, provide of theirs and mine. Be sure the *Talbott* be first discharged, for they will not tarry. There is much likewise to be paid to Mr. Beecher, which may stay a while.[5] There are other monies to be paid to Mr. Peirce, which must be provided. If all means fail, you may try Doctor Wright,[6] but I hope you have sold the land, and then that care is at an end. For Mr. Goffe, he hath failed exceedingly in his undertaking, so as he is in debt to many of us and hath had a great deal more of me than his due. Therefore pay him no more. I will send you the account for him and the rest whom I undertook for.[7]

I shall expect your mother and you and the rest of our company here the next spring, if God will. For directions for your passage I have written about it to your uncle D[owning] and your mother, and I am tired out with writing and much business. Commend my love and blessing to your brother Forth and your sister M[ary], my neice Matt:, and the rest of our family, and my kind salutations to all my good friends and neighbors who inquire of us, and to Mr. Nicolson.

For your sister Winthrop,[8] if she will come over, I will provide for her as mine own; if not, she hath a bond of four hundred pounds. Yet you know there is not so much due to her, for your brother had much money of me out of the four hundred pounds I had of him, besides what he ought to your sister Marye. Yet if it be to be had, I would pay it her, as it can be raised, but then she must give me a general release.

If money be brought to you or your uncle Downinge for goodman Lockwood, let Mr. Peirce be paid his bill of provisions for him and bring the rest with you.

For Forth's coming over, I leave it to my sister Painter her disposing.[9] If they come they shall be welcome. These afflictions we have met with need discourage none, for the country

2. Peirce, master of the *Lyon*, was much respected by Winthrop; Allerton, who had acted as business manager for the Plymouth colonists, was not reliable. For an attractive biography of Peirce, see George E. Littlefield, *Early Boston Booksellers, 1642-1711* (Boston, 1900), pp. 32-64.
3. John Revell, a wealthy backer, came to America with Winthrop but stayed only a few weeks.
4. Sir Richard Saltonstall, Isaac Johnson, and Thomas Dudley were probably, after Winthrop, the leading men of the colony.
5. Thomas Beecher was master of the *Talbot*, part of the Winthrop fleet.
6. Lawrence Wright, a physician, was a much-respected friend of Winthrop.
7. "Undertaking" in the sense of investing.
8. Henry's widow, Elizabeth.
9. The mother of Henry's widow, Priscilla Paynter, had been second wife to Thomas Fones, whose first wife was John Winthrop's sister.

is exceeding good, and the climate very like our own. Only people must come well provided and not too many at once. Pease may come if he will and such other as you shall think fit, but not many, and let those be good, and but few servants and those useful ones.

Take order that a copy of my relation, etc., be sent to Sir Nath[aniel] Barnardiston and my excuse of not writing to him and Sir Will[iam] Springe, with my salutations to them both, and if Sir Nath[aniel] hath put in no money, let him forbear still.

You must call to Mr. Andrewes in Bowe Lane for twenty pounds which Mr. Pincheon hath appointed for you, and you are to pay it and thirty pounds more to Mr. Rich[ard] Andrewes at the Mermaid in Cheapeside, but you must first inquire if it were lent to us, as we were promised at Hampton. It may be paid soon after Michaelmas next. There is also 208 pounds to be paid to Mr. Cradock or Mr. Woodward at his house in St. Barth[olomew] near the Exchange September 8 for which Mr. Johnson and I stand bound, but if it be not ready, I think Mr. Cradock will get it continued.[10]

Here is a barrel of meal of Bulbrooke's of Wenham. If I did not pay for it, let it be paid.

If you reckon with Mr. Wall, thus it stands. You received of him by Mr. Chamber (to whom I desire to be kindly commended)

	Ł	s.
The passage for himself, his wife, and a servant comes to	16	10
For one cow	15	2
For tunnage of his goods	11	
	42	12 s.

Demand the rest of him and certify me of it.

Hen[ry] Kingsburye hath appointed money to be paid to you by [blank].

Jo[hn] Warren hath appointed money to be paid to you by the bond he left with you. He owes besides ten pounds, besides his present provisions.

10. Matthew Cradock had preceded Winthrop as governor of the company.

Demand of Stone and Bragge of Neyland fifteen pounds. You have bond for it. Mr. Goffe's and my account stands thus:

He received of me in England at several payments	£642
More of me for my brother Downinge	107. 2 *s.*
You have paid him since by my direction from Hampton	[blank]
He is to discount for two mares and a horse (one Mr. Brande's) which died by the way	£27
He is allowed for 96 passengers at £4	£384
For twenty-four cows (ten being for my brother D[owning])	£361
For thirty-two ton of goods at £3	[blank]

I must end. The Lord God Almighty bless you and send you all hither in peace. Farewell, my dear son.

Your loving father,
Jo: Winthrop

Commend me to old Ponde and tell him both his sons are well and remember their duty to him. He must needs send his son John some more provisions, for much of that he brought was spoiled by the way. You must demand money of him. His reckoning stands thus:

His passage and goods come to	£27	
One cow	£15	
	£42	
I had of him	£10	4 *s.*
Rest due	£32	

Charlton July 23, 1630

For the country itself I can discern little difference between it and our own. We have had only two days which I have observed more hot than in England. Here is as good land as I have seen, there, but none so bad as there. Here is sweet air, fair rivers, and plenty of springs, and the water better than in Eng[land]. Here can be no want of anything to those who bring means to raise out of the earth and sea.

To my very loving son Mr. John Winthrop at Groton, Suffolk, deliver.

Winthrop wrote John, Jr., again three weeks later, but the letter provides little information about the activities that had engaged him in the interim. Extant reports that in time reached London give some indication of what Winthrop found to do. Those who had been sent to prepare houses and begin crops had neglected their responsibilities, and "so soon as Mr. Winthrop was landed, perceiving what misery was like to ensue through their idleness, he presently fell to work with his own hands and thereby so encouraged the rest that there was not an idle person then to be found in the whole plantation, and whereas the Indians said they would shortly return as fast as they came, now they admired to see in what short time they had all housed themselves and planted corn for their subsistence." Winthrop provided a good example, according to a 1632 account, by wearing "plain apparel, such as may well beseem a mean man, drinking ordinary water, . . . putting his hand to any ordinary labor with his servants. . . ." Nor did Winthrop neglect religion. He and Deputy Governor Dudley, Isaac Johnson, who was the wealthiest of the colonists, and the clergyman John Wilson created at Charlestown a church by covenant, like the one at Salem, with Wilson as the minister. But Winthrop's letter tells of more mundane affairs; it is chiefly a set of instructions. The original letter is Massachusetts Historical Society manuscript W. 7A. 46.

John Winthrop to John Winthrop, Jr.
August 14, 1630

Charlton in N:[ew] E:[ngland]
August 14, 1630

1. The *William and Thomas*, which arrived at the end of July, had been sent out with settlers by Thomas Hewson to establish a private plantation, possibly at Marblehead.
2. The relation is not extant (presumably it is the discourse referred to in the July 16 letter), and this journal may not be the famous one, *The History of New England.*

My good son:

I received your letters by Mr. Huson's ship[1] and do much rejoice and bless the Lord for the good news of all your welfares. For our condition here and our voyage hither, I wrote to you about a fortnight since by Mr. Revell, but more fully in a journal and relation[2] which I sent to your uncle Downing, yet I could [not] make any perfect relation for want of time and leisure, and I am still as much straightened as before, so as I must refer you and all my friends to my former report as it is. Withal I sent a card [chart] of our voyage at sea, which Captain Milborne drew for me. I wrote also how the Lord's hand had been very heavy upon our people in these parts and that which I conceived to be the reason why so many fell sick and so many died and what course you should take when your mother is to come hither, etc. I can now only write a word or two for direction about our affairs, and so I shall leave my blessing with you. First, for the land (if it be not already sold), you must sell it speedily, for much debt will lie upon us. For Mr. Appleton, take no money of him, for he can have no cows; there came not on shore one-half of them. I had fifteen pounds of Mrs. Sandes for a cow for her brother Goffe, but he could have none now. Ergo, if she will not have him have it at next return, let her have her money again.

Pay Mr. Goffe no more money, but require the remainder, and if he refuse to pay it, it were well his bond were put in suit. If you have money to spare, send over some more cows and goats, and bring one hundred pounds with you, or two.

The beef we had of Mr. Stretton[3] is as sweet and good as if it were but a month powdered. You shall know of other things by your mother's letters. We have powder and pieces enough but want flints and birdshot and store of chalk. But I must end. The Lord bless you and send you hither in safety. Farewell, my good son.

Your loving father,
Jo. Winthrop

To my very loving son Mr. John Winthrop at Groton, Suff[olk], deliver.

On August 23, 1630, the first meeting on American soil of the Governor and Company of the Massachusetts-Bay in New England was held. This was the monthly meeting of the governor and assistants required by the charter. Present were Governor Winthrop, Deputy Governor Thomas Dudley, Sir Richard Saltonstall, Roger Ludlow, Edward Rossiter, Increase Nowell, Thomas Sharpe, William Pynchon, and Simon Bradstreet. They provided for public support for the two ministers of the group under Saltonstall and for John Wilson, the minister of the church that Winthrop had helped found. The Salem

3. A butcher of Eastcheap.

church and the group that had already settled Dorchester also had ministers, two in Salem (including Higginson) and two in Dorchester.

Perhaps even before this meeting, the settlers of the Winthrop fleet gradually began to disperse. As Dudley's letter below explains, the group under Saltonstall settled at what became Watertown, and others settled at Roxbury, a few at Medford and Saugus. Winthrop remained at Charlestown, though by early September he must have become interested in the small peninsula (only about seven hundred acres) just to the south, which the Court of Assistants decided on September 7 to name "Boston." It had been called both Shawmut and Tramount or Trimount. Two days later, on September 9, Winthrop wrote again to his wife, telling her—and perhaps himself—that he had *not* made a mistake in choosing to come to America. His devotion to Margaret is still apparent, though he admits having neglected their agreed-upon times of spiritual communion with one another on Mondays and Fridays. The original letter is Massachusetts Historical Society manuscript W. 7A. 47.

John Winthrop to Margaret Winthrop
September 9, 1630

My dear wife:

The blessing of God all-sufficient be upon thee and all my dear ones with thee forever.

I praise the good Lord, though we see much mortality, sickness, and trouble, yet (such is His mercy) myself and children with most of my family are yet living and in health and enjoy prosperity enough, if the afflictions of our brethren did not hold under the comfort of it. The Lady Arbella is dead, and good Mr. Higginson,[1] my servant old Waters of Neyland, and many others. Thus the Lord is pleased still to humble us; yet he mixes so many mercies with His corrections as we are persuaded He will not cast us off, but in His due time will do us good, according to the measure of our afflictions. He stays but till He hath purged our corruptions and healed the hardness and error of our hearts and stripped us of our vain confidence in this arm of flesh that He may have us rely wholly upon Himself.

The French ship so long expected and given for lost is now come safe to us about a fortnight since, having been twelve

1. The Lady Arbella, Isaac Johnson's wife, died about September 1; Higginson, author of three letters above, died in August.

weeks at sea,[2] and yet her passengers (being but few) all safe and well but one, and her goats but six living of eighteen. So as now we are somewhat refreshed with such goods and provisions as she brought, though much thereof hath received damage by wet. I praise God, we have many occasions of comfort here and do hope that our days of affliction will soon have an end and that the Lord will do us more good in the end than we could have expected. That will abundantly recompense for all the trouble we have endured. Yet we may not look at great things here. It is enough that we shall have Heaven, though we should pass through Hell to it. We here enjoy God and Jesus Christ; is not this enough? What would we have more? I thank God, I like so well to be here as I do not repent my coming, and if I were to come again, I would not have altered my course, though I had foreseen all these afflictions. I never fared better in my life, never slept better, never had more content of mind, which comes merely of the Lord's good hand, for we have not the like means of these comforts here which we had in England, but the Lord is all-sufficient, blessed be His holy name. If He please, He can still uphold us in this estate. But if He shall see good to make us partakers with others in more affliction, His will be done. He is our God and may dispose of us as He sees good.

I am sorry to part with thee so soon, seeing we meet so seldom, and my much business hath made me too oft forget Mondays and Fridays. I long for the time when I may see thy sweet face again and the faces of my dear children. But I must break off and desire thee to commend me kindly to all my good friends and excuse my not writing at this time. If God please once to settle me, I shall make amends. I will name now but such as are nearest to thee: my brother and sister Gost[lin],[3] Mr. Leigh, etc., Castleins, my neighbor Cole and his good wife, with the rest of my good neighbors, tenants, and servants. The good Lord bless thee, and all our children and family. So I kiss my sweet wife and my dear children and rest.

> Thy faithful husband,
> Jo: Winthrop

I would have written to Maplestead if I had time. Thou must excuse me and remember me kindly to them all.
This is the third letter I have written to thee from n[ew] England.
September 9, 1630.

2. The *Gift* arrived August 20; it was sent by Thomas Goffe.
3. Jane Gostlin, wife of Thomas, was Winthrop's sister.

John Winthrop

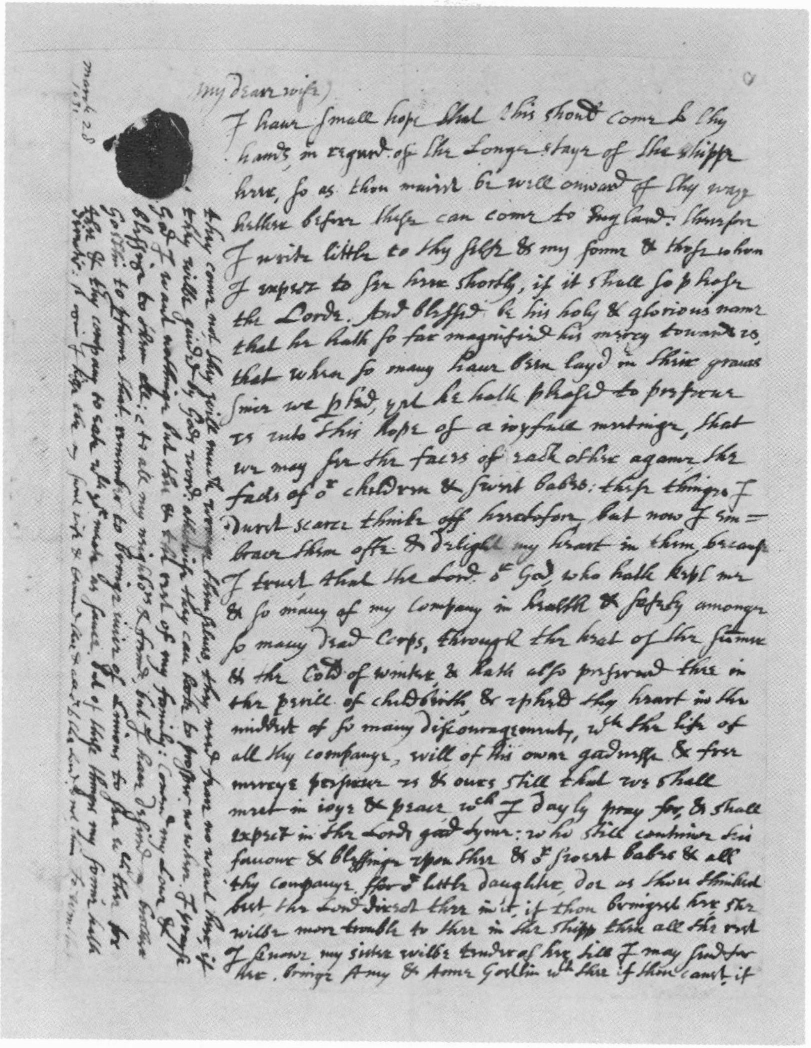
my dear wife)
I have small hope that this should come to thy
hands, in regard of the longe stay of the shippe
here, so as thou mayst be well onward of thy waye
hither before these can come to England: therefore
I write little to thy selfe & my sonne & those whom
I expect to see here shortly, if it shall so please
the Lorde. And blessed be his holy & glorious name
that he hath so far magnified his mercy towards us,
that when so many have been layd in their graves
since we parted, yet he hath pleased to preserve
us unto this hope of a ioyfull meetinge, that
we may see the faces of each other againe the
faces of our children & sweet babes: these thinges I
durst scarce thinke off heretofore but now I embrace them ofte & delight my heart in them, because
I trust that the Lord our God, who hath kept me
& so many of my company in health & safety amonge
so many dead Corps, through the heat of the summer
& the cold of winter, & hath also preserved thee in
the perill of childbirth, & upheld thy heart in the
middest of so many discouragements, with the life of
all thy companye, will of his owne goodnesse & free
mercye preserve us & ours still that we shall
meet in ioye & peace which I dayly pray for, & shall
expect in the Lords good tyme: who still continue his
favour & blessinge upon thee & our sweet babes & all
thy companye. ffor our little daughter, doe as thou thinkest
but the Lord direct thee in it, if thou bringest her she
will be more trouble to thee in the shipp than all the rest
I knowe my sister will be tender of her till I may send for
her. bringe Amy & Anne Gostlin with thee if thou canst. if

John Winthrop to Margaret Winthrop, March 28, 1634

On the same day Winthrop wrote again, mostly on business, to his son John. The letter shows clearly what a broad knowledge Winthrop had to have to serve as leader of the colony. The original letter is Massachusetts Historical Society manuscript W. 7A. 48.

John Winthrop to John Winthrop, Jr.
September 9, 1630

My good son:

The good Lord bless you ever.

I have written to your mother and to your uncle Downinge at large of all things here, to which I must refer you in regard of my much business and little leisure here.

I shall expect your mother and you and the rest of my company here next spring (if God will). I pray, take order (if it be possible) to make even reckonings with all before you come over and get a good ship and forty hogsheads of meal at least, well cleansed from the bran and laid abroad three or four days before it be packed, peas and oatmeal well dried as much as you can, good store of dry Suffolk cheese, brought loose or packed in very dry malt, butter and tried suet, sugar and fruit, pepper and ginger, store of coarse rugs both to use and sell, a hogshead of wine vinegar and another of verjuice, both in good cask and iron-bound. We have lost much by bad cask. Bestow everything in even hogsheads if you can, for it will save much in the charge of freight. Bring some good oil, pitch, and tar, and a good piece of an old cable to make oakum, for that which was sent is much lost. Some more cows would be brought, especially two new milch, which must be well mealed and milked by the way, and some goats, [and] especially sheep (if they can be had). Bring some store of garlic and onions, and conserve of red roses, alum and aloes, oiled skins, both calf and sheep, and some worsted ribbing of several sizes.

This is the third letter I have written to you from here. Commend me to all our friends, my love and blessing to your brother and sisters, your sister Winthrop, and cousin Matt,[1] my love and service to Mr. Gurdon and his wife, salutations to Mr. Jacie, Mr. Chamber, and the rest of the good ministers, Mr. Mott, and Mr. Brand. I laid out fifteen pounds to Mr. Goffe

1. Martha Fones, Winthrop's ward, had been engaged to marry John Winthrop, Jr., since February 1630. They were married in February 1631.

for a cow for his son. Commend me to all my good neighbors, Mr. Jarrold, William Ponde, and the rest. Those who were to have cows delivered here and failed must have their money again, my cousin [blank] of Rattlesden, twenty pounds. I can think of no other, but Mrs. Sandes fifteen pounds. Commend me to her, and if you see them at Graces, remember me to them. The Lord bless you. Farewell.

Your loving father,
Jo: Winthrop

September 9, 1630

On October 19, 1630, the first "General Court" was held in the Massachusetts Bay Colony. According to the charter, this court was to make laws for the plantation; indeed, according to the records, it was "for establishing of the government." Though the names of only the governor, deputy governor, and assistants are recorded, the provisions for government that were adopted were "fully assented unto by the general vote of the people, and erection of hands." This statement seems to indicate that many more than the assistants were permitted to vote. What was adopted was a provision giving freemen "the power of choosing assistants when they are to be chosen, and the assistants from amongst themselves to choose a governor and deputy governor, who with the assistants shall have the power of making laws and choosing officers to execute the same." The freemen were conceived by the charter as members of the company, and the present members were empowered to select additional members. What Winthrop and the assistants agreed to do was to permit all able-bodied men of the colony, except servants, to have a role in the government, to have the power to elect the legislative body, to become—in effect—citizens. And the records for the same date of October 19 list the names of 109 men who "desire to be made freemen." Seven months later, on May 18, 1631, 116 took the oath admitting them to freeman status.

Winthrop's letters do not tell of his move to Boston, made presumably in September. Winthrop may have been attracted to Boston by his friend Isaac Johnson, the prosperous co-

founder of the church covenanted at Charlestown. Johnson was
an old friend of the Reverend William Blackstone, who had lived
alone at Boston for several years. The advantage that Boston
offered was Blackstone's "excellent spring" of water; Charlestown's was less good. Johnson lived only until September 30;
his loss was a particularly serious one to the colonists, for he
was a much-admired leader. Communications between Charlestown and Boston remained close, with a ferry soon established.
Church services were held at Boston, and the remaining residents of Charlestown consequently had to cross over to attend.
Winthrop wrote from Boston to his wife at the end of
November. His tale was a sad one. The original letter is
Massachusetts Historical Society manuscript W. 7A. 49.

John Winthrop to Margaret Winthrop
November 29, 1630

My sweet wife:

The blessing of the Almighty be upon thee and thine forever.
There is a ship arrived at Plimmouth, some thirty miles from
us, which came from London the tenth of August and was
twelve weeks at sea in such tempests as she spent all her masts.[1]
Yet of sixty passengers she lost but one; all the rest (through
the Lord's great mercy) are safe and in health. Edy of Boxted,
who came in her,[2] told me a fortnight since that he had many
letters in the ship for me, but I hear not yet of them, which
makes me now (having opportunity to send to Plymouth) to
write these few lines to thee lest the ship should be gone before
I have received my letters and can return answer to them. Thou
shalt understand by this how it is with us since I wrote last (for
this [is] the third or fourth letter I have written to thee since I
came hither), that thou mayest see the goodness of the Lord
towards me, that when so many have died and many yet lan-
guish, myself and my children are yet living and in health. Yet
I have lost twelve of my family, viz., Walters and his wife and
two of his children, Mr. Gager and his man,[3] Smith of Buxall
and his wife and two children, the wife of Taylor of Haverill
and their child; my son H[enry] makes the twelve, and besides
many other of less note as Jeff[rey] Ruggles of Sudbury and
divers others of that town (about twenty), and one of L. Kedby

1. The *Handmaid* ar-
rived on October 29.
2. John Eddy lived in
Watertown till his death
at age ninety in 1684.
3. William Gager was
elected deacon of the
Boston-Charlestown
church at the election of
officers in late August; he
died less than a month
later.

his sons. The Lord hath stripped us of some principal persons; Mr. Johnson and his Lady, Mr. Rossiter, Mrs. Phillips, and others unknown to thee.[4] We conceive that this disease grew from ill diet at sea and proved infectious. I write not this to discourage thee but to warn thee and others to provide well for the sea, and, by God's help, the passage will be safe and easy, how long soever. Be careful (I entreat thee) to observe the directions in my former letters, and I trust that, that God, who hath so graciously preserved and blessed us hitherto, will bring us to see the faces of each other with abundance of joy. My dear wife, we are here in a paradise. Though we have not beef and mutton, etc., yet (God be praised) we want them not; our Indian corn answers for all. Yet here is fowl and fish in great plenty.

I will here break off, because I hope to receive letters from thee soon, and to have opportunity of writing more largely. I will say nothing of my love to thee and of my longing desires towards thee; thou knowest my heart. Neither can I mention salutations to my good friends other than in general. In my next I hope to supply all. Now the Lord our good God be with thee and all my children and company with thee. Grace and peace be with you all. So I kiss my sweet wife and all my dear children and bless you in the Lord. Farewell.

> Thy faithful husband,
> Jo: Winthrop

Boston in Mattachusets
November 29, 1630
Thou must excuse my not writing to my son Jo[hn] and others of my friends at this time, for I defer it till I receive my letters. [In another hand] To Mar[garet] Win[throp] the elder at Groton deliver.

4. Edward Rossiter, one of the West Country people who settled at Dorchester, was an assistant of the Massachusetts Bay Company; Mrs. Phillips's husband was minister of the Watertown church.

1631

No letters were written during the winter of 1630–31, for there was no opportunity for letters to be transported back to England between the end of November and the end of March, when the *Lyon*, which had arrived in Massachusetts in mid-February, returned. The winter was a very difficult one. The early records of Charlestown provide a picture of what life was like: "... as the winter came on, provisions began to be very scarce ... and people were necessitated to live upon clams, and mussels, and ground-nuts, and acorns, and these got with much difficulty, in the winter time. Upon which the people were very much tired and discouraged, especially when they hear that the governor himself had the last batch of bread in the oven." More information about that dreadful winter comes from the letters that follow.

Five letters that crossed on the *Lyon* (and the draft of another) have survived, a very remarkable number, and in them the experiences of the new settlers in attempting to survive are vividly described. Perhaps the most surprising survival is from a man named Pond, the son of William Pond, a seemingly illiterate workman on Winthrop's English estate; his wife Judith had been a servant to Winthrop's father. The identity of the letter writer cannot be precisely determined, since the letter is unsigned and there were two brothers in Massachusetts. Whichever he was, he was in his thirties when he came to America. Though obviously unaccustomed to writing—his handwriting is quite difficult to decipher—he tried to write a letter to his father. His letter contains so much information that it was probably given to John Winthrop, Jr., who brought it back to America with him. As a result, it survives. No letter gives a better sense of what it was like for an Englishman to arrive in the new land. Pond's naïveté, his readiness to compare his American experiences with his English memories, and his frankness in explaining personal hardships make his letter very revealing. The original letter is Massachusetts Historical Society manuscript W. I. 84.

John [?] Pond to William Pond
March 15, 1630/1

Most loving and kind Father and Mother:

My humble duty remembered unto you, trusting in God you are in good health, and I pray, remember my love unto my brother Joseife, and thank him for his kindness that I found at his hand at London, which was not the value of a farthing. I know, loving Father, and do confess that I was an undutiful child unto you when I lived with you and by you, for the which I am much sorrowful and grieved for it, trusting in God that He will so guide me that I will never offend you so any more, and I trust in God that you will forgive me for it, and my writing unto you is to let you understand what a country this new Eingland is where we live.

Here are but few eingeines [Indians], and a great sort of them died this winter. It was thought it was of the plague. They are a crafty people and they will cozen and cheat, and they are a subtle people, and whereas we did expect great store of beaver, here is little or none to be had, and their Sackemor John weigheth it,[1] and many of us truck with them and it layeth us many times in eight shillings a pound. They are proper men and clean-jointed men, and many of them go naked with a skin about their loins, but some of them get eingellische menes [Englishmen's] parell [apparel].

And the country is very rocky and hilly and some champion [open] ground, and the soil is very fleet [shallow], and here is some good ground and marsh ground, but here is no Michaelmas [autumnal] spring. Cattle thrive well here, but they give small store of milk. The best cattle for profit is swines, and a good swine is here at five pounds price and a goat is worth three pounds, a gardene [garden?] goat. Here is timber good store and acorns good store, and here is good store of fish, if we had boats to go eight or ten leagues to sea to fish in. Here are good store of wild fowl, but they are hard to come by. It is harder to get a shot than it is in ould eingland. And people here are subject to disease, for here have died of the scurvy and of the burning fever two hundred and odd, besides many layeth lame, and all Sudberey men are dead but three and the women and some children. And provisions are here at a wonderful rate.

1. Sagamore John, an Indian chief, lived in what is now Malden.

Wheat meal is fourteen shillings a bushel and peas ten shillings and malt ten shillings and eindey seid [Indian seed] wheat is fifteen shillings and their other wheat is ten shillings, butter twelve pence a pound, and cheese is eight pence a pound, and all kinds of spices very dear and almost none to be got, and if this ship had not come when it did, we had been put to a wonderful straight, but thanks be to God for sending of it in.[2] I received from the ship a hogshead of meal, and the governor telleth me of a hundredweight of cheese, the which I have received part of it. I humbly thank you for it. I did expect two cows, the which I had none nor I do not earnestly desire that you should send me any because the country is not so as we did expect it. Therefore, loving Father, I would entreat you that you would send me a firkin of butter and a hogshead of malt unground, for we drink nothing but water, and a coarse cloth of four-pound price, so it be thick. And for the freight, if you of your love will send them, I will pay the freight, for here is nothing to be got without we had commodities to go into the east parts amongst the eingeines [Indians] to truck, for here where we live is no beaver, and here is no cloth to be had to make no apparel, and shoes are at five shillings a pair for me, and that cloth that is worth two shillings eight pence a yard is worth here five shillings. So I pray, father, send me four or five yards of cloth to make us some apparel, and, loving Father, though I be far distant from you, yet I pray you remember me as your child, and we do not know how long we may subsist, for we cannot live here without provisions from ould eingland. Therefore, I pray, do not put away your shopstuff, for I think that in the end if I live it must be my living, for we do not know how long this plantation will stand, for some of the merchants that did uphold it have turned off their men and have given it over. Besides, God hath taken away the chiefest stud in the land, Mr. Johnson and the lady Arabella his wife, which was the chiefest man of estate in the land and one that would have done most good.

Here came over twenty-five passengers and there come back again four score and odd persons and as many more would have come if they had wherewithal to bring them home, for here are many that came over the last year, which was worth two hundred pounds afore they came out of ould eingland that between this and Michaelmas will be hardly worth thirty

2. Peirce's ship *Lyon.* The prices cited are three to fifty times the usual price in England. See James E. Thorald Rogers, *A History of Agriculture and Prices in England,* 8 vols. (Oxford, 1866-1902), vol. 6. But English prices were also very high that year.

pounds, so here we may live if we have supplies every year from ould eingland; otherwise we cannot subsist. I may, as I will work hard, set an ackorne [acre] of eindey [Indian] wheat and if we do not set it with fish and that will cost twenty shillings, and if we set it without fish they shall have but a poor crop.

So, Father, I pray consider of my cause, for here will be but a very poor being and no being without, loving Father, your help with provisions from ould eingland. I had thought to have came home in this ship, for my provisions were almost all spent, but that I humbly thank you for your great love and kindness in sending me some provisions, or else I should and mine have been half famished, but now I will, if it please God that I have my health, I will plant what corn I can, and if provisions be no cheaper between this and Michaelmas and that I do not hear from you what I was best to do, I purpose to come home at Michaelmas.

My wife remembers her humble duty unto you and to my mother and my love to my brother Joseife and to Sarey myler. Thus I leave you to the protection of almighty God.

from Walltur Toune in new eingland   [no signature]
the 15 of March 1630[/1]

We were wonderful sick as we came at sea with the smallpox. No man thought that I and my little child would have lived, and my boy is lame and my girl too, and there died in the ship that I came in fourteen persons. To my loving father William Ponde at Etherston[3] in Suffolcke give these.

Much the fullest account of the early days of the colony is that written by Thomas Dudley between March 12 and March 28, 1631. Born at Northampton in 1576, Dudley was a man of broad experience. He had served as page to the Earl of Northampton, clerk to a judge, and military officer. After becoming a puritan he served as steward to the young Earl of Lincoln, who had studied at Queen's College, Cambridge, with the puritan John Preston and his tutor. The earl's family was much identified with puritanism and the Bay Company; the earl's sisters included the Lady Arbella, wife of Isaac Johnson,

3. Edwardston, near Groton.

both of whom migrated with the Winthrop fleet, and the Lady Susan, whose husband, John Humphry, had been treasurer of the Dorchester Company in 1623. (The Humphrys migrated in 1634.)

Dudley was deputy governor when he wrote his letter, an office he held for thirteen years; he also served as governor for four years. His children included Anne, wife of Simon Bradstreet and a poet of distinction, and Joseph, who served as governor for a time in the 1680s and also in the early 1700s. Among the most notable if not the most agreeable leaders of the colony, he lived on until 1653, when he was seventy-six.

Dudley's letter was first printed at Boston in 1696 by Joshua Scottow in *Massachusetts, Or the First Planters of New England.* Below is the text as it appears in John Farmer's version, published in the *Collections* of the New Hampshire Historical Society in 1834. Farmer located a manuscript in an early seventeenth-century hand, now no longer extant. The prefatory epistle and the first paragraph of the text below are from Thomas Hutchinson's edition, in his *Original Papers*, since the Farmer manuscript lacked these portions. Dudley addressed his letter to Bridget, Countess of Lincoln; she was the daughter of Lord Say and Sele, another puritan nobleman, who considered coming to America and supported plantations in Connecticut and New Hampshire.

The letter is a strange one. An attempt at a complete and self-contained report, it provides much valuable information not reported elsewhere, but it also includes some misinformation that is hard to account for. Its picture of the hardships of the 1630 settlers is probably its most valuable feature.

Thomas Dudley to the Lady Bridget, Countess of Lincoln
March 12 and 28, 1630/1

To the Right Honorable my very good lady, the Lady Bridget, Countess of Lincoln,

Madam:

Your letters (which are not common nor cheap) following me hither into New England and bringing with them renewed testimonies of the accustomed favors you honored me with in the old have drawn from me this narrative retribution, which (in respect of your proper interest in some persons of great note amongst us) was the thankfullest present I had to send over the seas. Therefore I humbly entreat your honor this be accepted as payment from him who neither hath nor is any more than

> Your honor's old thankful servant,
> Thomas Dudley

Boston in New England
March 12, 1630[1]

For the satisfaction of your honor and some friends and for the use of such as shall hereafter intend to increase our plantation in New England, I have in the throng of domestic, and not altogether free from public, business, thought fit to commit to memory our present condition and what hath befallen us since our arrival here, which I will do shortly, after my usual manner, and must do rudely, having yet no table nor other room to write in than by the fireside upon my knee in this sharp winter, to which my family must have leave to resort, though they break good manners and make me sometimes forget what I would say, and say what I would not.

. . .[1] Sachem in New England whom I saw the last summer. Upon the river of Naponset,[2] near to the Mattachusetts fields,[3] dwelleth Chicka Talbot, who hath between fifty and sixty subjects. This man least favoreth the English of any sagamore (for so are the kings with us called, as they are sachems southwards) we are acquainted with, by reason of the old quarrel between him and those of Plymouth, wherein he lost seven of his best men, yet he lodged one night the last winter at my house in friendly manner. About seventy or eighty miles westward from these are seated the Nipnett men,[4] whose sagamore we know not, but we hear their number exceed any but the Pecoates[5] and the Narragansets,[6] and they are the only people we yet hear of in the inland country. Upon the river of Mistick is seated Sagamore John, and upon the river Sawgus, Sagamore James, his brother, both so named by the English. The elder brother John is a handsome young [one line missing] conversant with us, affecting English apparel and houses and speaking well of our God. His brother James is of a far worse disposition, yet repaireth often to us. Both these brothers command not

1. The Farmer manuscript begins here.
2. North of the present Quincy and Milton.
3. In the present Quincy.
4. A weak tribe inhabiting central Massachusetts.
5. The Pequots, a warlike tribe that lived in eastern Connecticut, were largely destroyed in the war of 1637.
6. They lived in Rhode Island and were not hurt by the 1616 plague that reduced most of the Indian populations.

above thirty or forty men, for aught I can learn. Near to Salem dwelleth two or three families subject to the sagamore of Agawam, whose name he told me, but I have forgotten it.[7] This sagamore hath but few subjects and them and himself tributary to Sagamore James, having been before the last year (in James his minority) tributary to Chicka Talbott. Upon the river Merimack is seated Sagamore Passaconaway, having under his command four or five hundred men, being esteemed by his countrymen a false fellow and by us a witch. For any more northerly I know not, but leave it to after relations. Having thus briefly and disorderly, especially in my description of the bays and rivers, set down what is come to hand touching the [one line missing].

Now concerning the English that are planted here, I find that about the year 1620 certain English set out from Leyden, in Holland, intending their course for Hudson's River,[8] the mouth whereof lyeth south of the river of the Pecoates but ariseth, as I am informed, northwards in about forty-three degrees and so a good part of it within the compass of our patent. These, being much weather-beaten and wearied with seeking the river, after a most tedious voyage arrived at length in a small bay, lying northeast from Cape Cod,[9] where, landing about the month of December by the favor of a calm winter such as was never seen here since, began to build their dwellings in that place, which now is called New Plymouth, where after much sickness, famine, poverty, and great mortality (through all which God by an unwonted Providence carried them) they are now grown up to a people healthful, wealthy, politic, and religious. Such things doth the Lord for those that wait for His mercies. These of Plymouth came with patents from King James and have since obtained others from our sovereign King Charles, having a governor and council of their own.[10] There was about the same time one Mr. Wesen,[11] an English merchant, who sent divers men to plant and trade who sat down by the river Wesaguscus, but these, not coming for so good ends as those of Plymouth, sped not so well, for the most of them dying and languishing away, they who survived were rescued by those of Plymouth out of the hands of Chicka Talbott and his Indians, who oppressed these weak English and intended to have destroyed them and the Plymoutheans also, as is set down in a tract written by Mr. Winslow of

7. It was Masconnomo. John's Indian name was Wonohaquaham; he ruled an area encompassing the present Malden, Everett, Revere, and Chelsea. James, or Monowompate, ruled Saugus, Lynn, and Marblehead. Both brothers and most of their people died of smallpox in 1633.
8. See Samuel Eliot Morison, "The *Mayflower's* Destination and the Pilgrim Fathers' Patents," *Publications* of the Colonial Society of Massachusetts 38 (1946-51): 387-413. Morison concludes that the Pilgrims were planning to settle in the jurisdiction of the Virginia Company in the Hudson River area.
9. Plymouth, of course, is to the west of Cape Cod.
10. The first patent was from the Virginia Company; the second was from the Council for New England, Sir Ferdinando Gorges' group.
11. Thomas Weston commanded the settlement at Weymouth in 1622.

12. Winslow's *Good News from New-England* (1624).
13. Little is known of Wollaston; Bradford mentions him briefly. Thomas Morton and others remained at Mount Wollaston.
14. Especially guilty was Thomas Morton, until the men of Plymouth put a stop to his activities.
15. The Lincolnshire group included Dudley, Richard Bellingham, John Leverett, William Coddington, Atherton Hough, and John Cotton.
16. The London group included Winthrop, Isaac Johnson, Matthew Cradock, Thomas Goffe, and Sir Richard Saltonstall; the West Countrymen included John Humphry, John Endecott, and Simon Whetcomb. For a discussion of Cradock, first governor of the Massachusetts Bay Company, see Valerie Pearl, *London and the Outbreak of the Puritan Revolution* (Oxford, 1961), pp. 185-87.
17. New style 1629.
18. Dudley's chronology is not wholly accurate. The Lincolnshire and London men joined with the Westerners after Endecott had left for America.
19. The *Arbella*, the *Jewell*, the *Talbot*, and the *Ambrose* were the four; the eight were the *Mayflower*, the *Whale*, the *Hopewell*, the *William and Francis*, the *Trial*, the *Charles*, the *Success*, and the *Gift*; the two early

Plymouth.[12] Also since, one Captain Wollastone with some thirty with him came near to the same place and built on a hill, which he named Mount Wollaston, but being not supplied with renewed provisions, they vanished away as the former did.[13] Also divers merchants of Bristow and some other places have yearly for these eight years or thereabouts sent ships hither at the fishing times to trade for beaver, where their factors dishonestly for their gains have furnished the Indians with guns, swords, powder, and shot. [14]

Touching the plantation which we here have begun, it fell out thus. About the year 1627 some friends, being together in Lincolnshire,[15] fell into some discourse about New England and the planting of the gospel there, and after some deliberation we imparted our reasons by letters and messages to some in London and the West Country,[16] where it was likewise deliberately thought upon, and at length with often negotiation so ripened that in the year 1628[17] we procured a patent from his majesty for our planting between the Matachusets Bay and Charles River on the south and the river of Merimack on the north, and three miles on either side of those rivers and bay, as also for the government of those who did or should inhabit within that compass, and the same year we sent Mr. John Endicott and some with him to begin a plantation[18] and to strengthen such as he should find there, which we sent hither from Dorcester and some places adjoining, from whom the same year receiving hopeful news, the next year, 1629, we sent divers ships over with about three hundred people and some cows, goats, and horses, many of which arrived safely. These by their too large commendations of the country and the commodities thereof invited us so strongly to go on that Mr. Wenthropp of Suffolke (who was well known in his own country and well approved here for his piety, liberality, wisdom, and gravity) coming in to us, we came to such resolution that in April 1630 we set sail from old England with four good ships. And in May following, eight more followed, two having gone before in February and March and two more following in June and August, besides another set out by a private merchant.[19] These seventeen ships arrived all safe in New England for the increase of the plantation here this year 1630, but made a long, a troublesome and costly voyage, being all windbound long in England and hindered with contrary winds after they set sail, and so scattered with mists and tempests that few of them arrived together. Our four ships which set out in April arrived here in June and July, where we found the colony in a sad and unexpected condition, above eighty of them being dead the winter before, and many of those alive weak and sick. All the corn and bread amongst them all [were] hardly sufficient to feed upon a fortnight, insomuch that the remainder of 180 servants we had the two years before sent over, coming to us for victuals to sustain them we found ourselves wholly unable to feed them by reason that the provisions shipped for them were taken out of the ship they were put in, and they who were trusted to ship them in another failed us and left them behind, whereupon necessity enforced us to our extreme loss to give them all liberty, who had cost us about 16 or 20 pounds a person, furnishing and sending over.

But bearing these things as we might, we began to consult of the place of our sitting down, for Salem, where we landed, pleased us not.[20] And to that purpose some were sent to the Bay[21] to search up the rivers for a convenient place, who upon their return reported to have found a good place upon Mistick [River], but some other of us seconding these to approve or dislike of their judgment, we found a place [that] liked us better, three leagues up Charles River,[22] and thereupon unshipped our goods into other vessels and with much cost and labor brought them in July to Charlestowne, but there receiving advertisements by some of the late arrived ships from London and Amsterdam of some French preparations against us (many of our people brought with us being sick of fevers and the scurvy, and we thereby unable to carry up our ordnance and baggage so far) we were forced to change counsel and for our present shelter to plant dispersedly, some at Charles Towne, which standeth on the north side of the mouth of Charles River; some on the south side thereof, which place we named Boston (as we intended to have done the place we first resolved on);[23] some of us upon Mistick, which we named Meadford; some of us westwards on Charles River, four miles from Charles Towne, which place we named Watertowne;[24] others of us two miles from Boston in a place we named Rocksbury;[25] others upon the river of Sawgus between Salem and Charles Towne;[26] and the western men four miles south from Boston at a place we named Dorcester.[27] This dispersion troubled some of us, but

departures were the *Lyon* and the *Mary and John*.

20. The original plan seems to have been for all except the West Country group to settle together. See Darrett B. Rutman, *Winthrop's Boston: A Portrait of a Puritan Town, 1630-1649* (Chapel Hill, N.C., 1965), pp. 24-40 and 280-83.

21. "The Bay" refers to Boston Harbor. The exploring party included Winthrop. See Winthrop, *The History of New England*, ed. James Savage, 2 vols. (Boston, 1853), 1:32.

22. At Newtown, later Cambridge.

23. A large group was expected from Boston, Lincolnshire. Two families went over in the Winthrop fleet, including William Coddington, a founder of Boston. John Cotton, the puritan minister of old Boston, did not come until 1633.

24. The group was led by Sir Richard Saltonstall and the Reverend George Phillips. Phillips and the Reverend John Wilson were the only clergymen to come in 1630, except for the two ministers of the separate West Country, Dorchester group.

25. This group was led by the wealthy William Pincheon or Pynchon. In 1636 he founded Springfield.

26. This group founded what became Lynn.

27. This group was led by Roger Ludlow, Endecott's brother-in-law. In 1636 he founded Windsor, Connecticut. Others in this group in 1630 were the ministers John Maverick and John Warham.

28. Settlement had been made on this river between Maine and New Hampshire as early as 1623.

29. John Revell never returned; William Vassall returned for a year in 1635; Francis Bright, who had come with Higginson and Skelton, may have been opposed to the church practices established in the Bay Colony. The assistants, according to the charter, were to be elected to serve as an executive council; later by a general vote of the people they became a legislative assembly, which served also to elect the governor and the deputy governor. See Morgan, *Puritan Dilema*, pp. 89-92.

30. The first was on July 30. On this day was founded at Charlestown what was to become the first church of Boston. John Wilson was ordained teacher, Increase Nowell ruling elder, and William Aspinwall deacon. Winthrop noted in his journal, "We used imposition of hands, but with this protestation by all, that it was only a sign of election and confirmation, not of any intent that Mr. Wilson

help it we could not, wanting ability to remove to any place fit to build a town upon, and the time too short to deliberate any longer, lest the winter should surprise us before we had builded our houses. The best counsel we could find out was to build a fort to retire to, in some convenient place, if an enemy pressed thereunto, after we should have fortified ourselves against the injuries of wet and cold. So ceasing to consult further for that time, they who had health to labor fell to building, wherein many were interrupted with sickness and many died weekly, yea almost daily; amongst whom were Mrs. Pinchon, Mrs. Coddington, Mrs. Philips, and Mrs. Alcock, a sister of Mr. Hooker's, insomuch that the ships being now upon their return, some for England, some for Ireland, there was, as I take it, not much less than an hundred (some think many more), partly out of dislike of our government, which restrained and punished their excesses, and partly through fear of famine, not seeing other means than by their labor to feed themselves, which returned back again. And glad were we so to be rid of them. Others also afterwards hearing of men of their own disposition, which were planted at Pascataway, [28] went from us to them, whereby though our numbers were lessened, yet we accounted ourselves nothing weakened by their removal. Before the departure of the ships, we contracted with Mr. Peirce, master of the *Lion* of Bristow, to return to us with all speed with fresh supplies of victuals, and gave him directions accordingly.

With this ship returned Mr. Revil, one of the five undertakers here for the joint stock of the company, and Mr. Vassall, one of the assistants, and his family, and also Mr. Bright, a minister, sent hither the year before. [29] The ships being gone, victuals wasting, and mortality increasing, we held divers fasts in our several congregations, [30] but the Lord would not yet be deprecated, for about the beginning of September died Mr. Gager, a right godly man, a skilful chirurgeon, and one of the deacons of our congregation, and Mr. Higginson, one of the ministers of Salem, a zealous and a profitable preacher, this of a consumption, that of a fever, and on the thirtieth of September died Mr. Johnson, another of the five undertakers (the Lady Arrabella, his wife, being dead a month before). This gentleman was a prime man amongst us, having the best estate of any, zealous for religion and greatest furtherer of this plantation. He made a most godly end, dying willingly, professing his life better spent in promoting this plantation than it would have been any other way. He left to us a loss greater than the most conceived.

Within a month after, died Mr. Rossiter, another of our assistants, a godly man and of a good estate, which still weakened us more, so that there now were left of the five undertakers but the governor, Sir Richard Saltonstall, and myself, and seven other of the assistants. [31] And of the people who came over with us, from the time of their setting sail from England in April 1630 until December following, there died by estimation about two hundred at the least. So low hath the Lord brought us! Well, yet they who survived were not discouraged, but bearing God's corrections with humility and trusting in his mercies, and considering how after a greater ebb he had raised up our neighbors at Plymouth, we began again in December to consult about a fit place to build a town upon, leaving all thoughts of a fort because upon any invasion we were necessarily to lose our houses when we should retire thereunto, so after divers meetings at Boston, Roxbury, and Waterton, on the twenty-eight day of December, we grew to this resolution: to bind all the assistants (Mr. Endicott and Mr. Sharpe excepted, which last purposeth to return by the next ships into England) to build houses at a place a mile east from Waterton, near Charles River, the next spring and to winter there the next year, that so by our examples and by removing the ordnance and munition thither, all who were able might be drawn thither and such as shall come to us hereafter to their advantage be compelled so to do, and so if God would, a fortified town might there grow up, the place fitting reasonably well thereto. [32]

I should before have mentioned how both the English and Indian corn being at ten shilling a strike [bushel] and beaver being valued at six shilling a pound, we made laws to restrain the selling of corn to the Indians and to leave the price of beaver at liberty, which was presently sold for ten and twenty shillings a pound. I should also have remembered how the half of our cows and almost all our mares and goats, sent us out of England, died at sea in their passage hither, and that those intended to be sent us out of Ireland were not sent at all, all which together with the loss of our six months' building, occasioned by our intended removal to a town to be fortified, [33]

should renounce his ministry he received in England." *History*, 1:38-39.
31. Endecott, Ludlow, Nowell, Pynchon, Coddington, Simon Bradstreet (who settled at Charlestown), and Thomas Sharpe of Boston.
32. This was Newtown, later Cambridge.
33. For a time a fortified town was planned between Boston and Roxbury; later it was to be at the "new town," later Newtown. But this plan, too, was abandoned. See Rutman, *Winthrop's Boston*, pp. 29-32.

weakened our estates, especially the estates of the undertakers, who were 3 or 4000 pounds engaged in the joint stock, which was now not above so many hundreds,[34] yet many of us labored to bear it as comfortably as we could, remembering the end of our coming hither and knowing the power of God, who can support and raise us again, and useth to bring his servants low that the meek may be made glorious by deliverance (Psalm 112).

In the end of this December departed from us the ship *Handmaid* of London, by which we sent away one Thomas Morton, a proud, insolent man who has lived here divers years and had been an attorney in the West Countries while he lived in England.[35] Multitude of complaints were received against him for injuries done by him both to the English and Indians, and amongst others for shooting hail shot at a troop of Indians, for not bringing a canoe unto him to cross a river withal, whereby he hurt one and shot through the garments of another, for the satisfaction of the Indians wherein and that it might appear to them and to the English that we meant to do justice impartially, we caused his hands to be bound behind him and set his feet in the bilboes and burned his house to the ground, all in the sight of the Indians, and so kept him prisoner till we sent him for England, whither we sent him, for that my Lord Chief Justice there so required that he might punish him capitally for fouler misdemeaners there perpetrated, as we were informed.

I have no leisure to review and insert things forgotten but out of due time and order must set them down as they come to memory.

About the end of October this year 1630, I joined with the governor and Mr. Maverecke[36] in sending out our pinnace to the Narragansetts to trade for corn to supply our wants, but after the pinnace had doubled Cape Cod, she put into the next harbor she found,[37] and there meeting with Indians, who showed their willingness to truck, she made her voyage there and brought us one hundred bushels of corn at about 4s. a bushell, which helped us somewhat. From the coast where they traded they saw a very large island four leagues to the east,[38] which the Indians commended as a fruitful place, full of good vines and free from sharp frosts, having one only entrance into it, by a navigable river, inhabited by a few Indians, which for a trifle would leave the island if the English would set them upon the main, but the pinnace, having no direction for discovery, re-

34. Ten men who had agreed to put up the necessary capital for the Company in exchange for commercial rights in furs, the making of salt, furnishing arms, and the transportation of passengers and goods. The ten were Winthrop, Saltonstall, Johnson, Dudley, and Revell, all of whom came in 1630, and Matthew Cradock, Nathaniel Wright, Theophilus Eaton, Thomas Goffe, and James Young.
35. Morton, later author of *The New English Canaan* (1637), had returned from England in 1629.
36. Samuel Maverick, an old planter discussed above, showed great hospitality to visitors. He was unsympathetic with the government and the churches of Massachusetts.
37. Perhaps at Chatham.
38. Probably Rhode Island, where Newport is now located.

turned without sailing to it, which in two hours they might have done. Upon this coast they found store of vines full of grapes dead ripe, the season being past, whither we purpose to send the next year sooner to make some small quantity of wine, if God enable us, the vines growing thin with us and we not having yet any leisure to plant vineyards.

But now having some leisure to discourse of the motives for other men's coming to this place or their abstaining from it, after my brief manner I say this: that if any come hither to plant for worldly ends that can live well at home, he commits an error, of which he will soon repent him. But if for spiritual and that no particular obstacle hinder his removal, he may find here what may well content him, viz.: materials to build, fuel to burn, ground to plant, seas and rivers to fish in, a pure air to breathe in, good water to drink till wine or beer can be made, which, together with the cows, hogs, and goats brought hither already, may suffice for food, for as for fowl and venison, they are dainties here as well as in England. For clothes and bedding, they must bring them with them, till time and industry produce them here. In a word, we yet enjoy little to be envied but endure much to be pitied in the sickness and mortality of our people. And I do the more willingly use this open and plain dealing, lest other men should fall short of their expectations when they come hither, as we to our great prejudice did, by means of letters sent us from hence into England, wherein honest men out of a desire to draw over others to them wrote somewhat hyperbolically of many things here. If any godly men, out of religious ends, will come over to help us in the good work we are about, I think they cannot dispose of themselves nor of their estates more to God's glory and the furtherance of their own reckoning, but they must not be of the poorer sort yet, for divers years, for we have found by experience that they have hindered, not furthered, the work. And for profane and debauched persons, their oversight in coming hither is wondered at, where they shall find nothing to content them. If there be any endued with grace and furnished with means to feed themselves and theirs for eighteen months, and to build and plant, let them come over into our Macedonia and help us,[39] and not spend themselves and their estates in a less profitable employment, for others, I conceive they are not yet fitted for this business.

39. See Acts 16:9. Paul saw a vision of a man of Macedonia beseeching him, "Come over to Macedonia and help us." The Bay Company seal shows an Indian saying, "Come over and help us," an allusion to the missionary purpose of the colony.

Touching the discouragements which the sickness and mortality which every first year hath seized upon us, and those of Plymouth as appeareth before, [they] may give to such who have cast any thoughts this way (of which mortality it may be said of us almost as of the Egiptians, that there is not an house where there is not one dead, and in some houses many). The natural causes seem to be in the want of warm lodging and good diet to which Englishmen are habituated at home, and in the sudden increase of heat which they endure that are landed here in summer, the salt meats at sea having prepared their bodies thereto, for those only two last years died of fevers who landed in June and July; as those of Plymouth who landed in the winter died of the scurvy, as did our poorer sort, whose houses and bedding kept them not sufficiently warm, nor their diet sufficiently in heart. Other causes God may have, as our faithful minister Mr. Wilsoune [40] (lately handling that point) showed unto us, which I forbear to mention, leaving this matter to the farther dispute of physicians and divines.

Wherefore to return: upon the third of January died the daughter of Mr. Sharpe, a godly virgin, making a comfortable end after a long sickness. The plantation here received not the like loss of any woman since we came hither, and therefore she well deserves to be remembered in this place, [41] and to add to our sorrows, upon the fifth day came letters to us from Plymouth, advertising us of this sad accident following. About a fortnight before, there went from us in a shallop to Plymouth six men and a girl, who in an hour or two before night on the same day they went forth, came near to the mouth of Plymouth Bay, but the wind then coming strongly from the shore kept them from entering and drove them to seawards, and they having no better means to help themselves, let down their killick [anchor] that so they might drive the more slowly and be nearer land when the storm should cease. But the stone slipping out of the killick and thereby they driving faster than they thought all the night, in the morning when they looked out they found themselves out of sight of land, which so astonished them, the frost being extreme and their hands so benumbed with cold that they could not handle their oars, neither had any compass to steer by, that they gave themselves for lost and lay down to die quietly, only one man who had more natural heat and courage remaining than the rest continued so long looking for land that

40. John Wilson was minister of the church for thirty-seven years.
41. Such comments as this one suggest that Dudley's letter was intended to be a report of a semi-official nature.

the morning waxing clearer, he discovered land and with difficulty hoisted the sail, and so the wind a little turning, two days
after they were driven from Plymouth Bay, they arrived at a
shore unknown unto them.[42] The stronger helped the weaker
out of the boat and, taking their sail on shore, made a shelter
thereof and made a fire, but the frost had so pierced their
bodies that one of them died about three days after their landing, and most of the others grew worse, both in body and courage, no hope of relief being within their view. Well, yet the Lord
pitying them and two of them who only could use their legs
going abroad, rather to seek than to hope to find help, they met
first with two Indian women, who sent unto them an Indian
man, who informed them that Plymouth was within fifty miles
and offered together to procure relief for them which they gladly accepting, he performed and brought them three men from
Plymouth (the governor and council of Plymouth liberally re-
warding the Indian and took care for the safety of our people),
who brought them all alive in their boat thither, save one man,
who with a guide chose rather to go over land but quickly fell
lame by the way, and getting harbor at a trucking house the
Plymoutheans had in those parts; there he yet abides.[43] At the
others' landing at Plymouth, one of them died as he was taken
out of the boat; another (and he the worst in the company)
rotted from the feet upwards where the frost had gotten most
hold and so died within a few days. The other three, after God
had blessed the chirurgeon's skill used towards them returned
safe to us. I set down this the more largely partly because the
first man that died was a godly man of our congregation, one
Richard Garrad, who at the time of his death more feared he
should dishonor God than cared for his own life, as also because
divers boats have been in manifest peril this year, yet the Lord
preserved them all, this one excepted.

Amongst those who died about the end of this January, there
was a girl of eleven years old, the daughter of one John Ruggles,
of whose family and kindred died so many that for some reason
it was matter of observation amongst us, who in the time of
her sickness expressed to the minister and to those about her
so much faith and assurance of salvation as is rarely found in
any of that age, which I thought not unworthy here to commit to memory, and if any tax me for wasting paper with recording these small matters, such may consider that little

42. On Cape Cod.
43. At Sandwich.

mothers bring forth little children, small commonwealths matters of small moment, the reading where of yet is not to be despised by the judicious, because small things in the beginning of natural or politic bodies are as remarkable as greater in bodies full grown.

Upon the fifth of February arrived here Mr. Peirce with the ship *Lyon* of Bristow, with supplies of victuals from England, who had set forth from Bristow the first of December before.[44] He had a stormy passage hither and lost one of his sailors not far from our shore, who in a tempest having helped to take in the sprit sail, lost his hold as he was coming down and fell into the sea, where after long swimming he was drowned, to the great dolor of those in the ship, who beheld so lamentable a spectacle without being able to minister help to him, the sea was so high and the ship drove so fast before the wind, though her sails were taken down. By this ship we understood of the fight of three of our ships and two English men-of-war coming out of the straits with fourteen Dunkirks [pirate ships], upon the coast of England as they returned from us in the end of the last summer, who through God's goodness with the loss of some thirteen or fourteen men out of our three ships, and I know not how many out of the two men-of-war got at length clear of them. The *Charles*, one of our three,[45] a stout ship of three hundred ton, being so torn that she had not much of her left whole above water.

By this ship we also understood the death of many of those who went from us the last year to Old England, as likewise of the mortality there, whereby we see are graves in other places as well as with us.

Also to increase the heap of our sorrows, we received advertisement by letters from our friends in England and by the reports of those who came hither in this ship to abide with us (who were about twenty-six) that they who went discontentedly from us the last year, out of their evil affections towards us, have raised many false and scandalous reports against us, affirming us to be Brownists in religion and ill affected to our state at home and that these vile reports have won credit with some who formerly wished us well. But we do desire and cannot but hope that wise and impartial men will at length consider that such malcontents have ever pursued this manner of casting dirt to make others seem as foul as themselves and that our godly

44. Winthrop had sent him back for provisions, and his arrival in February meant much to the colonists. Among the twenty or so passengers to arrive in the *Lyon* at this dreadful time was Roger Williams. 45. The others were the *Whale* and the *Success*.

friends, to whom we have been known, will not easily believe that we are not so turned from the profession we so long have made in our native country. And for further clearing, I truly affirm that I know no one person who came over with us the last year to be altered in judgment and affection, either in ecclesiastical or civil respects since our coming hither, but we do continue to pray daily for our sovereign lord the king, the queen, the prince, the royal blood, the council, and whole state, as duty binds us to do and reason persuades others to believe, for how ungodly and unthankful should we be if we should not thus do, who came hither by virtue of his majesty's letters patent, and under his gracious protection, under which shelter we hope to live safely and from whom [whose] kingdom and subjects we now have received and hereafter expect relief. Let our friends therefore give no credit to such malicious aspersions but be more ready to answer for us than we hear they have been. We are not like those which have dispensations to lie, but as we were free enough in Old England to turn our insides outwards, sometimes to our disadvantage, very unlike is it that now (being *procul a fulmine* [far from the thunderbolt][46]) we should be so unlike ourselves. Let therefore this be sufficient for us to say and others to hear in this matter.

Amongst others who died about this time was Mr. Robert Welden, whom in the time of his sickness we had chosen to be captain of one hundred foot, but before he took possession of his place, he died the sixteenth of this February and was buried as a soldier with three volleys of shot.[47] Upon the twenty-second day of February, we held a general day of thanksgiving throughout the whole colony for the safe arrival of the ship which came last with our provisions.

About this time we apprehended one Robert Wright, who had been sometimes a linen draper in Newgate Market and after that a brewer on the Bankside and on Thames Street. This man we lately understood had made an escape in London from those who came to his house to apprehend him for clipping the king's coin [one or two words missing] had stolen after us. Upon his examination, he confessed the fact and his escape, but affirmed he had the king's pardon for it, under the broad seal, which he yet not being able to prove, and one to whom he was known charging him with untruth in some of his answers, we therefore committed him to prison, to be sent by the next ship into England.

46. An echo of an adage of Erasmus; see *Ciceronian Dialogues,* Colloquy 999.
47. Just as the government supported a medical man, William Gager, and ministers, it also employed experienced soldiers to organize a militia.

Likewise we were lately informed that one Mr. Gardiner, who arrived here a month before us (and who had passed here for a knight by the name of Sir Christopher Gardiner all this while[48]) was no knight but instead thereof had two wives now living in an house at London, one of which came about September last from Paris in France (where her husband had left her years before) to London, where she had heard her husband had married a second wife and whom by inquiry she found out, and they both condoling each other's estate, wrote both their letters to the governor (by Mr. Pierce who had conference with both the women in the presence of Mr. Allerton of Plymouth[49]), his first wife desiring his return and conversion, his second, his destruction for his foul abuse and for robbing her of her estate, of a part whereof she sent an inventory hither, comprising therein many rich jewels, much plate, and costly linen. This man had in his family (and yet hath) a gentlewoman whom he called his kinswoman and whom one of his wives in her letter names Mary Grove, affirming her to be a known harlot, whose sending back into Old England she also desired, together with her husband. Shortly after this intelligence, we sent to the house of the said Gardiner (which was seven miles from us) to apprehend him and his woman, with a purpose to send them both to London to his wives there, but the man, who having heard some rumor from some who came in the ship that letters were come to the governor requiring justice against him was readily prepared for flight, so soon as he should see any crossing the river or likely to apprehend him, which he accordingly performed, for he, dwelling alone, easily discerned such who were sent to take him half a mile before they approached his house, and with his piece on his neck went his way, as most men think northward, hoping to find some English there like to himself, but likely enough it is, which way soever he went, he will lose himself in the woods and be stopped with some rivers in his passing, notwithstanding his compass in his pocket, and so with hunger and cold will perish before he find the place he seeks. His woman was brought unto us and confessed her name and that her mother dwells eight miles from Beirdly in Salopshire and that Gardiner's father dwells in or near Gloucester and was (as she said) brother to Stephen Gardiner, Bishop of Winchester,[50] and did disinherit his son for his twenty-six years' absence in his travels in France, Italy, Germany, and Turkey; that he had (as

48. Gardiner was probably acting as agent for Sir Ferdinando Gorges, who continued to have an active interest in the Massachusetts Bay area. See Richard A. Preston, *Gorges of Plymouth Fort* (Toronto, 1953), pp. 289-90.
49. Isaac Allerton was business manager for the Plymouth colonists.
50. A confusion; this Gardiner had been dead for seventy-five years.

he told her) married a wife in his travels, from whom he was divorced, and the woman long since dead; that both herself and Gardiner were both Catholiques till of late but were now Protestants; that she takes him to be a knight but never heard when he was knighted. The woman was impenitent and close, confessing no more than was wrested from her by her own contradictions, so we have taken order to send her to the two wives in Old England to search her further.

Upon the eighth of March, from after it was fair daylight until about eight of the clock in the forenoon, there flew over all the towns in our plantations so many flocks of doves, each flock containing many thousands and some so many that they obscured the light, that passeth credit if but the truth should be written, and the thing was the more strange because I scarce remember to have seen ten doves since I came into this country. They were all turtles, as appeared by divers of them we killed flying, somewhat bigger than those of Europe, and they flew from the northeast to the southwest, but what it portends I know not.[51]

The ship now waits but for wind, which when it blows, there are ready to go aboard therein for England Sir Richard Saltonstall, Mr. Sharpe, Mr. Coddington, and many others,[52] the most whereof purpose to return to us again, if God will. In the mean time, we are left a people poor and contemptible, yet such as trust in God and are contented with our condition, being well assured that He will not fail us nor forsake us. I had almost forgotten to add this, that the wheat we received by this last ship stands us in thirteen or fourteen shillings a strike, and the peas about eleven shillings a strike, besides the adventure,[53] which is worth three or four shillings a strike, which is an higher price than I ever tasted bread of before.

Thus, Madam, I have as I can told your honor all our matters, knowing your wisdom can make good use thereof. If I live not to perform the like office of my duty hereafter, likely it is some other will do it better.

Before the departure of the ship (which yet was wind-bound) there came unto us Sagamore John and one of his subjects requiring satisfaction for the burning of two wigwams by some of the English, which wigwams were not inhabited but stood in a place convenient for their shelter when upon occasion they should travel that ways. By examination we found that some

51. These pigeons were reported by many other early New Englanders. See Hammond's letter, below.
52. The *Lyon* left on April 1. Neither Sharpe nor Saltonstall returned. Saltonstall's young son Richard remained in Watertown; an early letter of his is below. William Coddington returned in 1633 but left for Rhode Island in 1637 because of the Antinomian controversy.
53. The amount due to the adventurers or investors in the company.

English fowlers, having retired into that which belonged to the subject and leaving a fire therein carelessly, which they had kindled to warm them, were the cause of burning thereof, for that which was the Sagamore's, we could find no certain proof how it was fired, yet lest he should think us not sedulous enough to find it out and so should depart discontentedly from us, we gave both him and his subject satisfaction for them both.

The like accident of fire also befell Mr. Sharpe and Mr. Colborne [54] upon the seventeenth of this March, both whose houses, which were as good and as well furnished as the most in the plantation, were in two hours' space burned to the ground, together with much of their household stuff, apparel, and other things, as also some goods of others who sojourned with them in their houses, God so pleasing to excercise us with corrections of this kind as he hath done with others, for the prevention whereof in our new town, intended this summer to be builded, we have ordered that no man there shall build his chimney with wood nor cover his house with thatch, which was readily assented unto, for that divers other houses have been burned since our arrival (the fire always beginning in the wooden chimneys) and some English wigwams which have taken fire in the roofs covered with thatch or boughs.

And that this ship might return into Old England with heavy news, upon the eighteenth day of March came one from Salem and told us that upon the fifteenth thereof there died Mrs. Skelton, the wife of the other minister there, who, about eighteen or twenty days before, handling cold things in a sharp morning, put herself into a most violent fit of the wind colic and vomiting, which continuing, she at length fell into a fever and so died as before. She was a godly and an helpful woman, and indeed the main pillar of her family, having left behind her an husband and four children, weak and helpless, who can scarce tell how to live without her. She lived desired and died lamented, and well deserves to be honorably remembered.

Upon the twenty-fifth of this March, one of Waterton having lost a calf and about ten of the clock at night hearing the howling of some wolves not far off, raised many of his neighbors out of their beds, that by discharging their muskets near about the place where he heard the wolves, he might so put the wolves to flight and save his calf. The wind serving fit to carry the report of the muskets to Rocksbury, three miles off, at such a

54. William Colburn became an important Bostonian and ruling elder of the first church.

time, the inhabitants there took an alarm, beat up their drum, armed themselves, and sent in post to us to Boston to raise us also. So in the morning, the calf being found safe, the wolves affrighted, and our danger past, we went merrily to breakfast.

I thought to have ended before, but the stay of the ship and my desire to inform your honor of all I can hath caused this addition, and everyone having warning to prepare for the ship's departure tomorrow, I am now this twenty-eighth of March, 1631, sealing my letters.

Another surviving letter sent back to England in late March was from John Masters, who had come to Massachusetts with his wife and five children in the Winthrop fleet. In England Masters had been steward to Sir Richard Saltonstall, with whom he presumably came to America. He addressed his letter to Lady Barrington, whose late husband had been a close friend of Winthrop. Her brother was the father of Oliver Cromwell and her sister the mother of John Hampden, famous for his opposition to the policies of Charles I. Masters is too courteous, too much aware of his addressee's station in life; his restraint prevented him from writing a really valuable letter, though his efforts to see New England as he imagined English lords and ladies might is significant. Masters remained in the colony till his death in 1639. The original letter is British Museum manuscript Edgerton 2645, folio 245.

John Masters to Lady Barrington
March 14, 1630/1

Right worshipful:

My good Lady Barrington and Sir Thomas Barrington with Mr. Robert Barrington and my good Lady Lampleath, and to the right worshipful Sir Gilbte Garrett and his good Lady and to Sir William Massome and his good Lady with all the rest of the gentlemen and gentlewomen in all your families, grace and peace be multiplied in our Lord Jesus Christ to you all. Right worshipful and well-beloved, I know not how sufficiently to style you, nor yet how to greet you as you deserve at my

hands, nor yet as your worthiness requires, but having so much
experience of taking in good part my rudeness in speaking, I
make bold to trouble you in writing, but your great kindness
and respect of me, that am so unworthy, makes me to muse
how to do it, but I pray you to accept of the acknowledgment
of all your kindness by way of thankfulness. And because you
desired me to write of this country and said you would believe what I should write I would fain grant your desire therein.
And because I could not write before I had some experience
of the country, I thought it fit to defer it until now.

The country is very good and fit to receive lords and ladies,
if there were more good houses, both for good land and good
water and for good creatures to hunt and to hawk, and for
fowling and fishing, and more also, our natures to refresh in,
and if you or any of yours will come here, I know you might
have good cheer, but because the right worshipful Sir Richard
Saltonstall hath put me in place to oversee his great family,
with his worthy son, and that his business being so great as it
is, I cannot write so large as I would, for besides his great family, he hath many cattle and kine, and horse and swine, and
some goats and poultry. He hath also much building at his own
house, and fencing, plowing, and planting, and also to help
build the new city,[1] and first for a house for God to dwell in.
These things will require my best diligence because that
Sir Richard will be long absent, and, therefore, seeing that he
is now come over, to advise with the wise, to advance the glory
of God, in planting the Gospel here, and to help forward those
that intend the good of this country. Therefore, I pray you, to
confer with him of the same, for I have made bold to acquaint
him with the acquaintance of your worships, and then Sir Richard will inform you of all the particulars that can be said of
this country, so much of it also as will bring over my Lady
Lampleath, and Sir George her husband, and some others of my
good Sir Francys Barrington's lineage, that I may lay myself
down at their feet, to do them some service for that extraordinary love and kindness and respect that I received from my
good Sir Francys and my good lady, which I fear I shall never
be able to requite. I am unwilling to take off my hand from
writing in paper, but if I could write you any better matter.
But I hope hereafter to answer your letters, which will make
me much more all your debtors. My God and my Lord and

1. Presumably a town in-
tended for purposes of
defense, to have been
built between Boston
and Roxbury; Dudley re-
fers to it also. It was
never built.

your God bless you all and yours, with all heavenly blessings and heavenly graces until we all meet in heaven in our places. Amen.

> Your friend in all service, till death end.
> John Masters

Watertowne, near Charles river,
New England: March 14th, 1630[1].
To the right worshipfull Lady Barrington at Hatfield, Broadway, or to Sir William Mirsome at Oates in Essex, these be presented in England.

Four months after his last letter to his wife, Winthrop could write again. Since he expected Margaret and his son John to leave England in the spring, he was not sure that his letter would reach them. They were delayed by the difficulties that the younger John Winthrop had met in selling Groton Manor: the governor believed that it was worth 5760 pounds, but no one was interested in paying anything near this price. Margaret in the meanwhile waited impatiently. In late spring she wrote to her step-son that she had visited with the Reverend John Wilson, who had returned to England on the *Lyon* to bring his wife to America, and Wilson, she reported, "speaks very well of things there, so as my heart and thoughts are there already. I want but the means to carry my body after them." Only in late August did Margaret, John Jr., and other members of the Winthrop family (and the Reverend John Eliot) set sail for America; they arrived in Massachusetts in early November. The original letter is Massachusetts Historical Society manuscript W. 7A. 50.

John Winthrop to Margaret Winthrop
March 28, 1631

My dear wife:

I have small hope that this should come to thy hands, in regard of the long stay of the ship here, so as thou mayest be well onward of thy way hither before these can come to England.

Therefore I write little to thyself and my son and those whom I expect to see here shortly, if it shall so please the Lord. And blessed be His holy and glorious name that He hath so far magnified His mercy towards us that when so many have been laid in their graves since we parted, yet He hath pleased to preserve us unto this hope of a joyful meeting, that we may see the faces of each other again, the faces of our children and sweet babes. These things I durst scarce think of heretofore, but now I embrace them oft and delight my heart in them, because I trust that the Lord our God, who hath kept me and so many of my company in health and safety among so many dead corpses, through the heat of the summer and the cold of winter, and hath also preserved thee in the peril of childbirth,[1] and upheld thy heart in the midst of so many discouragements, with the life of all thy company, will of His own goodness and free mercy preserve us and ours still that we shall meet in joy and peace, which I daily pray for and shall expect in the Lord's good time, who still continues His favor and blessing upon thee and our sweet babes and all thy company. For our little daughter, do as thou thinkest best. The Lord direct thee in it. If thou bringest her, she will be more trouble to thee in the ship than all the rest. I know my sister will be tender of her till I may send for her. Bring Amy and Anne Gostlin with thee if thou canst.[2] If they come not, they will much wrong themselves. They need fear no want here if they will be guided by God's Word. Otherwise they can look to prosper nowhere. I praise God I want nothing but thee and the rest of my family. Commend my love and blessing to them all, and to all my neighbors and friends, but I have desired my brother Gostlin to perform that. Remember to bring juice of lemons to sea with thee for thee and thy company to eat with your meat as sauce. But of these things my son hath direction. So again I kiss thee, my sweet wife, and commend thee and all ours to the Lord, and rest thine.

Jo: Winthrop

March 28
1631

1. A daughter, Anne, was born April 29, 1630, a month after Winthrop left for America. She died on the voyage when she came with her mother.
2. They did not come.

Another of this cluster of letters that travelled together, written the same day as the previous one, was from John Winthrop to his son, whose task of selling his father's property when finally completed brought 4200 pounds. Winthrop was, as usual, franker in writing to his son than to his wife. His references to "this strange land, where we have met many troubles and adversities" seem to suggest that he may have shared the conviction of the members of the company remaining in England that Massachusetts had proved unsuitable as a location for a colony. Emmanuel Downing, Winthrop's closest associate in England except for his family, had written the previous December, "Our friends here, yea those of best judgement, wish you bestow not much cost in building where you are, but do advise that you do speedily send about the discovery of some fitter place more to the south, where you may enjoy greater comfort in respect of milder winters and fruitfuller and earlier harvests, with more safety from foreign invasions." He recommended Rhode Island or the Hudson River area.

The original Winthrop letter is Massachusetts Historical Society manuscript W. 7A. 51.

John Winthrop to John Winthrop, Jr.
March 28, 1631

My good son:

The blessing of the Almighty be upon thy soul and life forever.

Among many the sweet mercies of my God towards me in this strange land, where we have met many troubles and adversities, this is not the least, and that which affords much comfort to my heart, that he hath given me a loving and dutiful son. God all-sufficient reward thee abundantly for all thy care and pains in my affairs and for all that love and duty thou hast showed to thy good mother. I doubt not but thou shalt find it in outward blessings, for thou art under the promise of having thy days prolonged, but I desire especially thou mayest find it in the manifestation of the good will of the Lord towards thee and in those spiritual blessings which may fatten thy soul.

This ship staying so long here, I am almost out of hope that my letters should come to thy hands, for though I think very long till I see you all here, yet I would rather you stayed, though it were two or three months, to come with Mr. Peirce, partly because of his skill and care of his passengers and partly that we might be the better provided of housing, etc., to entertain you, for we are much straightened yet that way, and we have had divers houses burnt, and now within these two days Mr. Sharpe and Mr. Colburne, both of our town, had their houses burnt to the ground and much goods lost. Thus it pleaseth the Lord still to humble us. I doubt not but he will do us the more good at the last.

I have written to your uncle D[owning] concerning all our business, fearing you should be come away. I have sent the assignment sealed. I left all my bonds and writings in my cupboard at Groton, or else at London.

Bring no provisions with you but meal and peas and some oatmeal and sugar, fruit, figs, and pepper, and good store of saltpeter, and conserve of red roses, and mithridate [an antidote to poison], good store of pitch and ordinary suet, or tallow. Bring none but wine vinegar, and not much of that, and be sure that the cask be good, store of oiled calves' skins of the largest, and the strongest welt leather shoes and stockings for children, and hats of all sizes. If you could bring two or three hundred sheepskins and lambskins with the wool on, dyed red, it would be a good commodity here, and the coarsest woolen cloth (so it be not flocks) and of sad colors, and some red, millstones, some two foot and some three foot over, with brasses ready cast and rings, and mill bills, store of shoemaker's thread, and hobnails, chalk, and chalkline, and a pair or two or more of large steel compasses, store of coarse linen, some birdlime.[1]

When you have cleared all things in England, if you have any money left, you may bring some with you (not above one hundred pounds) and the rest leave with your uncle D[owning] or dispose of it as your own occasions may require. Any wise, Matt. must have four hundred pounds, and there will be much due to your sister Winthrop[2] which were be best to be left in England. But you must advise with your uncle D[owning] about these things, for I am so full of business here as I can't think of mine own affairs as I should. You must also

1. A very full invoice of goods shipped on the *Lyon* shows that son John brought to his father, for example, 32 hogsheads of meal, 5 of peas, 2 of vinegar, and 2 barrels of pitch. An extant bill indicates that the vinegar was wine vinegar and that it cost 47 shillings per hogshead. See *Winthrop Papers*, 3: 41-45.
2. Henry's widow, Elizabeth.

consider what you would have for yourself and how you would employ it.

I never had letter yet from your brother F[orth].[3] If he intends to come hither, it were good he sold his land and paid his sister her one hundred pounds, which he promised when I put over his land to him. You shall need bring no more cows, for I have enough. The good Lord bless you and bring you and all my company hither in safety. So I rest.

> Your loving father,
> Jo: Winthrop

Massachusetts
March 28, 1631.

I hope the Lord hath provided a good husband for your sister Winthrop. Mr. Coddington is well affected to her.[4] If he proceed, I wish you to further it, for he is a godly man and of good estate.

To my very loving son Mr. John Winthrop at London deliver. If he be come away, my brother Downing may open this letter.

The last of the extant letters of March 1631 has survived only as a draft. It concerns an unwelcome immigrant to Massachusetts who was being returned to England. Thomas Dudley devoted a paragraph of his letter to the same incident. The records show that the man returned had been officially pardoned, but doubtless the discovery of his crime was only a pretext for returning him. The early court records on file in the clerk's office of the Supreme Judicial Court for the County of Suffolk (Massachusetts) include this manuscript. .

John Winthrop to Sir Nicholas Hyde
March 1631

Right Honorable:

Our humble duties to your good lordship presented. May it please you to understand that whereas one Robt. Wright, citizen and merchant-tailor of London, without our privity was come

3. No news had yet reached Winthrop of his son's death in late November.
4. Elizabeth did not marry John Coddington, later a follower of Anne Hutchinson.

into N[ew] E[ngland] and had settled himself in Charles
towne, we had intelligence that he was fled out of England for
treason, whereupon we caused him to be apprehended and upon
examination he confessed to us that about two years since he
had clipped some of the coin of our sovereign lord the king's
majesty, and the officers coming to search his house he fled
and so was not taken, but used means by his friends to obtain
his majesty's pardon, but forasmuch as he could produce no
record thereof before us, we thought it our duty to send him
over prisoner by this bearer Mr. Wm Peirce, master of the
ship *Lyon.* So we humbly take leave and rest.

> At your lordship's command
>   for his majesty's service,
> [John Winthrop]

[Endorsed by Winthrop]
Copy letter to Lord Chief Justice de Wright, March 1630[/1]

1632

After this cluster of March 1631 letters there are none to tell the story of the next ten months. Winthrop's journal suggests that the time was devoted to the organization of the colony, agriculture, house-building, and getting to know the land. The colonists built a thirty-ton bark, *The Blessing of the Bay*, for coastwise trading and exploring; they protected the colony, or thought they did, by banishing the "old planter" Thomas Walford, who had been in the Boston area before the Winthrop group, for his "contempt of authority and confronting officers," and Matthew Cradock's man Philip Ratcliff for what the colony's records call "uttering malicious and scandalous speeches against the government and the church of Salem." The colonists also demonstrated their high moral standards by whipping a colonist "for soliciting an Indian squaw to incontinency." No longer a feature of Winthrop's record is the cataloging of deaths, and he reports "a plentiful crop."

The improved conditions are reflected in the next letter, written by young Richard Saltonstall. Presumably his father, Sir Richard Saltonstall, had left John Masters in charge of his property because his son was only twenty-one. Son Richard remained in America only about a year longer than his father before he too returned to England. Later he settled in Ipswich. Not long before he returned in 1632, he wrote the letter below to Emmanuel Downing, who in time reappraised the potentialities of Massachusetts: Winthrop's brother-in-law came over in 1638. Saltonstall's letter once again shows the mixture of motives that created the Massachusetts Bay Colony. The original letter is at Melbourne Hall, Derbyshire.

Richard Saltonstall to Emmanuel Downing
February 4, 1631/2

Worthy Sir:

Since my arrival in New England I have endeavored to give a true and faithful relation of such things as came within mine observation and might answer the desires of such as expected letters from me. That which I know will be most grateful to you in regard of your desire of a common good and my debt unto you thereby, I will briefly set down. The country abounds with good creatures needful for sustentation of the life of man, and after some time of liberty from building, and enclosing of grounds for the safety of our cattle from the wolf, I doubt not but we shall raise good profit not only by our fishing trade (which is sufficiently known) but by hemp. flax, pitch, tar, potashes, soap ashes, masts, pipe staves, clapboard (and iron as we hope), for we find there are minerals, but for want of skill and time cannot yet certainly satisfy either ourselves or you of what kind they are.

Therefore, good sir, encourage men to come over, for here is land and means of livelihood sufficient for men that bring bodies able and minds fitted to brave the first brunts, which the beginnings of such works necessarily put men upon. Without hands nothing can be done nor anything with any great profit until multitudes of people make labor cheap. It is strange the meaner sort of people should be so backward, having assurance that they may live plentifully by their neighbors, and that the better sort of people should not help the poorer, with means to transport them, that in time might return their adventures [investments] with answerable advantage in any of the afore-named commodities, and divers others not mentioned. If gentlemen of ability would transplant themselves, they might in time much advance their own estates and not only supply the want we labor under of men fitted by their estates to bear common burdens and the gifts of their minds to nurse up this infant plantation but also might improve their talents and times for the honor and benefit of old England (to which we owe the fruit of our best endeavors) and their own eternal glory in being worthy instruments of propagating the Gospel to these poor barbarous people, the truest object of Christians' bowel-compassions that the world now affords. Oh that it might please God to move either the general state or at least (by the favor and encouragement of our gracious sovereign) some large-hearted men to contribute (if it were) but the tithe of what was bestowed upon Virginia for the educating of our poor Indians, in the supporting of their bodily necessities, till they might attain such abilities whereby they might feed themselves and others with spiritual food.

I pray you send over by some of your East Country merchants to get some few master-workmen for the ordering of our potash work. We have great store of hemp growing naturally in some parts of the country, a sample whereof you may call for from this bearer. Certainly the ground would admirably well agree with it planted that offers it unto us without our labors. The haste of the bearer enforceth me to take an abupt leave, and with my best respects to yourself and Mrs. Downing do rest

Your very loving friend,
Richard Saltonstall

From the Matachusetts Bay this 4th February 1631.
To my very worthy friend Emanuell Downing, Esq., at the Byshop's Head in Fleet Street near the Conduict deliver in London.
[Endorsed] Mr. Saltenstall's of the 4 of February 1631. Received 10 May 1632. Out of Massachusetts Bay.

Although only about seventy colonists came to Massachusetts Bay in 1631 and many of the 1630 colonists departed, some four hundred came in 1632, and by 1634 as many as two thousand were migrating each year. For a long time the members of the company remaining in England had to trouble themselves with the claims of Sir Ferdinando Gorges to New England, and in this connection Emmanuel Downing wrote an important letter to Sir John Coke, secretary of state and member of the Privy Council: "This plantation and that of Virginia went not forth upon the same reasons nor for the same end. Those of Virginia went forth for profit. . . . These went upon two other designs, some to satisfy their own curiosity in point of conscience, others (which was more general) to transport the Gospel to those heathen that never heard thereof. . . ."

These views of Downing's are somewhat reflected in a letter from the Reverend Thomas Welde. Welde had much to say about the practice of true religion and, by implication, much about the new Congregational way in Massachusetts, but nothing about converting the Indians. Before his arrival in Massachusetts on June 5, 1632, at the age of about forty-two, with his wife and four children, Welde had served since 1624 as a minister at Terling, in Essex. Deprived of his position for nonconformity, he was later arrested but fled to Amsterdam, where he preached at the Begynhof Church along with Thomas Hooker, Hugh Peter, and John Davenport, all of whom eventually came to America. Though the extant copy of the letter is dated 1633, it was clearly written earlier—between June 5 and sometime in July 1632, when Winthrop noted that it had been decided that Welde "should sit down with them of Roxbury," with John Eliot. Welde became a prominent church leader and was active in colony affairs. From 1641 to 1646 he served as agent for the colony in England, after which time he did not return to America. His highly rhetorical letter seems to have been intended for reading aloud to his former congregation at Terling.

Welde's letter and Thacher's below are both preserved in a curious manuscript at the British Museum. They are part of a volume of letters preserved and prepared for publication in the 1650s by Nehemiah Wallington, who apparently was unable to have his collection of "Profitable and Comfortable Letters" published. The collection begins with the Second Epistle of St. John and includes a good many by Wallington, a minister, himself. Wallington entitled Welde's letter "A Letter of Master Wells from New England to Old England to his people at Tarling in Essex. It is a letter setting forth the great mercies of God with praise and thanksgiving." This copy is British Museum manuscript Sloane 922, folios 167-74.

Thomas Welde to his Former Parishioners at Tarling
June/July 1632

Most dear and well beloved in Tarling, even all that love the Lord Jesus Christ's gospel, and myself, rich and poor, weak and strong, young and old, male and female, I [write] unto you all in one letter, wanting time to mention you all in particular, you being all dear unto me, yea, most dear to my heart in Jesus Christ, for whom I bow the knee to the Father of lights, longing to hear of your great welfare and spiritual growth in his dear son. From your presence though I be placed and must see your faces no more, yet I shall after a few weary days ended and all tears wiped away, and though happily never on earth yet in the New Jerusalem. And here though we cannot be suffered to live together, yet there we shall enjoy together sweet society in all fullness of perfection to all eternity. O blessed forever blessed be His holy name. And let the heaven and earth and sea and men witness of his favor to us and ours and sound out his glorious praises, yea, let all within us, without us, yea, all that we can, ring out the riches of His grace from sea to sea, from New England to Old, and from Old to New, for all His abundant mercies temporal, spiritual, and eternal, past, present, and to come, bestowed, continued, and renewed and multiplied on us all, in particular on me and mine, for he hath laden me and crowned me with mercies ever since our last embracing, drowned in tears for our sad departure, as Paul told his dear friend weeping because that they should see each others no more. To Holland, in Holland, from Holland, mercies, mercies; to New England, in New England, abundance of mercies. I have cause to stand and wonder, had I but a heart so affected, that I and all are passed the deeps and are alive and well. Yea, mercy, mercy in the Lord, inwardly, outwardly, in spite of devils and storms, as cheerful as ever, my wife all the voyage on the sea better than at land, and seasick but one day in eleven weeks,[1] at sea my children never better in their lives. They went ill into the ship but well there and came forth well as ever. Myself had not one ounce of seasickness, nor one motion or inclination thereunto, not all the way. Stand still and behold the salvation of the Lord. And not only I and all mine well and safe but all in the ship, being near eighty passengers, yea, some very aged,[2] twelve persons being all able to make well nigh one thousand years, some very young and hanging on the breast. Some women big with child, and one delivered of a lusty child within forty hours after she landed, she and the child well, and so continue to this day. Another woman in our ship of sixty years old who had labored of a consumption and strong cough of the lungs seven years is not only alive but came forth of the ship fully cured of the cough, as fresh as eagle that hath cast her bill and renewed her strength. I am the eyewitness of this, and we hope God may add to her fifteen years to her life.

And not only all safe in our ship but all safe in the ships that came this spring out of England laden with passengers, cattle, and goods, wherein not a man, woman, or child died by the

1. They had left London on March 9 in the *William and Francis*.
2. One was Stephen Bachiler, age seventy-one, a clergyman who expected to join another group of dissenters in a plantation that had collapsed. See his interesting story in V.C. Sanborn, "Stephen Bachiler and the Plough Company of 1630," Maine Historical Society *Collections*, 3rd ser. 2 (1906): 342-69.

way nor since that came to shore, nor any of them that came weakly to land, but abide strong through God's mercy to this day. Our ships being all in this admirable manner arrived, there was holden and that by authority a public solemn day of thanksgiving to God for his mercy, within seven days after landing,[3] from which I am persuaded God smelt a savor of rest, as in Noah's sacrifice when he came forth of the ark. Here we are come into as goodly a land as ever mine eyes beheld. Such groves, such trees, such an air as I am fully contented withal and desire no better while I live. Yea, I see assuredly with industry and self-denial men may subsist as well here as in any place. The plantation is now set upon fishing for a staple commodity; store of salt I see already for the fish and a ship to go to the salt islands for more where are mountains of salt for the fetching,[4] and shallops made and tackling provided to catch it withal and to send it into other countries to fetch in all other commodities. Here is also rape oil, which is like to be a sta come [staple?].[5] Here I find three great blessings, peace, plenty, and health in a comfortable measure. The place well agreeth with our English bodies that they were never so healthy in their native country. Generally all here as never could be rid of the headache, toothache, cough, and the like are now better and freed here, and those that were weak are now well long since, and I can hear of but two weak in all the plantation. God's name be praised. And although there was wanting at the first that provision at the first glut of people that came over two years since, but blessed be God, here is plenty of corn that the poorest have enough. Corn is here at five shillings six pence a bushel. In truth you cannot imagine what comfortable diet the Indian corn doth make and what pleasant and wholesome food it makes. Our cattle of all do thrive and feed exceedingly. I suppose that such as are to come need bring no more or little or no provision except malt (but no more of these things). I would have none aim at outward matters in such an attempt as this, lest the Lord meet him in the way as he met Balaam with a drawn sword, but at things of an higher nature and more spiritual nature.

O how hath my heart been made glad with the comforts of His house and the spiritual days in the same wherein all things are done in the form and pattern showed in the mount,[6] members provided, church officers elected and ordained, sacrament

3. Winthrop notes that this thanksgiving was for "the good success of the king of Sweden, and Protestants in Germany, against the emperor, etc., and for the safe arrival of the ships, they having lost not one person, nor one sick among them." *History*, 1: 94.

4. There were no such mountains; Higginson's remarks, above, were more reliable.

5. Rape seed oil never became a significant product.

6. The allusion is to God's prescription to Moses.

administered, scandals prevented, censured, fast days and holy feast days and all such things by authority commanded and performed according to the precise rule. Mine eyes, blessed be God, do see such administration of justice in civil government, all things so righteously, so religiously and impartially carried, I am already fully paid for my voyage who never had so much in the storms at sea as one repenting thought rested in my heart. Praised and thanked be God who moved my heart to come and made open the way to me. And I profess if I might have my wish in what part of the world to dwell I know no other place on the whole globe of the earth where I would be rather than here. We say to our friends that doubt this, Come and see and taste. Here the greater part are the better part. Here Mordecai speaketh kindly to the hearts of his people.[7] Here are none of the men of Gibea,[8] the sons of Belial, knocking at our doors, disturbing our sweet peace, or threatening violence. Here, blessed be the Lord God forever, our ears are not beaten nor the air filled with oaths, swearers, nor railers, nor our eyes and ears vexed with the unclean conversation of the wicked.[9] Here it is counted an honor by the worst to lay hold on the skirt of a Jew.[10] Here if any be, our sanballets [mockers] would thrust in themselves yet could not.[11] Here the rudest have a charge and dare not break it. I say the Lord continue and enlarge it still these sweet encouragements and make us walk worthy, and it is enough. I desire no more till I come in heaven. Conceive us not as if we went about to justify ourselves or dream of perfection.[12] No, God knows we think ourselves the poorest and unworthiest of all his servants, justly, else he might spew us out of his mouth. Only we desire to breathe after perfection and to know what is the rule and to walk in it. Nor as if we went about to condemn other places besides our own or other men besides ourselves. No. No. I assure you we look at our dear native country as the place where the Lord showed us mercy and to His holy ordinances there is the holy means of our God. If ever we had it, we had it there. We pray for your congregations public and private. We fast and pray for you. We love you dearly. You lie next to our hearts. Sorrow we are when we hear any evil betide you; glad when any good. We desire to do this forever. And let our tongue cleave to the roof of our mouth if we forget. You my beloved have the like affection towards us as we have towards you in the Lord, yet we cannot but mourn

7. See the Book of Esther, in which Mordecai's guidance of the conduct of his stepdaughter results in the Hebrews being protected from extermination.
8. They were inhospitable and hostile. See Judg. 19.
9. Nathaniel Ward, who spent twelve years in Massachusetts, wrote "I never heard but one oath swore, nor saw one man drunk, nor ever heard of three adulteresses, in all this time, that I can call to mind." *The Simple Cobler of Aggawam* (London, 1647), p. 61.
10. See Zech. 8: 23, where it is prophesied that the day will come when men will take hold of the skirt of a Jew and say, "We will go with you, for we have heard that God is with you."
11. See Neh. 4:1.
12. The dangers inherent in dreaming of perfection were especially well known to John Winthrop. See his letter to Sir Simonds D'Ewes, dated September 26, 1633 (below).

for the spots and blemishes that are among your meetings, which the Lord of his infinite mercy cleanse away. To return to my own particular at my first landing. I was so far from wanting a place of receipt that I was so importuned in four several places that it was a trouble to know what friend to gratify. At last I rested with Mr. Masell[13] at Charles Town, where now I am with my family most kindly entertained till I know where God shall dispose of me. I am most earnestly entreated to be in four several congregations, and all have sought by public and solemn fasting and prayer that God would move my heart thither if it be His will.

The blessing of God be with you all, my dear hearts. I desire now to hear from you, hoping that by this time the Lord hath provided some faithful pastor to teach and watch over you in the Lord. Once more farewell. The Lord comfort your hearts, bottle your tears, pardon your sins, supply your wants, work all your works for you, know your souls in adversity, and preserve you to His everlasting kingdom. Amen.

The name of John White has been prominently mentioned in these pages because of his role in the early stages of the settlement of Massachusetts. His work has been widely recognized by historians since his time, but he has never been given due credit by the general public. The explanation is simple: he never came to Massachusetts. Moreover, though he continued to look out for the welfare of the colonists, for example by collecting provisions to alleviate the hard times that the migrants suffered soon after they began crossing the water in numbers, he was not sympathetic with the new religious system of Bay puritanism, especially its rigidities. Ultimately, at the time of the Puritan Revolution, he became a presbyterian. The best testimonial of the affection in which the colonists held him is a letter from John Winthrop, written two years after the governor came to America. The original manuscript is at the Public Record Office, London, numbered C. O. 1/6, folio 63.

13. Perhaps Ralph Mousall, who came in 1630.

John Winthrop to Rev. John White
July 4, 1632

Reverend and worthy sir:

I salute you in the Lord, being much comforted to hear of
your health and in the hope at length to see and enjoy you here,
that you may reap some fruit of all your labors, care, and cost
bestowed upon this work of the Lord.

I wrote to you by the last return how I had undertaken to pay
them of Dorchester for Jo[hn] Gallop[1] and Dutch their wages,
which Mr. Ludlowe did accompt [account] to receive part here
and part in England, so as I marvel you should have any further
trouble about it. I have also paid Jo[hn] Elford the remainder
of his wages, being eleven pounds and other arrears here, so as I
think there is now nothing to be demanded for such reckonings.
I have disbursed above three hundred pounds for the Company's
engagements here, but I have some cattle and old kettles, etc.,
for it, and I hope more than enough to satisfy me.

I have much difficulty to keep John Galloppe here by reason
his wife will not come. I marvel at the woman's weakness, that
she will live miserably with her children there when she might
live comfortably here with her husband. I pray persuade and
further her coming by all means. If she will come, let her have
the remainder of his wages. If not, let it be bestowed to bring
over his children, for so he desires. It would be above forty
pounds' loss to him to come for her.

The surveyer of our ordnance is now returned home.[2] We
were loath to part with him, but his longing after his native
country would not be stilled. He hath received of me twelve
pounds, ten shillings, for a year and quarter service, and five
pounds I procured him from the Court (though I am forced to
disburse it.)[3] His diet he hath had of me with his lodging and
washing all the time he hath been here. Yet if his passage be
paid, he will not have above eight pounds left, which will not
suffice to apparel him and carry him into Germany. I pray, sir,
make use of your old faculty to help him with some small
matter more for his better accommodation.

1. Gallop had a small vessel
that served as a means of
communication among the
settlers along the coast; he
seems to have used it also
for fishing.
2. This man, one Jost
Weillust, was in charge
of the colony's fortifications and was also "Can-
noneer." See John Noble
and John F. Cronin, eds.,
*Records of the Court of
Assistants, 1630-1692*,
3 vols. (Boston, 1901-28),
2:11.
3. Winthrop frequently
spent his own funds in
this fashion.

John Gallop hath written to some of your neighbors for twelve dozen of cod lines. If he provide them and bring them to you, I pray deliver him this bill enclosed. If not, I desire you to furnish us so far as this bill will go and some cod hooks also.

Thus earnestly desiring your prayers and longing for your presence, I commend you to the Lord and rest.

> Yours assured in the Lord's work,
> Jo: Winthrop

Massachusets, July 4, 1632

I would send salutations to my brother and sister Painter but fear they are dead, for I have written divers letters to them but never received any.[4]

[Enclosure]

Brother Downing:

I pray pay unto this bearer by the allowance of Mr. John White of Dorchester twelve pounds. It is for fishing lines to be sent me into newe England. So I rest.

> Your loving brother,
> Jo: Winthrop

Massachusetts in N:[ew] E:[ngland]
July 4, 1632

To his reverend and very loving friend Mr. Jo: White, Minister of the Gospel in Dorchest, deliver.

John White never harvested the fruit of his labors by migrating to the colony that he helped to create. Thomas Welde was most welcome, for the colonists were eager to have pure churches and good preaching. But until John Cotton and Thomas Hooker crossed the Atlantic in 1633, the colony was without a minister with a first-class mind. Perhaps for this reason, John Winthrop and the Reverend John Wilson, Winthrop's minister, wrote in October 1632 to Dr. John Stoughton, a distinguished London clergyman whose two brothers were in Massachusetts. (In 1635 Israel Stoughton wrote his brother John an important surviving letter.) The invitation says next to

4. Neither was dead.

nothing about the Congregational church polity, though it makes clear that the writers are acting on behalf of the church. Stoughton did not accept the invitation. The original letter is at the Public Record Office, London, numbered C. O. 1/6, folio 67.

John Winthrop and Rev. John Wilson to Dr. John Stoughton
October 1632

Reverend and worthy sir:

We may be bold to let you know (upon certain intelligence which hath come to us) that we have heard (with much joy to our hearts) of the disposition of your thoughts towards us, or rather towards the Lord's work begun here for the spreading of the Gospel in these western parts of the world. Withal we have taken notice of that good report you have among the saints and of those gifts the Lord hath furnished you with for this service. Whereupon we thought good to let you understand and to give you what firm assurance we may of our strong desires towards you. We mean not of ourselves only but of the Church of Boston whereof we are, and although we dare not press you with importunity of arguments (being conscious of our own unworthiness of so great a blessing) to come into N[ew] E[ngland] and help us, yet we assure you it would much add to the comfort of ourselves and our encouragement in the hope of much success in this way the Lord hath set us in if we may please Him to send you unto us, by the return of this bearer, with a mind so prepared as upon your discerning the state of our congregation and the affections of our people towards you and our acquaintance with you and knowledge of your abilities, you might be joined to us in the office of the ministry. Now (good sir), we beseech you, that this may suffice to persuade your heart this motion proceeds from the truth of our desires towards you and the apprehension of our own want of such help as the Lord hath enabled you to afford us. And for all other matters which you shall desire to be informed of, to receive satisfaction from this bearer Mr. Peirce, our most faithful friend and brother in Christ, till whose return (by the good providence of the Lord) we shall sit down and expect your resolution. In the mean time we crave the help of your prayers, and so commending you and all yours to the Lord's most just and holy disposing in this and in all your occasions, with most hearty salutations we take leave and rest.

Yours truly in the Lord,
Jo: Winthrop
John Wilson

Boston in Massachusetts in N[ew] E[ngland]
October 1632
To our reverend and right worthy friend Mr. Doctor Stoughton deliver.

1633

Throughout the early years of the colony men of ability arrived in considerable numbers; many of them were immediately given positions of responsibility. Thus John Haynes, who arrived in 1633, was made governor in 1635; Richard Bellingham, who arrived in 1634, was made deputy governor with Haynes. (Bellingham was from Boston in Lincolnshire, where he had been borough recorder for eight years; in 1628 he was a member of Parliament.) Learned and effective ministers, too, continued to join the new commonwealth. The one man most identified with missionary work with the Massachusetts Indians is of course John Eliot, who came to America in 1631. Since John Wilson, minister of the Boston church, had returned to England to persuade his wife to join him in America, there was no clergyman for the Boston church. Winthrop, Dudley, and Nowell were acting as substitutes. Eliot therefore agreed to serve as a temporary replacement. When Wilson returned to Massachusetts in May 1632, Eliot was invited to join Wilson as a permanent minister. But he preferred to minister to the newly founded church at Roxbury, since some of its people were from his home area in England. Eliot was about twenty-seven at this time. Not until 1646 did he begin preaching to the Indians.

Eliot's letter below, which was discovered in 1951, is important for several reasons. First, though many of his later letters survive, this one is much the earliest known to exist, the next having been written fourteen years later in 1646. Secondly, it is the earliest known proposal by a member of the colony for the creation of a college. Eliot's estimate of five hundred pounds or less for the establishment of a college was very close to the amount that the General Court voted in 1636, four hundred pounds, and to John Harvard's bequest of about 375 pounds.

Eliot explains briefly how the colony was being governed. He makes Massachusetts Bay sound like a nearly sovereign state, and though he affirms the importance of English precedents in the conduct of courts, he also notes the existence of something new, a developing system of representative government. Originally the

General Court was the assembly of shareholders (called free-men) of the Massachusetts Bay Company. On October 19, 1630, 108 men had been admitted to the status of freemen, though they were not shareholders. They were thus franchised to elect the governor, the deputy governor, and the assistants or magistrates. This first step in the spread of political power to the people was followed in the spring of 1632 by the establishment of a limited form of representative government—two men from each town were to help in levying taxes.

Sir Simonds D'Ewes, to whom Eliot wrote, was not much older than he. One of the century's outstanding antiquarians, he had married into a wealthy family in 1626. Since his youth he had had puritan sympathies, and a particular interest of his was the Massachusetts Bay Colony, many of whose members he knew. As an antiquarian he was a great saver of papers; in all, six of the letters in this collection were written to D'Ewes. Though the Hammond and Browne letters below demonstrate that he toyed with the idea of moving to America, such a move was unlikely, for his interests were in English historical manuscripts. His great work is on the parliaments of Elizabeth I. In a portion of his autobiography, written about 1638, D'Ewes refers to those who went to Massachusetts "to avoid the burthens and snares which here were laid upon their consciences," but he also notes that "they go a little too far on the right hand."

Eliot's college proposal was made in response to a suggestion that D'Ewes had made in a letter to Winthrop. The letter had been carried to Massachusetts by William Hammond the younger. Though D'Ewes's letter has not survived, Eliot's postscript suggests its contents. Ironically, Eliot is far more revealing than is Winthrop, whose reply to D'Ewes is below. Perhaps Winthrop had asked Eliot to comment on the proposal in his behalf. Eliot's original letter is British Museum manuscript Harley 384, folios 256-57.

John Eliot to Sir Simonds D'Ewes
September 18, 1633

Right worshipful:

Both mine own and my wife's service remembered to your-self and to your beloved lady, etc. I humbly thank you for your kind remembrance of us, whereby both our hearts and bowels were refreshed, and whereas you desire a declaration of our present state, I will do it with the best plainness and brevity I can, and the rather because I conceive hope of the enjoyment of your presence here, and I will do nothing but what shall appear truth. For our young commonwealth, I suppose you know the state of our government by patent, that it consisteth of a governor, deputy governor, and eighteen assistants, that they have full power to do all manner of justice and have power of life and death, etc., so that in our courts which are every month, there is the image of all courts in England (pro re nata [as matters are]) for all businesses of all courts are judged by them. (I know not what power they have in cases of admiralty. I suppose that they have none but bind them to answer it in England.) But we have sweet and glorious justice and judgment among us, and all proceedings are according to the form of those courts in England, where such cases are judged. But, dear sir, we want able and learned men for assistants in this great work, for of this number mentioned we have but eight,[1] and what more God may provide we know not, yea and of them (though all of them be worthy and able men) yet some be not experienced lawyers, and such men are very useful in laying the foundation of this commonwealth, and, worthy sir, if God should move your heart to come to us, I am persuaded you would be an able builder in this work, and I doubt not but you would deserve highly at the hands of this poor commonwealth.

Our governor and all the Court are yearly elected by the body of freemen,[2] and changeable, according to their abilities and defects, but we have not yet changed our governor, because he is incomparable in wisdom, godliness, etc., and is deep in the hearts of all. But they say it's fit to change, lest it grow to a custom.[3] For military men we have some both able and expert, but more of them would be more comfort. For our churches, we walk in all things as near to the revealed will of God as we can, in all humbleness and peace, loving and praying for our native land, our gracious king, queen, posterity, privy council, etc., and for all magistrates, ministers, etc.[4] For our towns men take a little plot for yards and gardens and so dwell together, and farther off have what they can improve, as nigh as may be, and if any be rich, and able to take a farm, they may seek a place to their own content, and take five hundred acres if they will, provided it be a convenient distance from towns, that poor

1. Increase Nowell, William Pynchon, John Endecott, Roger Ludlow, William Coddington, John Winthrop, Jr., and Simon Bradstreet, plus John Humphry, who had not yet come to America.
2. The first group of freemen admitted after Winthrop arrived in New England included all or nearly all of the adult male members of the colony except servants. The old planters Blackstone, Conant, and Maverick were among those admitted. In 1631 the General Court ruled that in the future freemanship was to be restricted to church members. See *Massachusetts Records*, 1:87, and Edmund S. Morgan, *The Puritan Dilemma: The Story of John Winthrop* (Boston, 1958), pp. 84-92.
3. In 1635 Dudley was elected governor.
4. Eliot says little about the churches, apparently because he did not wish D'Ewes to know what was happening. When word got back to England of the development of Congregationalism, many were disturbed. See below, pp. 126, 194-95, 200.

men, and all men, be not wronged by it, and surely here is land enough and good enough for all that come, though ten thousand more should come.

We are at good peace with the natives, and they do gladly entertain us and give us possession, for we are as walls to them from their bloody enemies, and they are sensible of it and also they have many more comforts by us, and, I trust, in God's time they shall learn Christ. We have eleven several plantations, whereof eight be pretty competent towns.[5] Cattle do much increase in every kind. Ploughs begin to cut the ground, and one hath reaped a rich harvest. Mr. Humfry in London is the owner of it, who I doubt not can fully inform you.[6] For buildings we are already pretty convenient, and still increase. We have slate for our best coverings. We have brick excellent good, and next year we shall have tile (God willing). We can make good lime of oyster shells, which are as big as a man's foot. Our air is temperate, and both heat and cold is comfortably tolerable by the weakest, having warm houses. In a word, I know nothing but is comfortable to a contented mind.

Now for yourself to come, I do earnestly desire it, if God so move your heart, and not only for the commonwealth's sake but also for learning's sake, which I know you love and will be ready to further, and indeed we want store of such men as will further that, for if we nourish not learning, both church and commonwealth will sink, and because I am upon this point I beseech you let me be bold to make one motion for the furtherance of learning among us. God hath bestowed upon you a bountiful blessing. Now if you should please to employ but one mite of that great wealth which God hath given to erect a school of learning, a college among us, you should do a most glorious work, acceptable to God and man, and the commemoration of the first founder of the means of learning would be a perpetuating of your name and honor among us. Now because my proposition may seem to require great charges, I will be bold to propose a way which will make it attainable with little. First, here cannot be lands and revenues in present improved to maintain such a work. All the charge is the building of such a place as may be fit for such a purpose, and such learned men as be here and may come must of their own proper charge frequent those places at fit seasons for the exercising of learning,

5. See Hammond's list below, p. 111. The plantations presumably were Medford, Winnisimmet (Chelsea), and Agawam (Ipswich). Agawam was settled earlier in 1633 to prevent the French from occupying the place. See Albert H. Hall, "How Massachusetts Grew, 1630-1642," *Publications* of the Cambridge Historical Society 21 (1936): 19-49; William Hubbard, *A General History of New England* (Boston, 1848), p. 161, and Winthrop, *History*, 1:120.
6. Humphry's lands were near the Saugus River; he did not come to America till 1634.

and such young men as may be trained up must bear their own charges. Only we want a house convenient. Now the bare building of a house big enough for our young beginnings will be done with little charge. I doubt not but if you should set apart but five hundred pound for that work, it would be a sufficient beginning and would make convenient housing for this many years. Nay, four hundred or three hundred would do pretty well, and this privilege you would have by it, that you should not need to send aforehand (if you should come) to build a house for your habitation, for that would be ready to give you present entertainment, and then you may bestow your charges of building to your own content, where you shall choose, and this very thing may be a brace of hundreds in your way, and for your more easy performance of this work, without any trouble or molestation to yourself or other occasions of weight, do only this. Send a sure bill of payment of such a sum of money to be employed for such and such buildings, etc. I say send such a bill to our worthy governor and who else you will, and they will do the work presently and take payment in England by returning that bill and assigning it to be paid as they think fit for their use, or if you shall please to send so much ready money or so much in merchantable commodities, though it be troublesome. Now I beseech you, consider what an opportunity God hath put into your hand of doing good with that rich portion God hath given you, and if you should pass us by and miss the opportunity, you may lose what you have, and never have the like opportunity again. But I will say no more, only pray unto the Lord to move your heart unto it.

For your own coming, if God so move your heart, I desire to know of it, and I would do my best to write to you such directions as may do you some pleasure. Briefly thus much now: I advise you to bring not many servants, for they be a sure charge and trouble and an uncertain gain. Bring only some few carpenters and masons for your own building and no more, a joiner, etc., but such serving men as you bring for your comfortable attendance, I advise that they be as fair conditioned as you can but poor and such as cannot work, and then you shall keep them, for if they be either rich and workful they will desire freedom, but bring few such for they be ill members in our young commonwealth. I speak it that [you] may not be left destitute of servants, and many, you know, are fit to attend a gentleman that are not fit for labor, yea, and brave ingenious men they be.

As for the bargain you have made with William Hammond for two heifers it is a most indifferent bargain. It will be (by God's blessing) a comfort to the poor man and a sure commodity to yourself, and if you should send to prepare you a good stock on the same terms, you should do well, and here be many honest godly men that would willingly be your servants in it, and I have formerly this summer written to the same purpose to Mr. Barrington,[7] advising him to that very course, and it's the most sure gainful course, and the best way to buy them is to send a bill of payment, and here may be cattle bought as cheap as they can be brought,[8] and your bill will be taken for them and to be paid upon the return of it. It is a sure and easy way. But one word more about the forenamed business: I doubt not but you are well acquainted with many worthy gentlemen which are favorers of learning and will be ready to show some tokens of their bounty this way. If therefore you please to stir up others by your own example and persuasions to join with you in such a glorious work, it will still be to us a great favor and comfort to yourself, I doubt not. But I would not be troublesome nor overbold with your worship, but thus leave you to the Lord's gracious direction and blessing, praying for your prosperity and welfare and eternal happiness.

> Your worship's humbly to be
> command any service I can in Christ,
> John Eliot

September 18

Right dear and worthy sir:

I had fully finished this your letter before I had opportunity to see your letters to our worthy governor, and the sight of them have kindled a new fire in my bosom to be more earnest with your worship to set to your hand even to your own project. I humbly thank you for your tender care of us and for your great respect to our name in the defense of it against the gainsayers.[9] I humbly thank you for putting us in mind of such

7. Son of Lady Barrington, addressed in John Master's letter, above.
8. Compare Hammond's comments, below.
9. Presumably Gorges and his supporters.

weighty and necessary matters. For my own part I have often spake of the writing a history, and some do record the most memorable passages, but none yet have set themselves apart for it, and for a library and a place for the exercise of learning, it's my earnest desire and prayer that God would stir up the heart of some well wishers to learning to make an onset in that kind, and indeed, sir, I know none every way more fit than yourself. I beseech you therefore, consider of it, and do that which may comfort us, and whereas a library is your first project, and then a college, I conceive upon our experience that we shall most need convenient chambers to entertain students at first, and a little room, I fear, will hold all our first stock of books, and as they increase we may enlarge the room. But with us in our young beginnings men want purses to make such buildings, and therefore public exercises of learning be not yet set on foot, though we have many learned men, both gentlemen and ministers, but had we a place fitted we should have our terms and seasons for disputations and lectures, not only in divinity but in other arts and sciences and in law also, for that would be very material for the welfare of our commonwealth.

And now I will say no more but pray that the Lord would move your heart (which yet I hope is already moved) to be the first founder of so glorious a work as this is.

Eliot alludes to William Hammond and the bargain D'Ewes had made with him. More is said about this transaction in a letter that Hammond's father sent to D'Ewes. A man of fifty-eight, the older Hammond had been a tenant of D'Ewes. Having come to America probably in 1630, he had settled at Watertown. Hammond's letter is written clearly but his spelling is picturesque, and he wrote in a Suffolk dialect. He was a simple man, and his letter quite lacks self-consciousness, after a few preliminary apologies. Consequently he was able to discuss unaffectedly whatever had caused him to marvel, such as the new and strict moral code created by the colonists. Hammond's original letter is British Museum manuscript Harley 386, folios 34-35.

William Hammond to Sir Simonds D'Ewes
September 26, 1633

Sir Simmyones:

I am something bold to write unto your worship desiring your worship to pardon me my writing unto your worship is to certify your worship in something concerning new Eingland in amereyca. My son telleth me that your worship did give him twenty pounds to buy you a couple of bullocks here to breed a stock. They are wonderful dear here. There is none to be gotten but at a great price. A cow is worth here twenty-five pounds; a calf of this year is worth here ten pounds, and none to be gotten; a mare is worth here thirty pounds. There came over this year many people and brought no cattle with them. I went to Master Governor and told him of it and I did deliver him a letter that your worship sent him and he did read it, and he doth much rejoice and so do all the assistants that your worship is such a good willer to new eingland. I told him how you took my son twenty pounds to buy two bullocks, and I told him that I had inquired in the plantations for two bullocks for your worship, and I would have bought two of him but he had none, but he hath promised me that he will help me to two for your worship. He is to have some come from vergenya, and as soon as they come, he telleth me I shall have two, and there is a gentleman hath promised me two as soon as they come. But resolve that I will not fail you of a couple, for if I cannot have them in our plantation I will go to plimworth [Plymouth] for them. That is forty mile from us.

I think it good to certify your worship something of the country. We dwell in a place which is called marthateutyeis bay. It is a place full of islands that the sea compassed them in, and we have many good harbors for the ships to ride in. First, for the country, it is a very good air, for we have none sick here. We have much champaign ground, many hills which are rocky, much marsh ground with fresh rivers, many great ponds two or three miles about, and great store of fresh fish in them: perch, roach [chub?], and pikes, and other fish which we know not the names; great store of timber but no bushes,[1] and as for fish, some three leagues at sea from us they will go out with a shallop, and in a day and a night some time three men or boys will

1. The Indians destroyed the underwood to make hunting easier.

catch three or four hundred of codfish or a great fish, we call it a bass, very good fish, and we have great store of mackerel, and we have a fish we call it a holy back [halibut]. Some of them are nigh as big and as long as a man, and it is a handful thick, and we have great store of oshetures [oysters]. Some are ten inches long. Fowl here are good store, as geese and duck and teal and some swans and cranes and here are great store of heath pheasants [heath hens], and when it is an acorn year here our pigeons abound.[2] You may think that I do tell you an untruth: this time three years we all in the country did see so many pigeons as might have loaded two or three ships. For two hours we did behold them. They did fly for six miles of breadth, so thick that they covered the air that we did think that the first flight was twenty miles afore the last came. Those that did not see them might think it was not true, but it is very true that I write to your worship. We have a river some thirty miles from us is called mereynick [Merrimack] river. There is a great store of sturgeon. We have many go a-fishing for some thither but the engeines [Indians] catch them for them. Here is good store of deer; were it not for the wolves here would be abound, for the does have most two fawns at once, and some have three, but the wolves destroy them, and they kill our goats and our pigs. Had we but a kennel of great hounds we should hunt them from our plantations. Our cattle thrive very well here.

We have here eight hundred trained soldiers,[3] and we have good captains, and we have a fort, and here are twenty pieces of ordnance. We have some eight towns and villages: one town called Salume, and one called Dorchester; one called Roxberey; one called Bostan; one called Saugus;[4] and one called Charles towne; one called new toune; and one called waltur toune.[5] We have good laws here. We have, thanks be to God, a wise, religious governor, and every month we have a court, and there all causes are heard, and witness cometh in, jury panelled, and if men deserve the law, they have [it]. If not, they are cleared. We have few that are drunk, and here is no swearing, for if they be drunk or swear if it be known, they are punished. We have good teaching. Here it pleased God to send over hither this year three good ministers, Mr. Hocker, and Mr. Cotton, and Mr. Ston,[6] three excellent teachers, and as for the eingeines, we have but few amongst us. They are quiet, but the governor, if they do offend, have them fetched before him and admonish

2. The same passenger pigeons mentioned above by Dudley.
3. Citizen-soldiers, trained by experienced captains who were brought over for the work.
4. In 1637 it was renamed Lynn.
5. Watertown was frequently so spelled.
6. Thomas Hooker, John Cotton, and Samuel Stone had arrived only three weeks before.

them and if that any of them steal, the sagamore that is over them bring them to the court and there they are punished. They go naked with a skin or a blanket about them. Thanks be to God, it is like to be a flourishing plantation, and as for the buying of two bullocks for your worship, I will do it without [delay]. If we had but four mares, they would be a great stay for the country. We have five team of bullocks and horse in the country, but they are nothing to serve the country for plowing.[7] Ould eingland corn grow well here. Barley, oats, and rye here was this year very good. Thus I leave writing to your worship, leaving your worship to the protection of almighty God, from waltur toune in new eingland in amereyca, your worship to command me.

Wiliam Hammond

To the right worshipful Sir Simmyuns Deuese, knight, at sente Edmondes, bereye, give this.

7. Compare William Wood's statement made the same year that "there are fifteen hundred head of cattle, besides four thousand goats, and swine innumerable." *New Englands Prospect* (Boston, 1865), p. 54.

Compared with Eliot's and Hammond's respectful letters, Winthrop's is abrupt. The governor was a busy man. More realistic than Eliot, he was reluctant to encourage D'Ewes in his thoughts on migration. The most important features of Winthrop's letter are his belief that perfection is not to be reached in this world and his care not to say much about certain aspects of the colony's "practices and judgment." He merely alludes to departures from the practices of the Church of England, perhaps the limitation of church membership to those who could provide evidence that they had saving faith. But like Eliot, Winthrop considers the new ways of the colony solidly established through uniformity of opinion about what the ideal should be; it follows from "the state of things, as we see them." Winthrop's original letter is British Museum manuscript Harley 388, folio 186.

Worthy Sir:

Yours by young Hammond I received and cannot but most
thankfully accept your kind remembrance of me, and your
good affection to this work, which the Lord's own hand hath
begun and upheld hitherto, and in the prosperity whereof some
blessing and comfort may redound to all the churches of Christ.
For our estate here both politic and ecclesiastical I know you
are already sufficiently informed and although we cannot profess a perfection in either (which is not to be looked for in this
world) yet it is such as the Lord's holy and wise servants (such
as he hath vouchsafed to bestow upon us both formerly and
now of late) do approve of and accordingly do join with us in
the same course. I mean especially those two reverend and faithful ministers Mr. Cotton and Mr. Hooker, who lately arrived
here with their families in as good health (praised be God) as
when they came forth, although Mrs. Cotton was delivered of a
son at sea, who was since baptized on shore and named Sea-
borne.[1]

For your advice about our affairs, I am much beholden to
your care of us and do concur with your opinion in the most,
as our practice doth declare, and shall be somewhat rectified
by your advice at present and more as our means may be enlarged, but in the last, both our practice and judgment differ
from yours, but I suppose we should soon be agreed if you were
here to see the state of things, as we see them. I think [it] not
fit to enter into particulars because letters are subject to mis-
carry, but you can conceive my meaning. I cannot enlarge
towards you as your love deserves. I hope you will consider my
occasions and many letters which I must write. How you should
employ any stock here, except you send some faithful man to
manage it, I cannot advise you. Only you may drive a trade with
the Lord here in helping forward the work of the Gospel by

1. Cotton's first child was
not baptized at sea be-
cause there was no settled
congregation on the ship.
Congregationalism taught
that to be considered a
minister, a clergyman had
to have a congregational
charge. Imagining a min-
ister without a congre-
gation was, according to
William Ames, "as ridicu-
lous as trying to imagine a
husband without a wife."
John H. Eusden, ed., *The
Marrow of Theology*
(Boston, 1968),
pp. 209-10.

sending over some poor godly families with a year's provision, which I account one of the best works which may be performed at this season. If you will please to raise a colony here in that manner (which would not be difficult for yourself with such godly friends as you may have to join with you), I would take off any further trouble from you about it, but I leave it to your consideration.

So with my hearty salutation and due respect to yourself and your lady, I commend you to the Lord and take my leave. I rest yours to do you service in the Lord.

Jo: Winthrop

Massachusetts, N[ew] Eng[land]
September 26, 1633
To the right worshipful my honored friend Sir Simond Dewes Knight, High Street of the County of Suff[olk] shire, to be delivered.

1634

Winthrop was far more generous with his comments in a letter written in the following spring. Here he explains clearly both the representative nature of the commonwealth's political government and the semi-democratic nature of the church government. He also tells a story that shows how the settlement of New England was creating some friction between colonies. The letter is addressed to Sir Nathaniel Rich, a prominent member of the Virginia Company in the 1620s, who had assisted the Massachusetts Bay Company in its dealings with Gorges. Later he was involved in the colony established off the coast of the Yucatan peninsula. He died in 1636. Winthrop's original letter is in the Public Records Office, London, numbered G.D. 15, no. 421.

John Winthrop to Sir Nathaniel Rich
May 22, 1634

Worthy sir:

That you are pleased among your many and weighty employments to spend so many serious thoughts and good wishes upon us and the work of the Lord in our hands, I must needs acknowledge it among other the special favors of God towards us and an undoubted testimony of your sincere love towards us, which makes me the more careful to satisfy your desire of being truly informed of our estate (this being the first safe means of conveyance since I received yours in October last.)

You may please therefore to understand that first, for the number of our people, we never took any survey of them, nor do we intend it, except enforced through urgent occasion (David's example sticks somewhat with us[1]), but I esteem them to be in all about four thousand souls and upward, in good health (for the most part) and well provided of all necessaries, so as (through the Lord's special providence) there hath not died above two or three grown persons and about so many children all the last year, it being very rare to hear of any sick

1. David's counting his troops brought down God's wrath. See 1 Chron. 21:1-8.

of agues or other diseases, nor have I known of any quartan ague[2] among us since I came into the country.

For our subsistence here, the means hitherto hath been the yearly access of newcomers, who have supplied all our wants for cattle and the fruits of our labor, as board, pale, smith's work, etc. If this should fail, then we have other means which may supply us as fish, viz., cod, bass, and herring, for which no place in the world exceeds us if we can compass salt at a reasonable rate. Our grounds likewise are apt for hemp and flax and rape seeds and all sorts of roots, pumpkins, and other fruits, which for taste and wholesomeness far exceed those in England. Our grapes also (wherewith the country abounds) afford a good hard wine. Our ploughs go on with good success; we are like to have twenty at work next year. Our lands are aptest for rye and oats.[3] Our winters are sharp and long. I may reckon four months for storing of cattle, but we find no difference whether they be housed or go abroad. Our summers are somewhat more fervent in heat than in England. Our civil government is mixed; the freemen choose the magistrates every year (and for the present they have chosen Tho[mas] Dudley, esquire, governor), and at four courts in the year three out of each town (there being eight in all) do assist the magistrates in making of laws, imposing taxes, and disposing of lands. Our juries are chosen by the freemen of every town. Our churches are governed by pastors, teachers, ruling elders, and deacons, yet the power lies in the whole congregation and not in the presbytery further than for order and precedency.

For the natives, they are near all dead of the smallpox, so as the Lord hath cleared our title to what we possess.

I shall now acquaint you with a sad accident which lately fell out between our neighbors of Plimouth and some of the Lord Saye his servants at Pascat[aqua]. They of Pl[imouth] having engrossed all the chief places of trade in N[ew] E[ngland], viz., Kenebeck, Penobscot, Narigancet, and Conecticott, have erected trading houses in all of them.[4] The Lord's pinnace going with three men and a boy to trade at Kenebeck, were forbidden, and, persisting in their purpose, two of the magistrates of Pl[imouth], viz., Jo[hn] Alden and Jo[hn] Howlande and about nine more, came up to them in their pinnace and sent three men in a canoe to cut the cables of the Pas[cataqua] pinnace (her

2. Malaria.
3. When immigration stopped after 1640, there was a depression. See Darrett B. Rutman, "Governor Winthrop's Garden Crop: The Significance of Agriculture in the Early Commerce of Massachusetts Bay," *William and Mary Quarterly*, 3rd ser. 20 (1963): 396-415.
4. Between 1631 and 1636 the Plymouth colony shipped more than ten thousand pounds' worth of fur to England. See William Bradford, *Of Plymouth Plantation*, ed. Worthington C. Ford, 2 vols. (Boston, 1912), 2:229-30.

master, one Hockin, having given them provoking speeches)
and stood in their own pinnace with their pieces charged and
ready to shoot. After they had cut one cable Hockin came up
and asked them if they meant to cast away his vessel, etc., and
sware withal that he would kill him that should come to cut the
other, whereupon (the canoe being driven away with the
strength of the stream) they took out him that steered her and
put in another and sent them again to cut the other cable,
which while one was doing (for it was cut), Hockin shot one of
them in the canoe dead, upon which one of Pl[imouth] men
out of their pinnace shot at Hockin and killed him upon the
place, whereupon another of Hockin's company, coming up
upon the deck one of Pl[imouth] men asked Howland if he
should kill him also, but he forbade him, saying he feared
there had been too many killed already. The pinnace being then
driven on shore and in danger, the Pl[imouth] men saved her
and put one of their own men into her to carry her homewards
towards Pasc[ataqua]. Upon the report of this we were much
grieved that such an occasion should be offered to our enemies
to reproach our profession and that such an injury should be
offered to those honorable persons who for love of us and for
furtherance of our beginnings here had so far engaged themselves with us, so as we wrote to them to know the truth of the
matter and whether they would advow it. They wrote to us
again relating the matter in effect as I have expressed, with justification of the fact, etc.; yet declaring their sorrow that it had
happened so sadly otherwise than they intended. But they did
not doubt but [that] their grant would bear them out. Upon this
we refuse to hold communion with them till they give better
satisfaction, and having the said Alden before us at a General
Court, we took security of him for his forthcoming and wrote
to them what and wherefore we had done it, and upon their
answer that themselves would do justice in the cause, we re-
mitted him to them as having no jurisdiction in it to try it ourselves. All that we aim at is that they may come to see their sin
and repent of it, which if they shall do, I would entreat you to
intercede with the Lords for them that the injury and discour-
tesy may be passed by upon such satisfaction as they can make.

I can think of nothing more at present to acquaint you with.
So desiring the continuance of your care and prayers for us as

we wish and rejoice in the success of your like undertakings to the southward, I take leave and rest.

> Yours ever to be commanded in the Lord,
> Jo: Winthrop

Boston Massachu[se]ts N[ew] E[ngland]
May 22, 1634
Here are six ships lately arrived with passengers and cattle. Most of them came in six weeks' space. We have settled a plantation twenty miles to the northward, near Merimacke. Mr. Parker is to be minister there.[5]

Letters from New England survived for a variety of reasons. Many survived because the recipient was a collector of documents, some because they dealt with important matters, others by chance. Even letters of no consequence have something to tell about the colonists. Here is Governor Winthrop writing to his trusty shipmaster; Winthrop knew that one should send only first-class merchandise across the expanse of the ocean. A photocopy of the original letter is at the Massachusetts Historical Society; the location of the original letter is not known.

John Winthrop to Thomas Graves
June 5, 1634

Mr. Graves:

I pray bring me a pair of mill stones, peak stones, seven foot broad and of thickness answerable. They are for a windmill,[1] and upon sight hereof this shall be sufficient warrant to my brother Downinge to deliver you money for them. So I rest.

> Your loving friend,
> Jo: Winthrop

Massachusetts
N[ew] England, June 5, 1634
Mr. Pincheon[2] desires you to bring him six chalder of sea coal.
[Endorsed, in another hand] Mr. Downing in Lenckoun End Felds, by the Goulden Lion's tower.

5. Thomas Parker and others settled at Agawam, later Ipswich.

1. Boston's first windmill was one that had been set up near Newtown, but there, Winthrop reports, "it would not grind but with a westerly wind." The second windmill, perhaps the one for which Winthrop was ordering the stones, was built in 1636. See Winthrop, *History*, 1:104, 234.

2. William Pynchon, an early member of the Massachusetts Bay Company who later was the founder of Springfield.

When Winthrop preached his famous sermon "A Modell of Christian Charity" on his way to America, he declared that one of the colony's aims was to create "a due form of government both civil and ecclesiastical." Sir Simonds D'Ewes had advice for Winthrop on this subject in 1634. Despite Winthrop's unwillingness to let him know the character of the New England churches, D'Ewes had somehow found out. The New England Way, as it came to be called, was congregational, not episcopal; it made no use of the Book of Common Prayer; and it was beginning to question the validity of ordinations to the ministry in the Church of England. Winthrop shows that he was fully aware how far Massachusetts Bay had departed from the ways of old England in the four years since its creation; he also shows great confidence in the rightness and righteousness of the new ways. Winthrop's original letter is British Museum manuscript Harley 388, folios 186-88.

John Winthrop to Sir Simonds D'Ewes
July 21, 1634

Much honored Sir:

Yours per William Hamond I received, acknowledging myself so much bound to you that you are pleased to take all occasions to manifest your good will to our colony and to myself in particular [so] that I would gladly have bestowed much pains in satisfying your desire concerning the estate of our country and affairs, and I did hope upon the discharge of my place to have good leisure to that end, but our new governor (my brother Dudly) dwelling out of the way,[1] I am still as full of company and business as before. But for the natives in these parts, God's hand hath so pursued them as, for three hundred miles' space, the greatest part of them are swept away by the smallpox, which still continues among them.[2] So as God hath hereby cleared our title to this place, and those who remain in these parts, being in all not fifty, have put themselves under our protection and freely confined themselves and their interest within certain limits.

For your counsel of conforming ourselves to the Church of England, though I doubt not but it proceeds out of your care of our welfare, yet I dare not thank you for it, because it is not

1. Thomas Dudley lived at Newtown.
2. The epidemic of 1616-17 killed all but about seventeen thousand New England Indians. The Massachusetts tribe's population dropped from three thousand to five hundred in the fifteen years before 1630. See Vaughan, *New England Frontier*, pp. 28-29, 54.

conformable to God's will revealed in His Word. What you may do in England where things are otherwise established, I will not dispute but our case here is otherwise, being come to clearer light and more liberty, which we trust by the good hand of our God with us and the gracious indulgence of our King we may freely enjoy it.

So desiring you to excuse my brevity and to continue your good will towards us, I commend you with your good lady and all yours to the gracious protection and direction of the Lord, and so I take leave and rest at your service in the Lord.

Jo. Winthrop

Boston, N[ew] E[ngland],
July 21, 1634
To the right worshipful Sir Simond Dewes knight at Lavenham in Suff[olk] deliver.
Leave this with Mr. Gurdon or with Mr. Rogers of Dedham.[3]
To the right worshipful his much honored friend and cousin Sir Simeon Dewes at Lavenham in Suff[olk] deliver.

The flood of migration to New England was not ignored in the mother country. In 1634 Archbishop Laud received a report from Henry Dade, commissary of Suffolk, that ships were about to sail for New England with persons whom he believed to be "either indebted persons or persons discontented with the government of the Church of England." He noted that "If suffered to go in such swarms [he believed as many as six hundred were to go], it will be a decrease of the king's people here, an increase of the adversaries of the episcopal state, and will also be an overthrow of trade." Presumably as a consequence the Privy Council ordered the detention of eight vessels that were ready to leave for New England. The Council then ordered the masters of the ships to give bonds of one hundred pounds that worship services according to the Book of Common Prayer would be held daily on board ship (the puritans found much of the prayer book, even the very concept of a book of prayers, highly objectionable), and that they would not receive persons who had not taken the oaths of allegiance and supremacy (the puritans considered God, not the king, supreme).

3. Brampton Gurdon was an old friend of Winthrop; the Reverend John Rogers was a famous Puritan preacher. The letter has two addresses, in different hands.

The efforts to keep puritans—who were judged to be dangerously subversive—from migrating were unsuccessful, because the officials given responsibility for ascertaining the loyalty of those who planned to migrate were often sympathetic with puritanism. Other kinds of restrictions were more successful, and as a result it became very expensive to ship many kinds of merchandise to the new land. The situation is well described in a petition made by "the planters of New England" sometime around 1634. This document was accompanied by a list of the liberties granted to the Bay colonists by the charter and a list of the liberties that the colonists were being denied. The original manuscript is in the Public Record Office, London, numbered C.O. 1/8, folios 112-14.

The Planters of New England to King Charles I
1634 [?]

To the King's Most Excellent Majesty
The Humble Petition of the Planters of New England

Most humbly show

That a restraint hath formerly been made that no ship intending for the plantations in New England shall have liberty to go that voyage until they have license from the lords of his majesty's Privy Council, which hath been a means to enrich the agents that procured such license but hath impoverished the planters and merchants who have paid for the same, and much time hath passed before such licenses could be obtained, the voyages of the ships have by that means been hindered, the passengers' estates much weakened, and much of their goods have been spoiled by the long stay of the ships after they have been freighted before they could be cleared.

That a restraint hath been to transport to the said plantations necessaries for foods, apparel, and munion [munition], without which and some supply (as yet) from this kingdom those planters cannot comfortably subsist nor be secure from enemies.

That the searchers after some ships have been laden have caused them to be unladen and unpacked and broken up their goods, to the great charge and damage of the owners thereof, that great customs taxes have been laid upon such goods and merchandise as have been transported to those parts, so that some things could not be carried thither by reason of the great impost laid on them, although not otherwise prohibited, which hath been a great discouragement to the planters.

Now for as much as this kingdom being supplied from foreign parts with divers necessaries which in itself it hath not, may very probably in short time be supplied with the same from New England, which in case of restraint elsewhere will be for the great security of this nation, as namely with cordage, cables, sails, canvas, pitch, and tar (there being great store of pitch trees) and likewise good masts (there being goodly mast trees, big enough to fit the tallest ship in England) as also with all sorts of timber fit for navigation, which is so decayed in this nation that within these seven last years it's advanced to near double value.

The petitioners humbly pray that the merchants and planters in the several places of New England and of this kingdom may have freedom to transport to the said plantations all their portable estates which by law are not forbidden, with all other necessaries for food, apparel, tackle, and munition and other things fitting for the plantation and that the said merchants and planters may have privilege to freight ships for the said plantations without any license, tax, or penalty whatsoever, and that all goods and merchandise for the supportation and encouragement of the said planters may be free of all customs and imposts exportable and importable to and from the same, and that the grant of the petitioners' humble desires may receive a speedy dispatch in regard the season for the Newfoundland voyage is now approaching, which opportunity being lost, the charge of transportation to the said plantations will be almost double.

And the petitioners shall daily pray, etc.

A Particular of the Liberties Granted to the Planters of New England, Their Factors, and Agents, by His Majesty's Letters Patent Dated 4 March Anno 4th Carolus

1. Liberty to transport as many of his majesty's liege people as are willing to go to New England except such as should be restrained by special name.
2. Liberty to transport all shipping.
3. Liberty to transport armor, weapons, ordnance, munitions, powder, shot, corn, victuals, and all manner of clothing, imple-

ments, furniture, beasts, cattle, horses, merchandises, and all other things necessary for the plantation for use and defense with the people.

4. Liberty to go custom-free for the same by the space of seven years from the date of the patent.

5. Liberty to be custom-free for the space of twenty-one years for all goods and merchandise exported or imported except only paying five per cent.

6. That the sight of the letters patent or duplicate or the enrollment shall be to the Treasurer, Chancellor, Barons of the Exchequer and to all customers, farmers, searchers and other Officers a sufficient discharge and warrant in that behalf for exportation or importation of goods at five pounds per cent.

That the Planters of New England, Their Factors and Agents Have Been Barred of the Liberties Granted by Letters Patent

1. That a general restraint hath been used against all his majesty's liege people bound for New England until an oath taken by them and a certificate of conformity brought and especially for subsidy men or valuable unto subsidy men who must be at the charge of license.

2. That no shipping, no, not those that are built in New England and belonging to the planters there can be suffered to depart for that plantation without license first obtained at great charge.

3. That no armor, weapons, ordnance, powder, shot, corn, victual, clothing, beasts, cattle, horses, or merchandise can be transported without license first obtained.

4. That greater customs and impositions are required for goods imported and exported than five per cent of the planters, etc.

5. That other warrants are required of the planters, etc., than the showing of the letters patent, duplicate or enrollment.

6. That nine pence per head hath been taken and is usually paid and taken for each passenger before he can be at liberty to depart.

7. That the ship *James* ready to set sail, being laden according to the course by the custom formerly allowed of for lading New England ships had her goods taken all out again by the searchers and detained months not relieved but upon redemption at eighty pounds' charge beside the loss and spoil of part of the goods.

⚜ Despite their independence and their creation of new structures, the men of Massachusetts Bay continued to rely on the old country for many things. Thus, in the fall of 1634 John Winthrop, Jr., accompanied by the Reverend John Wilson, went on a mission to England. Winthrop's wife had died in childbirth not long before, and he handed over his house and household in Ipswich, where he had lived for a year after helping to found it, to the Reverend Nathaniel Ward. Winthrop's primary tasks were to encourage emigration to the Bay and to make purchases for the colony. Perhaps, since the New Englanders valued families highly, he was also looking for a wife.

The governor wrote to young John, and two letters survive. In the first, Winthrop refers to the famous incident of Endecott and the cross in the ensign, later to be made the subject of a story by Nathaniel Hawthorne. What seems to have happened is that the Salem militia carried in drill a flag with a red St. George's Cross in a white canton, the so-called King's Colors. Endecott defaced the flag, apparently at the urging of Roger Williams, by cutting out part of the cross, which he considered a relic of antichrist because it had been given to the king of England by the pope. The matter was much disputed, with Thomas Hooker writing a paper in opposition to Endecott. Finally the General Court sidestepped the real issue of idolatry and censured Endecott for failing to recognize that authority in such matters rested with the government, not the individual. Endecott was barred for one year from holding any public office. The views of Williams and Endecott did, however, prevail, and from 1636 to 1686 the Massachusetts Bay Colony used a flag without a cross. The use of a distinctive flag is a mark of the colony's individuality and sense of independence.

The original letter is Massachusetts Historical Society manuscript W. 7A.

John Winthrop to John Winthrop, Jr.
November 6, 1634

1. Presumably the Reverend John Wilson. The name Warner was meant to serve as a disguise, since Wilson might "be troubled and detained" in England, according to Winthrop's journal. (*History*, 1:183).

My dear son:

I hope the Lord hath carried you safe to E[ngland] with our most dear Mr. Warner[1] and the rest of our good brethren and friends. There is nothing befallen since your departure, but

Mr. Peirce came from Naragansett three days after, with five hundred bushels of corn only.[2] At the Court it was informed that some of Salem had taken out a piece of the cross in their ensign, whereupon we sent forth an attachment to bring in the parties at the next Court, where they are like to be punished for their indiscreet zeal, for the people are generally offended with it. Mrs. W. was at first very much affected with her husband's departure, but she is now well pacified. I intend to send this letter by Captain Underhill, who hath leave to go see his friends in Holland.[3] If he come to you, he can inform you of all things here. As I was writing this, Rich[ard] came in and told me the dog had killed an old wolf this morning in our neck: she made more resistance than both the former. I have many things to write to you about, for such necessaries as are to be provided and sent over, but this occasion is sudden, and I cannot think of them but shall write more largely by Mr. P[eirce] if the Lord will. Yourself know what will be needful, and therefore may consider accordingly. Remember copperas white and green[4] and two or three pounds of Paracellsus plaster,[5] and some East Indian bezoar, store of sail cloth, nails, cordage, pitch, tallow and wick, steel spades and shovels, two hand saws and small axes, the best of all whatever they cost. Commend us to all our good friends where you be come: Mr. W. and the rest, your uncles, aunts, etc. Advise Mr. W. to keep close by all news, and make haste back. The good Lord bless and prosper you that we may see your face with joy. Your mother, etc., salute and bless you. Farewell.

[John Winthrop]

November 6, 1634
To my loving son Mr. John Winthrop deliver, at Mr. Downinge his chamber in the Inner Temple Lane, London.

The leading minister of the Massachusetts Bay Colony during its first decade was John Cotton, author of five letters in this collection. Born in 1584, Cotton studied at Cambridge University. Following his graduation he became a fellow of Emmanuel College, soon famous for its puritanism, and there he remained for nearly ten years. One of his colleagues at

2. Presumably he was trading with the Indians of what is now Rhode Island.
3. On March 22, 1630/1, the Court of Assistants had ordered that "every person within their town (except magistrates and ministers) as well servants as others be furnished with good and sufficient arms allowable by the captain or other officers" and on the following April 12 that "every captain shall train his company on Saturday in every week." Captain Underhill headed a company at Boston and Roxbury. See *Records of the Court of Assistants*, 2:12, 13, 18.
4. Used in drying, tanning, and making ink and medicine.
5. Plaster containing minerals.

Emmanuel was Thomas Hooker, who eventually migrated to America on the same ship as Cotton. In 1612 Cotton became vicar of St. Botolph's Church at Boston in Lincolnshire, an unusually large and beautiful church. There he established a reputation as a great and learned preacher. (Some of the sermons of Cotton's years at St. Botolph's eventually found their way into print, after Cotton had come to America.) In 1615 he became more determined in his puritanism and as a result created within his parish a group that covenanted together "to follow after the Lord in the purity of his worship." Thus a kind of Congregationalism was established within a Church of England parish.

At St. Botolph's Church Cotton managed to practice his puritanism for some time without harassment. Even when the stained glass and statuary of the church was destroyed in 1621, Cotton kept his post. In the last years of the 1620s he became interested in the Massachusetts Bay venture, and though as already noted he reprimanded his old friend Samuel Skelton, then at Salem, for what appeared to Cotton to be religious radicalism, he was sufficiently sympathetic with the 1630 migration to preach at Southampton to Winthrop's group, which included many Lincolnshire folk. The sermon was published the same year as *Gods Promise to his Plantation.*

Soon after, Cotton was ill with malaria for nearly a year, during which he stayed with the Earl of Lincoln, a good friend to the Bay colonists. While he was ill, his Boston parish was served by his wife's cousin, Anthony Tuckney. On Cotton's recovery but before he could return to Boston, word reached him that he was being sought for his puritanism by that most strenuous opponent of nonconformity, Bishop William Laud. Cotton went into hiding. He thought for a time that he might go to Holland, which offered some kind of protection, but Thomas Hooker's experiences there were not encouraging. So in May of 1633 he resigned his position at St. Botolph's, in June he took ship for New England, and in October, a month after his arrival, he became teacher of the church at new Boston, with John Wilson as pastor.

Soon after he arrived in New England John Cotton began something like a career of justifying himself and his ecclesiastical ideas, and in time he produced such major works as *The Way of the Churches of Christ in New-England.* In the year following his move to America he wrote back to an unidentified puritan clergyman still in England to set forth his reasons for coming to America. His explanation does not invoke a divine cosmic plan that existed for the future of America, such as the second generation was to cite in justification of the "Fathers of New England." Cotton was far more practical. The original letter survives in the Massachusetts Archives, and though the archival original is the basis for the transcript that follows, I have benefited from the readings of the editors of the *Hutchinson Papers* (Albany, 1865), who consulted the manuscript when it was in better condition that it now is.

John Cotton to an Unidentified Clergyman
December 3, 1634

Reverend and beloved brother in our blessed savior:

That which you observe touching the wonderful goodness of the Lord to my wife and child, in the midst of deep dangers, I desire never to forget it,[1] but to walk (as the Lord shall be pleased to help me) according to that abundant faithfulness of his to one so undeserving all my days. Help me with your faithful prayers so to do, that as by the prayers of yourself and other brethren, I acknowledge the former mercy to have been granted to me, so by the same a faithful and fruitful use of it may be granted to me likewise. Otherwise I may say it with shame, I see a frame of spirit in myself ready to turn every grace of God into unprofitableness, yea and forgetfulness of the most high God, the God of our salvation. Howsoever God dealt otherwise with my cousin Tuckney[2] and which might give unto some whom it nearly concerned a seasonable advertisement, yet I am persuaded it was in much faithfulness to her that God took her away to prevent the disquietness and discouragement of her spirit, which the evils ensuing, evils hastening upon the town, would have brought upon her.[3] The Lord is wise and gracious and knoweth how to deliver his out of the hour of temptation. Blessed for ever be his name in Christ.

The questions you demand, I had rather answer by word of mouth than by letter, yet I will not refuse to give you account of my brother Hooker's removal and mine own, seeing you require a reason thereof from us both. We both of us concur in a

1. Cotton's first wife having died in 1631 or 1632, leaving him childless, Cotton married again in 1632. This second wife gave birth to a son, Seaborn, on the way to America.
2. The wife of Anthony Tuckney, Cotton's successor at St. Botolph's, had died.
3. I have not been able to ascertain what Cotton refers to.

threefold ground of our removal. 1. God having shut a door against both of us from ministering to him and his people in our wonted congregations and calling us by a remnant of our people and by others of this country to minister to them here, and opening a door to us this way, who are we that we should strive against God and refuse to follow the concurrence of his ordinance and providence together, calling us forth to minister here. If we may and ought to follow God's calling three hundred miles, why not three thousand? 2. Our savior's warrant is clear and strong (as we conceive) in our case, that when we are distressed in our course in one country (*ne quiddicam gravius* [not to speak of something more severe]), we should flee to another. To choose rather to bear witness to the truth by imprisonment than by banishment is indeed sometimes God's way, but not in case men have ability of body and opportunity to remove, and no necessary engagement for to stay. Whilst Peter was young he might gird himself and go wither he would, John 21.18, but when he was old and unfit for travel, then indeed God called him rather to suffer himself to be girt of others and led along to prison and to death.[4] Nevertheless in this point I conferred with the chief of our people, and offered them to bear witness to the truth I had preached and practiced amongst them even unto bonds, if they conceived it might be any confirmation to their faith and patience, but they dissuaded me that course, as thinking it better for themselves and for me and for the church of God to withdraw myself from the present storm and to minister in this country to such of their town as they had sent before hither, and such as were willing to go along with me or to follow after me, the most of the [illegible] choosing rather to dwell in the [a line and a half illegible] there. What service myself and brother Hooker might do to our people or other brethren (especially in close prison, which was feared) I suppose we both of us (by God's help) do the same and much more and with more freedom from hence as occasion is offered, besides all our other service to the people here, which yet is enough and more than enough to fill both our hands, yea and the hands of many brethren more, such as yourself, should God be pleased to make way for your comfortable passage to us. To have tarried in England for the end you mention, to appear in defense of that cause for which we were questioned, had been (as we conceive it in our case) to limit witness-bearing to the

4. Cotton's elderly adviser John Dod, referred to later in this letter, is said to have advised Cotton by saying, "I am old Peter, and therefore must stand still and bear the brunt, but you, being young Peter, may go whither you will and ought being persecuted in one city, to flee unto another." See Cotton Mather, *Magnalia Christi Americana* (Hartford, 1855), 1:263.

cause (which may be done more ways than one) to one way only, and that such a way as we do not see God calling us unto. Did not Paul bear witness against the levitical ceremonies and yet choose rather to depart out of Hierusalem because the most of the Jews would not receive his testimony concerning Christ in that question (Acts 22. 18) than to stay at Hierusalem to bear witness to that cause unto prison and death? Not that we came hither to strive against ceremonies (or to fight against shadows): there is no need of our further labor in that course; our people here desire to worship God in spirit and in truth, and our people left in England know as well the grounds and reasons of our sufferings against these things as our sufferings themselves, which we beseech the Lord to accept and bless in our blessed savior. How far our testimony there hath prevailed with any others to search more seriously into the cause, we do rather observe in thankfulness and silence than speak of to the prejudice of our brethren.

3. It hath been no small inducement to us to choose rather to remove hither than to stay there that we might enjoy the liberty not of some ordinances of God but of all, and all in purity. For though we bless the Lord with you for the gracious means of salvation, which many of your congregation do enjoy (whereof our own souls have found the blessings and which we desire may be forever continued and enlarged to you), yet seeing Christ hath instituted no ordinance in vain (but all to the perfecting of the body of Christ) and we know that our souls stand in need of all to the utmost, we durst not so far be wanting to the grace of Christ and to the necessity of our own souls as to sit down somewhere else under the shadow of some ordinances when by two months' travail we might come to enjoy the liberty of all.

To your second question, how far ministers are bound to bear witness against corruptions cast upon the face of God's ordinances, it is too large a point for me to give answer to in the heel of a letter. But thus much briefly: witness is to be borne against corruptions 1. By keeping a man's own garments clean; I mean his own outward practice. Revelation 16. 15. 2. By declaring the whole counsel of God to his people, not shunning any part of it, as reasonable occasion is offered, to prevent sin in them. Acts 20. 26, 27. By avoiding appearances of evil as well as evil itself. I Thessalonians 5.22. Eleazerus durst not eat mutton or bread or any other clean food when it had an appearance of eating swine's flesh but chose death rather than deliverance by such means. II Maccabees chapter 6, verses 21 to 25, whose story though it be apocryphal yet the example is authentical as being ratified by the apostle's testimony amongst the rest of like nature, Hebrews 11. 35, where by the others he speaketh of, he meaneth not other women but other men, for the word is ἄλλοι, masculine. Howsoever, Peter's dissembling is evidently blamed by Paul in a like case, when by his example he countenanced the imposing of ceremonies upon the Gentiles, to whom God never gave them. Galatians 2. 11 to 14.

4. By contending for the truth in an holy manner, when others with us against it. Jude 3.4.5. By giving account of our faith before magistrates if they call us to it publicly requiring to be informed of our doctrine and manner of life. I Peter 3. 14. Otherwise, if they call us to know our opinions in private (intending to bring us into trouble) or publicly rather as captious questioners than judicial governors, in such a case I suppose we may conceal our minds and put our adversaries upon proof as our savior did, John 18. 19, 20, 21. But why do I spend time and words to you in these things, who know them as well as I can tell you. I rather desire you may be kept in a peaceable way of bearing witness to the truth (if the will of God be such) than exposed to hazards by such confessions as might prejudice your liberty. My poor requests are to heaven for you, as I desire you might not forget me and mine and all us here. Now the God of peace and power guide and support your spirit in all your holy endeavors, bless and prosper your labors, and keep you as a chosen vessel in the shadow of his hand, through him that hath loved us.

Present my humble service to my right honorable lord,[5] as also my dear affection to Mr. Ball, Mr. Slater, and all the brethren with you, especially to Mr. Dod, Mr. Cleaver, Mr. Winton, Mr. Cotton,[6] with earnest desire of the continuance of all their prayers (with your own) in our behalf. So I rest.

Your very loving brother in our blessed savior,
J[ohn] C[otton]

Boston: Dec
3 1634

5. The Earl of Lincoln.
6. The puritan clergymen John or Thomas Ball, John Dod, and Robert Cleaver. The other men were presumably also puritan ministers.

While in London, John Winthrop the younger received two letters from John Endecott. Taking advantage of Winthrop's experience in settling English estates, Endecott asked him to work with Thomas Reade in selling his house in England. In so doing, Winthrop met Reade's sister Elizabeth, nineteen years old, and in July John and Elizabeth were wed. Elizabeth's mother and the Reverend Hugh Peter had married in 1625, when the clergyman was twenty-seven and Mrs. Reade a fifty-year-old-grandmother. Endecott had known Peter in England; indeed, Peter had signed Endecott's 1628 instructions concerning his duties at Salem. In 1635 there was a reunion, when Peter came to America with his step-daughter and her new husband; they arrived in October. Mrs. Peter did not join her Massachusetts family until two years later. The original letter that presumably led to the younger Winthrop's marriage is in the Robert C. Winthrop collection of deeds, agreements, and correspondence relating to Ipswich, Massachusetts, 1633-84, in the James Duncan Philips Library, Essex Institute, Salem, Massachusetts.

John Endecott to John Winthrop, Jr.
December 8, 1634

Dearest Sir:

I writ unto you by Mr. Babb,[1] wherein I gave you full commission to sell my house. And I do by this second it again, desiring you to sell it to an honest man, else not to sell it. The price I writ was 250 pounds, what above you can. And if you see good you may abate some of it. I have given order to Thomas Read, who is now in England, to find out a chapman if he can as also to Mr. Peters in Holland, and have written to him to make you acquainted with their proceedings that there be no wrong done to any. If God should so order that you can sell it I pray you do so much as to certify so much by letter to Mr. Peters in Holland who is at Roterdam.[2]

There is no news here. All your friends are well. We had the greatest snow fell the nineteenth of the ninth month that I have seen yet since I came into the land. The cross is much stood for,

1. Shipmaster of the *Griffin*, traveling between England and Massachusetts.
2. Hugh Peter became minister at Salem, where Endecott lived, till 1641, when Peter returned to England as agent for the colony. A close friend of the Reverend John White and a subscriber to the New England Company before he went to America, Peter had a distinguished career after his return to England in the puritan Commonwealth. He was executed after the restoration of monarchy in 1660. See Raymond P. Stearns, *The Strenuous Puritan, Hugh Peter, 1598-1660* (Urbana, Ill., 1954).

John Winthrop, Jr.

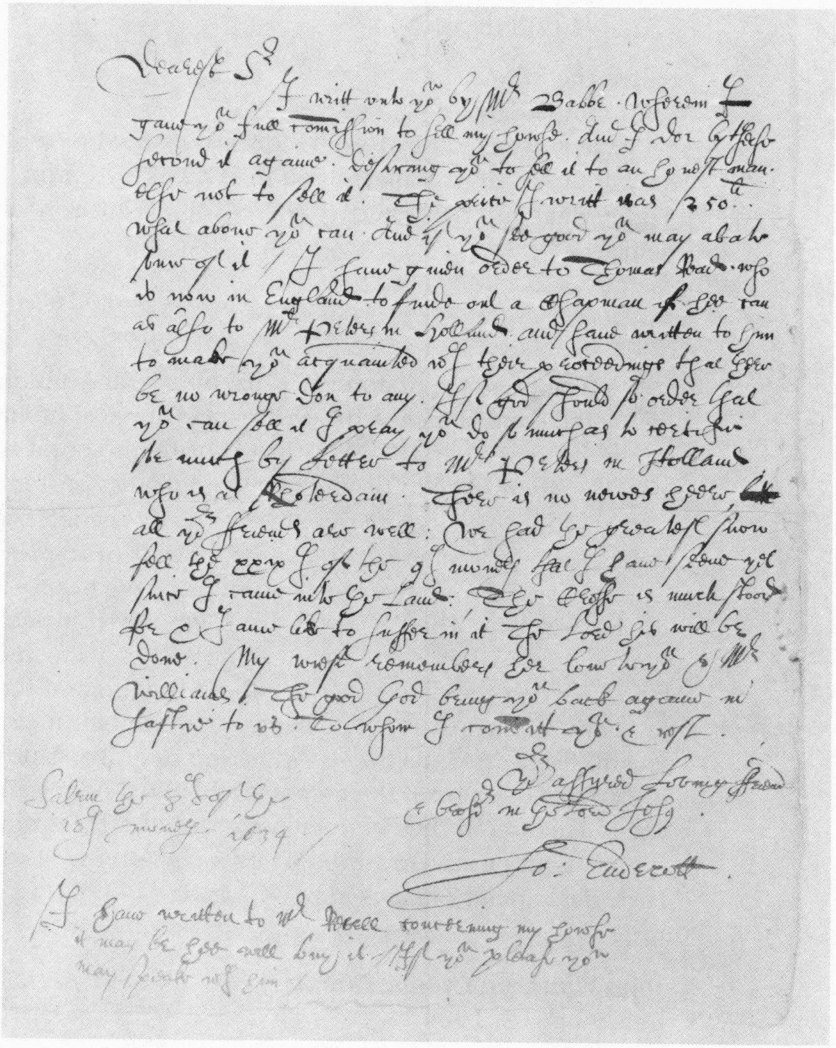

Deareste Sr

I writt unto you by Mr Babbe wherein I gave you full commission to sell my howse. And I doe by these recall it againe. Desiring you to sell it to an honest man, else not to sell it. The price I writt was 250li. What above you can. And if you see good you may abate some of it. I have given order to Thomas Read who is now in England to finde out a Chapman if hee can as also to Mr Peters in Holland, and have written to him to make you acquainted with their proceedings that there be no wronge don to any. If god should so order that you can sell it I pray you doe so much as to certifie the same by letter to Mr Peters in Holland who is at Rotterdam. There is no newes heere but all your friends are well: wee had the greatest snow [illegible] the [illegible] of the 9th moneth that I have seene since I came into the Land. The Cattle is much [illegible] I am like to suffer in it. The Lord his will be done. My wife remembers her love to you and Mrs Williams. The good God bring you back againe in saftie to us. To whom I commit you and rest.

Your assured loving friend
[illegible]
Io: Endecott

Salem the 8 of the 10th moneth 1634

I have written to Mr [illegible] concerning my howse it may be hee will buy it. If you please you may speake with him.

John Endecott to John Winthrop, Jr., December 8, 1634

and I am like to suffer in it. The Lord His will be done. My wife remembers her love to you and Mr. Williams.[3] The good God bring you back again in safety to us. To whom I commit you and rest.

> Your assured loving friend and brother in the Lord Jesus,
> Jo: Endecott

Salem the 8th of the
10th month 1634

I have written to Mr. Revell[4] concerning my house. It may be he will buy it. If you please you may speak with him.
To my dear and right worthy friend John Winthrop, Jr., Esquire, deliver.

The presence of John Winthrop's son in London created the conditions for the writing and survival of another letter. In December 1634 Winthrop wrote his absent son an affectionate, newsy letter, including a long list of items to be purchased for use in America. In every way the letter gives a strong sense of the circumstances and needs of the New Englanders. It also contains a brief account of the events leading to the Pequot War. The Pequot Indians, who lived in the lower Connecticut Valley, were the most aggressive tribe in New England. Friction increased between these Indians and Massachusetts and Connecticut colonists who visited their area for several years after the events Winthrop describes below. Finally in 1637 soldiers from the colonies and allied Narraganset Indians slaughtered the Pequots in a series of attacks along the Connecticut coast. Governor Winthrop's letter is Massachusetts Historical Society manuscript W. 7A. 54.

John Winthrop to John Winthrop, Jr.
December 12, 1634

My good son:

The Lord bless thee ever.

I wrote to you by Captain Underhill, who went hence in Mr. Babb's ship, since which time here arrived a ship from Barn-

3. Probably John Wilson, who returned to America at the same time as the younger Winthrop.
4. John Revell, who was in Massachusetts briefly in 1630.

stable of two hundred ton, Mr. Packers, master. She brought about twenty passengers and forty cattle. She lost but two and yet was seventeen weeks outward bound, whereof five in Ireland. She now returns empty with Mr. Peirce, by whom I send these.

All things continue as when you left us, only Mrs. Warham is dead,[1] and Mr. Hooker's young son (who died of the smallpox, which are very rife at Newtowne); and two men of our town, Willys and Dowtye, and two lads were cast away in a great tempest at N[ew] E[ngland] on Friday, November 21, in the night, between Noddles Island and Boston, in a small boat which they had overladen with wood. Myself and divers others were in the same tempest, not without some peril, but the Lord preserved us. Mr. Sewall's boat was then in the cove at the head of Cape Anne and broken to pieces, but the men and goods saved.[2] The pestilent fever hath taken away some at Plimouth, among others Mr. Prence the governor his wife and Mr. Allerton's wife.[3] We met the last week to consider about the business of the ensign at Salem and have written a letter to my brother Downing wherein under our hands we signify our dislike of the action and our purpose to punish the offenders.[4]

[in margin] This enclosed, to Mr. Warner, is to your bedfellow in the ship.

I wrote to you in my former letter about divers things which we should have need of, which I will here insert also with addition of some others.

The Pekods sent two embassies to us: the first time they went away without answer. The next time we agreed a peace with them (for friendly commerce only which was that they desired, having now war with the Dutch and [the] Narrigansett[s]) upon these terms, viz., that they should deliver us those men who killed Captain Stone, etc.,[5] and surrender up to us their right in Conectecott, which they willingly agreed unto, and offered us a great present of wampompeag [wampum] and beaver and otter with this expression, that we might with part thereof procure their peace with the Narigansetts (themselves standing upon terms of honor not to offer anything of themselves).

Winter hath begun early with us: the bay hath been frozen all over but is now open again, and we had a snow last week [of] much depth in many places. It came with so violent a storm as it put by our lecture for that day.[6] I wish that in your

1. Wife of the Reverend John Warham of Dorchester.
2. Another version of the story is in Winthrop's *History*, 1:179. Henry Sewall, father of the judge and diarist Samuel, later settled in Newbury.
3. Thomas Prence was first elected governor this year; Isaac Allerton was the colony's business agent.
4. Winthrop was eager to prevent scandal that might damage the colony's reputation.
5. The death of John Stone, a Virginian, took place on the Connecticut River, where he was trading.
6. John Cotton lectured every other Thursday at the Boston church.

return you would observe the wind and weather every day that we may see how it agrees with our parts.

Mr. Warde continues at your house this winter, and Mr. Clerk (to give him content) in his own.[7] Mr. Cl[erk] finds much fault with your servants John and Sarah and tells me they will not earn their bread and that Ned is worth them all.

Spades and shovels.

Felling axes and other small axes.

Nails of six, ten, and twenty.

Piercer bits.

Scythes for grass, and two brush scythes.

Copperas white and green.

Emplastrum Paracellsi two or three pounds.

Emplastrum dominion.

Trading cloth, good store if money may be had.

Brown threads and hair buttons and a hogshead of twine for herring nets.

Shoes two-soled strong, and the best Irish stockings, and wash leather stockings.

Strong cloth suits, unlined, and linen suits of canvas.

Suet, tallow, and wick.

A carpenter, and a husbandman, and a ropemaker, and a cooper.

Some muskets.

Store of brimstone.[8]

A brake for hemp.

Bring the more of all necessaries because this is the last we shall have without custom.[9]

7. Nathaniel Ward; John Clark was one of the founders of Ipswich.
8. Sulfur for making gunpowder.
9. Massachusetts Bay was granted freedom from customs duties in its first seven years.
10. Thomas Wiggin and William Hilton were both involved in trading between New and old England.

If my brother Tindale would let you have one hundred pounds, you may give him assurance of so much in cattle here to be presently set out for my wife and her children, with the increase or for two hundred pounds if he will.

Commend us to all our good friends, your aunt Dow[ning] and uncle G[ostlin] and aunts, those at Maplested, Graces, Assington, Groton, Charterhouse, Sir Rich[ard] S[altonstall] and his son, etc., and all the rest as you have occasion, Mr. Kirby, etc., and Mr. Howes, and make haste back, and if there be any matter of importance, write by the first fishing ships. Direct your letters to Captain Wiggin or Mr. Hilton.[10]

Your mother and the rest are in health (I praise God.) We all
salute you. The good Lord direct, keep, and bless you. Farewell, my good son.

[John Winthrop]

December 12, 1634
To my dear son Mr. John Winthrop at the house of Mr. Down-
ing in Lincolns Inn Field near the Golden Lyon Tavern,
London, deliver.

A second letter of John Endecott's has survived, written
only two weeks after the previous extant one from him.
Though the letter itself is slight and of no great importance, the
story behind it makes the sometimes unpleasantly puritanical
puritans seem more human. Endecott was a rigid puritan—in the
words of a biographer, "stern and irascible, a man of iron will
and of little human sympathy." He had not always been so. As
a young man Endecott had fathered a child out of wedlock.
After he crossed the sea to New England he continued to take
responsibility for the boy, who was named for his father, but
he would not have the boy in Salem to bring disgrace upon him.
With the assistance of his friends Emmanuel Downing and Hugh
Peter, he negotiated with Dr. Samuel Read, a physician, for
Roger Dandey of Holborn, London, to see that the boy was
educated and later properly apprenticed. John Endecott's
letter is at the Houghton Library, Harvard University.

John Endecott to Dr. Samuel Read
December 25, 1634

Dear Sir:

I was bold formerly to address one letter unto you concerning
one Roger Dandy in Shoe Lane at the Cockpitt yard. The
business I doubt not you know, and myself ashamed to write
of. I beseech you according to my former request, which is the
same I make you now again, that you will be pleased to end
that business. You shall receive forty pounds of Mr. Emanuell

Downing, Esquire, one of the attorneys of the Court of Wards, or more if it be needful. If you can agree cheaper, I shall think myself much bound unto you. Only I would not by any means have the boy sent over. Mr. Peter hath taken order for the money. If there be anything wherein I may do you service here, I shall not be backward. The Lord in mercy keep you, to whose blessed protection I commit you and rest.

Your most obliged friend to command,
Jo: Endecott

I pray you call for a writing of Roger Dandy. It is a deed of sale of a house now fallen into my hands.[1]
Salem the 25th of the tenth month.
Received February 16, 1635.
Answered the 2nd of May, 1637.[2]
To my worthy friend Doctor Samuell Read deliver these.
At the Frying Pan in New High Street Hill, London.[3]

Many famous Puritan ministers came to New England, but some that were much hoped for did not, among them John Robinson, pastor to William Bradford and others of the Plymouth colony in Holland; William Ames, to whom many of the Bay Colony's ministers looked for intellectual leadership; and Dr. John Stoughton, the prominent London preacher whose two brothers went to America. The letter of invitation to Stoughton survives because it was among the documents that were seized in his house by the government in 1635, when he was thought to be involved in some puritan master plan. Two other letters from New England were taken in the same way and thus survive: one from Dr. Stoughton's brother Israel and one from James Cudworth, a former parishioner of Dr. Stoughton's already in Scituate when he wrote.

Cudworth had probably come to Massachusetts, to Boston, in 1632. Perhaps he had travelled with Timothy Hatherly, to whom Scituate land was granted in 1634, for Cudworth settled there. Scituate was in the jurisdiction of the Plymouth colony. Relations between Plymouth and Massachusetts Bay had been good ever since Deacon Samuel Fuller of Plymouth had in 1629 attended the sick among the Salem settlers with his medical

1. See Endecott's letter to John Winthrop, Jr., above.
2. Evidently Dr. Read's notes. He was a poor correspondent.
3. In another hand.

knowledge. The Plymouth leaders believed that they had taught the men of the Bay much about the Congregational way, and the ability of the Plymouth colonists to sell cattle and provisions to the group to their north was mutually advantageous. Many families left the Massachusetts Colony to settle in the lands of the Plymouth Colony, Cudworth among them. In 1636, he was one of the two Scituate men appointed to revise the proposed laws of Plymouth; later he served as deputy governor and as leader of the Plymouth soldiers in King Philip's War.

Cudworth's letter once again demonstrates how different the new church order and discipline were from the ways known in England. It also shows the determination of the colonists to keep Massachusetts strictly religious and religiously strict. Cudworth's letter is at the Public Record Office, London, numbered C. O. 1/8, folios 110-11.

James Cudworth to Dr. John Stoughton
December 1634

Citewat [Scituate] the ——of December 1634
Dear and worthy sir:

My bounden duty and earnest affections in the bowels of love to you remembered, and also to my most dear mother. The Lord, who is the searcher of the heart and trier of the reins knows that I do unfainedly desire the peace, prosperity, and welfare both of your souls and bodies as of mine own. These are to let you understand that I have received your godly and pious letter, full of grave and wholesome exhortations, which argues your unfained desires and continual endeavors for the good of my soul, and, indeed, I have cause if ever any had to bless the Lord that ever I saw you, for under God you have been the greatest instrument of good to me in the world, and since my absence from you the care you had of me with your pains in a laboring with me is frequent in my mind and does take a deep impression in my soul and has been an instrumental cause of working me nearer unto and walking closer with the Lord, and more and more to see the vanity of all these outward things and that fullness that is Christ Jesus.

I desire that you will be as frequent in your letters as you may, for I find a great deal of sweetness in them, for they put a great deal of quickening life and edge unto my affections, and you know the best in this life are subject to grow cold in our perfection that we daily need some exhortation and consolation, both to provoke to the practice of holy things and to support us in the time of temptation or affliction, that we may wade through all the difficulties of this short life with cheerfulness of heart, laboring to make some benefit to our souls of all the Lord's dealings with us, whether they be mercies that they may allure us or chastisements that they may correct and amend us our judgments, that may terrify us our afflictions, that they may refine us, so that at length we may be more than conquerors over all our corruptions so that we may serve the Lord with the whole man and worshipping him according as he has revealed in his holy word, walking in the way and order of the gospel, standing for the purity of his ordinances, and as Moses would not part with nor leave a half behind for of those he was to serve his God, so not to part with one of the ordinances but to be ready to lay down our lives for them, for with those we must serve our God. I am very sorry to hear of your sickness. My prayers shall and have been continually to the Lord for you. I shall entreat you to bear with patience what the Lord shall lay upon you, laboring to make a sanctified use of all his dealings and in all things submitting your will unto his, and then all things shall work together for the best unto those that love him.

Also I understand that there is like to be twenty pounds lost by Walter Gamblinge. If it be so, I know it is the Lord's doing, and if I consider what have I that I have not received from the Lord, nay, what have I deserved, surely nothing but eternal wrath and condemnation, therefore let him do with his own as seemeth good in his eyes. I thank the Lord it is no trouble but rather case of rejoicing when I weigh a temporal loss with a spiritual gain, when the Lord is pleased even to befole[?] me there that I could not manage my affairs with comfort, even as if the Lord should say, "It is but a folly to attempt anything afoot. Here, I will take away thy abilities. Thou shalt not be able to go through stich [?] with anything here, but thou must go far from thine own land and father's house and there will I reveal myself to thee, and there shalt thou honor, worship, and serve me as I shall reveal to thee out of my sacred word." I do ingeniously freely confess to you now, the Lord has brought me hither and in a small measure made me acquainted with his ways and how and in what manner he will be worshipped in. Although here be many difficulties to be undergone, yet I account it an excellent mercy that the Lord has brought me to see that which my forefathers desired to see but could not: to see so many churches walking in the way and order of the gospel, enjoying that Christian liberty that Christ has purchased for us.

And to relate to you that which yet I have not, concerning the estate of New England. Here are these churches. 1, Plymouth, where Mr. Smith is pastor,[1] no Teacher. 2, Bostone, Mr. Willson, Pastor; Mr. Cotton, Teacher. 3, Dorchester, Mr. Wareham, Pastor; Mr. Mavoricke, Teacher. 4, at Rockes Burey, Mr. Weeldes, Pastor; Mr. Elyot, Teacher. 5, at Charles towne, Mr. Jeames, Pastor, and my cousin Simes is now gone thither to be their Teacher.[2] 6, at Newtowne, Mr. Hoocker, Pastor; Mr. Stone, Teacher. 7, at Wattertowne, Mr. Philipes, Pastor. 8, at Sagus, where Mr. Somphereyes [Humphry] lives, Mr. Bachelor, Pastor. 9, at Salem, their Pastor, old Mr. Skelton, is dead. There is Mr. Williames, who does exercise his gifts but is in no office.[3] 10, at Ipsidge [Ipswich], a plantation made up this year, Mr. Ward, Pastor, Mr. Parker, Teacher.[4]

Now those plantations that are not yet settled and are newly begun, are three: Duckes burey, where Mr. Colyer dwells, no Pastor nor Teacher. Ours, Cittewate, to whom the Lord has been very gracious and his providence has been admirably seen, our being, to bring us our Pastor, whom we so long expected, Mr. Lathrope, who the Lord has brought to us in safety, whom we find to be a holy, reverend, and heavenly-minded man.[5] And the other is Beare Cove, where is no Pastor nor Teacher.[6]

Now one thing I would entreat you, that if you do know any of your friends and acquaintances that come over hither, that you would direct them to our plantation, the nature of the place being as in my former letters you shall find and is still, though now I have seen more of the plantations than then I had, and yet it finds place in my affections before any. And with all such as you shall advise to sit down with us, we would entreat you they may be such as you judge to be fit to be received into church fellowship. Also, if it should please God to bring you into this land amongst us, I would entreat you for your own good not to come engaged to any people till you come here yourself and see the nature of the place where you are to sit down, together with the condition of the people.

1. Ralph Smith, Plymouth's first settled minister, came to Plymouth from Salem in 1629; he left in 1636.
2. The arrival of Thomas James, who came to New England in 1632, permitted the separation of the people of Boston and Charlestown into two churches. See Winthrop, *History*, 1:112-13, 170-71.
3. Roger Williams had been acting teacher since some time in 1633; in July 1635 he was duly elected teacher.
4. Both the famous Nathaniel Ward, author of *The Simple Cobler of Aggawam*, and Thomas Parker came to New England in 1634, when the town of Agawam, later Ipswich, was founded.
5. Duxbury, across Plymouth Bay from Plymouth, was the first settlement in the colony to have a church separate from Plymouth's, in 1632. At Scituate John Lathrop was the first minister; he had been a separatist in England and came with thirty followers. See Massachusetts Historical Society *Collections*, 2nd. ser. 1 (1814): 163-71.
6. Bearcove, or Barecove, became the town of Hingham.

One thing I cannot but relate and that not only with grief, for and with fear of what will be the event of a strange thing put in practice by some in the church of Salem, but by whom I hear not, and that is they have cut out the cross in the flag, or ensign, that they carry before them when they train. Indeed, it is contrary to the minds and wills of all that I can hear of. Captain Indicat, their captain, is a holy, honest man and does utterly abandon it, and who are the agents in it I cannot hear.

Now, as concerning my own particular, I thank the Lord I have wanted nothing since I came into the land. I have, I bless God, as yet the best house in the plantation. Though but a mean one, it contents us well. I planted corn, contrary to Mr. Hatherly's mind, which I know not how I should have done. I bless the Lord I have, I think, at least fifty bushels of corn, which is worth some twelve pounds so that I think I shall not need but shall have enough till next harvest. My house is the meeting house because it is the biggest, but we are but few as yet in number, not passing sixty persons.

As concerning my uncles,[7] blessed be God they are both in good health, and my uncle Thomas is to be married shortly, to a widow that has good means and has five children. Thus much I made bold to trouble you withal, being all for the present, only desiring to be remembered to all my brothers and sisters and all my friends, and my wife likewise desires her duty to you both, her love to the rest, and I would pray whereas I wrote for stuff for two coats—it was rashly done—that you would refrain till you have [money] of mine to pay yourselves withal. Only I must entreat you to be mindful the first ship that comes, to send my wife some clothes, for she looks her to come the first of April. So for the present I commit you to the protection of the Almighty and ever rest,

Your dutiful son till death,
James Cudworth

7. Thomas and Israel Stoughton.

To his very loving and kind father
Dr. Stoughton at his house in Alldermanbuy

1635

Cudworth's letter interested the English authorities who had
seized Stoughton's papers; they endorsed it "James Cudworth
to Doctor Staughton showing his private correspondence with
the irregular inconformable fugitive ministers beyond the seas
in New England," and underscored such offensive passages as
"the purity of His [God's] ordinances" and "the way and order of the gospel," and the whole of Cudworth's comment that
immigrants should be "fit to be received into church fellowship." Much has been made of the fact that only a fraction of
the Massachusetts Bay colonists became church members.
James Truslow Adams's comment is famous: "not more than
one in five of the adult males who went even to Massachusetts
[the most religious of the New England colonies] was sufficiently in sympathy with the religious ideas there prevalent to become a church member, though disenfranchised in so doing."
Adams seems to imply that joining a church was an action that
might be easily and casually undertaken. But there were many
barriers to church membership. For instance, one might believe
that he lacked evidence of conversion or that he could not face
a close scrutiny of his religious and moral life. Or he might be
reluctant to place himself under the discipline of the church.
Or he might judge that his inferior social status prevented him
from applying for membership. The surviving letters from
Massachusetts Bay, here assembled, are significant evidence
that the colony was intended by its leaders to have a religious
rationale. This rationale attracted additional leaders, most of
whom lent strong support to the rapidly developing structures
of both church and state.

Israel Stoughton, who wrote the next letter, was one of
the 1630 settlers; he helped found Dorchester. He was
elected to the General Court in 1634, when that body first became representative. Each town elected three deputies or committees. The system usually worked well because the freemen
were usually in agreement with the magistrates on basic issues:

they shared beliefs about religion and government. But minor disagreements were inevitable, and it was as a deputy that Stoughton came to grief, as his letter explains. It is one of the most revealing documents extant on the structure and workings of the Massachusetts government. The Massachusetts political structure was more democratic in principle than in practice, and Winthrop dominated the early years of Massachusetts Bay. The unconventional view of Winthrop provided by Stoughton's letter is part of its importance. The letter, written in the spring of 1635, survives because it, like Cudworth's above, was removed from John Stoughton's study when it was raided. The letter is in the Public Record Office, London, numbered C. O. 1/8, folios 49-52.

Israel Stoughton to John Stoughton
1635

Dear Brother: Grace and peace be with you and yours in Christ.

There coming this friend Mr. Patricson (Mr. Cradock's agent here)[1] so happily in the spring, I thought I would not omit to write a word, and but a word, because I hope to have many opportunities more this summer, though as yet we have not a ship come nor know not certainly whether we shall; only we hear of many and hope the best. We are generally in good health. I and my family have enjoyed our health, I bless God, with very little interruption from the beginning. Here are divers things whereof I would write more fully to you about, but I am willing to wait a while and shall do it hereafter. It is like you will hear of many of them more or less there, but I hope God will give you and others that fear God there wisdom to judge of things wisely and not believe all that is reported with all aggravations and additions as are usual in such cases.

1. Much you will hear, I suppose, about the cross in the banners, and many things true, for 'tis true Captain Indicot did deface it upon his own private head and is now left out of place of government and his fact publicly protested against by the greater part of the country, and the ministers and some of the magistrates too.[2] It is also true some of the magistrates with some ministers and divers of the people do apprehend it an idol, unlawful to be continued in so honorable a place and time

1. Matthew Cradock, governor of the company before Winthrop, owned lands at what is now Malden, but he did not come to America.
2. See above, introduction to Cudworth letter. The terms *magistrate* and *assistant* were used interchangeably.

to be abolished, and therefore do strongly incline that way, but 'tis also true the greatest part esteem no such danger in it but do desire to inform themselves well in the point and then to be zealous according to knowledge and all judgment, not being willing to abuse their Christian liberty to licentiousness before God nor yet to a needless making of friends enemies or to the provoking of those against us who are willing to let us alone.

So that now the truth is, this hath bred some evil blood in our body, and I fear will be a greater cross and more wildy to bear than the former. It hath already caused no little alienation of affection, strife, . . . censuring on their parts who are so zealous for the cross its rejection against, and almost condemning their brethren that have not been so opinionated and affected as themselves, and the truth is, if anything would have done it, that party that so deeply condemns the simple use of the cross in banners had overborn and crushed the other party though the bigger most by far. Such was their zeal and potency. But as yet it is not come to that point, for the conclusion is, counsel shall be further taken of God and the learned wise and godly there with you, and in the meantime there shall be a pause, and if there be any need of banners, those that will may use their old as they are, without any alteration, and the party that did that fact must stand upon his own bottom to answer for his attempt, for the greater part of ministers and country have washed their hands of it. Finally, for to end this matter, had not Mr. Hooker and the rest of the ministers stepped in and with great strength appeared against the contrary part, it had not been as it is, and yet I dare say the greater number of the magistrates are best pleased that it is thus and no otherwise as well as the people. I forebear to mention persons and particular passages, because I will give none offence nor occasion, but I suppose you may inform yourself by Mr. Patricson and Mr. Cradock if you shall desire more full relations.

2. Here hath been somewhat to do too about a negative voice, for the magistrates would that no law nor act of court should be current and established (excepting choice of magistrates) unless the greater number of magistrates present do also approve and consent to it, though all country and three of seven of the magistrates do like and desire it,[3] and they plead the patent allows them this power, and some also have well liked it. Others have not liked it, and now the greater number by far, I suppose five

3. For a discussion of the attitudes of these two groups, see Morgan, *Puritan Dilemma*, pp. 155-63.

or ten for one and of the ministers too, are of another mind. I know none that have read the patent (excepting magistrates) that esteem it their due, but yet many were willing to have condescended to it at the first, whose minds are now changed. The conclusion of that business is, it sleeps in silence and is so like, for it is concluded by some that the magistrates hereafter will never ask it nor the people never give it but only thus: that whereas now our courts for making laws consist of the body of the magistrates and three committees chose by every town to join with them that there shall be power of suspension on either party in cases where they agree not until the mind of the whole body of the country may conveniently be known, and then the issue to be on the major part's side according to the patent and so both tumultuousness and many mischiefs may be prevented. This was at first proposed and approved by ministers and country but not by magistrates.[4]

3. Here hath not been a little to do about myself, and though I am unwilling to make any large relation of my own things, yet because I know you will hear many things, I dare not omit to write something, both in faithfulness to you and myself. For I do not know how relations may be made which may much trouble you, unless you have some certainty. What therefore I write reckon it to be true impartially as you esteem of me impartial or otherwise. Take the relation thus.

When I came into the country, for one whole year after the government was solely in the hands of the assistants. The people chose them magistrates, and then they made laws, disposed lands, raised moneys, punished offenders, etc., at their discretion. Neither did the people know the patent nor what prerogative and liberty they had by the same. But there being some sums of money raised and a speech of more, it made some inquisitive into matters and particularly after the patent. About which time Mr. Wenthrop, governor, having the patent, did give way to the country upon their motion to see it, and all the magistrates (as in charity I must say) were willing to admit the people to join with themselves in the governance of the state, by three deputies for each town. So in May last year [1634] there was a general court, wherein things were so agitated. In which court I was by our town chose a committee, and by the committees chose the chief speaker on the country's behalf (there being three speakers), and indeed such was their good

4. In 1636 the General Court passed a statute that "no law, order, or sentence shall pass as an act of the Court without the consent of the greater part of the magistrates on the one part and the greater number of the deputies on the other part, and for want of such accord, the cause or order shall be suspended. . . ." *Massachusetts Records*, 1:170.

opinion of me (unworthy, I confess) that they would have chose me into an assistant's place but that they said they needed no more there for the present.[5] So that the court passed, and though there was a little opposition in one particular case, yet all ended in peace with manifestations of great love and the magistrates' good approbation of us that had in some points opposed and crossed them, at least some of boston, where Mr. Winthrop dwells.

Then there was a second court about August last,[6] not for choice of magistrates but for making laws, etc., where I was also both a committee and speaker (as before). In this court there were some more strait passages and specially about the negative voice, which fell to be my portion much to oppose, though not alone, in which court time Mr. Wenthrop and myself had accidentally some private discourse about the patent and the power of assistants and governor; so likewise had one Mr. Ludlow, an assistant, and dwelling in Dorcester, where I live. But the conclusion of the court was all peace and love, and no manifestations of anything to the contrary. Nay, Mr. Wenthrop having somewhat harshly and unadvisedly taken up a young man, a committee, came after in private to me and excused himself and professed to me that for that young man's part and mine, though we had much opposed him, yet the more he honored us both in his very heart, adding that he saw our aims and ends were good. So that court finished.[7]

Then there was again a third court that year, in March last, chiefly called about Captain Indcott his fact about the cross, where I was again a committee and a speaker but not the chief because Mr. Bellengum, a great man and a lawyer, was then a committee, and he was chief speaker.[8] Now after I was chose, great probability there was that the negative voice would be questioned, whereupon many lay hard upon me to give them my reasons in writing why I refused to yield it so as they had desired it, which I utterly refused a good while, till at length three men of our church came to me in the name of Mr. Warhum (our pastor)[9] to entreat it of me, saying that the ministers were to meet about it, and he much desired my reasons before they met, and they pressed my conscience that I sinned if I refused. Hereupon having but now half a day's time to do it in, I notwithstanding condescended and gave it (it being one sheet of paper), twelve reasons of my refusal to give them such a

5. That is, he would have been elected assistant or magistrate. At this time there were nine assistants in Massachusetts; the charter called for eighteen.
6. It met on September 3, 1634.
7. Winthrop's version is in his *History*, 1:168-69. John Cotton supported Winthrop by preaching on the authority of the magistrates.
8. Richard Bellingham, who had served as a member of parliament, came to Massachusetts in 1634. In 1641 he was elected governor and served several terms.
9. John Warham.

negative as they challenged. Now no sooner had Mr. Warum the thing but he (without my privity) carries it to the ministers, presents it at their meeting, which for aught I ever heard was well approved by every man of them. Sure I am, four of them did come to me and give me large thanks and applause for the thing, and Mr. Cotten, that had preached at first for the magistrates' having a negative (though afterwards yielded to a stopping voice only, such as before I expressed) desired the paper, took it home, and finding that some of the reasons to be grounded upon the patent, he, not well understanding the patent, did (as he professed to me) in the simplicity of his heart send them to Mr. Wenthrop to be resolved in some points of the patent, who as it seems by the sequel took such distaste at them and me for them that moved him to what follows.

The day of the court coming (for I knew not a tittle of ought until the minute of time that I was accused), in the morning he [Cotton] possesseth the governor with my book, so soon as ever we were met, all the country being put out save magistrates, committees, and ministers,[10] the governor and some of the magistrates charge me for writing a book against the magistrates and for denying them to be magistrates, and so fell into such bitter terms against me as was much, if it had been proved, for Mr. Wenthrop said of me, "This is the man that had been the troubler of Israel," and I was a worm (such an one as Mr. Hooker had spoke of in his sermon) and an underminer of the state, and yet, saith he, "Who but Mr. Stoughton is the eye of the country?" And, saith he, "I had from a special friend" (I suppose it was Dr. Wright[11]) a letter of good report of me, that I was a man worthy of his acquaintance, but I had never come at him (wherein I confess I have been something failing through shamefastness and a natural defect that way), yet I have been with him divers times and always showed him great respect as also and in truth he had done to me above my deserts. But now to the point. They charged my book for this and that. One thing was that I should say in it that I by my fact had freed the state so and so. Now this I utterly denied, that had not so written, and the book was read, and so read as that it did expressly so speak; at which I was amazed and desired to see it myself, and I confess there wanted a comma, but that being added they all confessed the sense was quite otherwise and so

10. The Bay version of executive session.
11. Dr. Lawrence Wright, a physician.

were silenced in that point. And it was so plain without a comma that no man excepted at that till Mr. Wenthrop, nor did any make such sense of it but he, and such as he had possessed. But then the main accusation which they stuck to was that I denied the assistants to be magistrates and made them but ministers of justice, etc., which charge I denied, and affirmed I never did deny them to be magistrates, though I also did say they were ministers of justice and might without dishonor be called ministers as well as magistrates both by the rule of the Word (Romans 13[12]) and secondly the custom of London, whose printed oath for all freemen styles the aldermen by the term and title: thus the mayor and all other ministers of the city and so comprehends the aldermen; third, and by the rule of the patent and with respect to the patent and to general courts assembled, for I had written thus in that (the reasons against the negative): the patent makes their power ministerial according to the greater vote of the general courts and not magisterial according to their own discretion. These were my very expressions, whereby I intended and meant that their power—call it ministerial or magisterial or magistratical (which you will)—was not so great that they could do ought or hinder ought simply according to their own wills, but they must eye and respect general courts, which by patent consist of the whole company of freemen. And this is in very deed the magistrates' own judgment and the judgment of every man in the land that hath expressed himself, and yet for this my expression they would have me to affirm they were no magistrates, and these my words should be a proof of it. Other words they took great offence at but instance no other but these two. I confess there were some others that were very plain English such as to some is offensive, but I know little reason it should be to any. Sure I am it was no other than such as I would allow and most desire from my meanest servant in any cause wherein he hath to deal with me.

But much ado there was, and because it was adjudged by some it would much please and pacify them if I would desire that it might be burned, at length for peace' sake and to show how little I esteemed ought of mine, I said let the book be burned if it please them; to give them content I regarded it not. So that business ended, yet so that they caused it to be recorded that such a thing was burned as weak and offensive.[13]

12. There rulers are referred to as ministers.
13. See *Massachusetts Records*, 1:135.

But still they were not pacified towards me but would have it be that I denied them to be magistrates, and for the further proof of that point, Mr. Wenthrop and Mr. Ludlow, of whom I spake before, did affirm to the court upon their credit (without oath) that I had in the time of the last court (before whom I had some conference with them as I told you before about their power and authority) said to them that the assistants were not magistrates. So that though I had constantly denied it and had also unknown to me then a witness that can upon oath testify that my words to Mr. Wenthrop did not so import nor were they any affirmation at all but merely thus: in answer to something he had said, which was that assistants had power simply by their places over our persons, goods and lives without any law of ours, I replied, "What, is it so? I had thought your power had been so and not so." The same witness also being an ear witness of my words to Mr. Ludlo and a very wise and godly young man (the same that I spake of before, that Mr. Wentrop snibbed [reprimanded] but after did somewhat recant), he, being a brother of our church, suspecting that Mr. Ludlo had forsworn himself (for he was not now a committee to hear) did go in private (before our two ministers, myself and another) to this Mr. Ludlo and begin to deal with him for what he had done until that he purged himself thus by saying he did not give in his witness upon oath.

And so the conclusion of the matter was that I by way of punishment of that whereof they charged me must be disallowed for bearing any office within the jurisdiction for three year,[14] which was by magistrates and committees. That is, the major part did then conclude that order, which was the main business of that court in March last, Captain Indicot's business being referred to the great general court of May. But the truth is the greatest part of the committees did yield thereto merely to give the magistrates content, purposing to reverse it again with the first opportunity. Mr. Bellengam made the same apology unto me in private. And many of the rest that did yield (for all did not) and that with tears, and one made public acknowledgment in open court afterwards that he had sinned and was sorry. I should be too tedious to you to relate the several private passages of Mr. Cotton's, of Mr. Hooker's, of Mr. Ward's, and other ministers about this business, who have been marvelously affected to see their dealings, especially Mr. Wenthrop's,

14. Stoughton's liberty was restored after Sir Henry Vane became governor in May 1636, and shortly afterwards he was elected an assistant. *Massachusetts Records*, 1:175.

who the truth is had too much forgot and overshot himself, as
I hear he hath confessed so much publicly the last court, before
all the country in general, and manifested the particulars to
those that were then committees privately, as I have been told.

Now followed the great general court in May, which continued two days for the whole body and is not yet ended,
(though prorogued) for magistrates and committees. This
general court one Mr. Haynes was chosen governor, a very godly
man of Mr. Hooker's charge.[15] Captain Indicot is left out, partly
for his business in the cross and partly for other matters. So also
our Mr. Ludlow is now no magistrate, though within six days
before it was most probable and almost past question that he
would be chosen governor (for we desire to change year by year
the governorship, but the assistants more rarely, yet sometimes,
lest it be esteemed hereditary). Now he is neither governor nor
assistant, so did divine providence dispose it. And I question
whether he will ever be magistrate more, for many have taken
great offence at him, the causes I forbear to relate,[16] but they
are both wise and godly men that are offended, and not many
much sorry.

And to tell you the truth (for it is like you may hear of it
from others), Mr. Wenthrop had very many hands against him
for being either governor (which some attempted) or assistant.
The causes it is like they know best that put in blanks.[17] I
suppose they were not his enemies, nor none of the most simple. He hath lost much of the applause that he hath had (for
indeed he was highly magnified), and I heard some say they put
in blanks not simply because they would not have him a magistrate but because they would admonish him thereby to look a
little more circumspectly to himself. He is indeed a man of men,
but he is but a man, and some say they have idolized him and
do now confess their error. My opinion is that God will do him
good by some, as also he hath done good to some by him. And
that he is a godly man and a worthy magistrate notwithstanding
some few passages, at which some have stumbled.

It may be it will be reported there (as some have not spared
to speak it here) that those that opposed him did it because he
was so zealous against the cross, for he esteems it a gross idol.
But though I be now no statesman, nor do I meddle with those
affairs, yet thus much I can upon my credit and by intimations
I have received inform you, that that was not at all the cause,

15. John Haynes served
one term only; he moved
to Connecticut in 1637.
16. The chief cause seems
to have been his protest
that the election of
Haynes was illegal. See
Winthrop, *History*, 1:188.
17. "It is likely that those
who put in blank ballots
know the reason."

for others were not so dealt by that were as zealous as he
(neither was his doings about me the only cause, though possibly that might a little further it, though I cannot say so expressly), but there was some other passages that have been done by
him, which being observed have made some willing to admonish
him in that manner whilst they do not well know how to do it
in a more convenient manner. But such is my opinion of the
man that some might more conveniently have dealt with him
in a more plain fashion, if they have any grievance. I say some
might. I do not say all.

This court Captain Indicot's business was transacted by the
whole country, and after some strong and hard labor brought
to the issue forementioned, wherein the ministers did their
parts as good midwives, or else it would not have been altogether so as it is.

This court also it was intended my business should have been
transacted by the whole body with a general vote before the
day, that they would do about it great matters. Aye, that they
would, said committees and most in general, but Captain
Indcot's business proved so tiresome and tedious that their
spirits and strength was spent, and though there was petition
made by the town (for my part I sit down in silence and desire with my whole soul that no more stir may be about it; I
look up to Him that knoweth all things, to whom myself and
all men must one day give account and receive wages, according
as our works have been) that I should have the interpretation
of my own words, which was in part granted, and I was called,
but because I did not give them so full satisfaction as some
desired, the thing rests yet as it did, only it is said by some it
shall be agitated by the magistrates and committees at their
next sitting. For the words whereof they charged me I can
make no interpretation of them because I cannot say I ever
uttered such words, but for my real opinion about the assistants' real power I spake in public court as much and more than
ever I spake before, and it was all accepted and taken well without contradiction.

But as I have been informed since something they would
have from me before they blotted out that order (which was the
thing petitioned for by the town, to have it blotted out and not
to stand to posterity to defame me as if I had held some ana-
baptistical opinion about magistrates, when they all knew I was
innocent and had not merited such infamy) that so the honor

of the court might be maintained.[18] This was all that any of them stood upon that ever I heard of. This large relation when I was once entered I could not forbear for reasons aforesaid. Now I leave you to judge when you have heard all as you shall see cause.

But now I beseech you these two things: first, that these things may be private, only where you shall see good cause, as to my mother for her satisfaction, to whom I cannot conveniently make a long relation, also to others of wise friends. If you should hear I were by any traduced and abused, as some or at least one (for I have not heard of more) hath much endeavored to take my good name away here, in a kind of zeal to Mr. Went[hrop], but the Lord forgive him, and if Dr. Wright should hear ought and first inquire of you, I know not what intimation and communion there is between him and Mr. Winthrop, but I do not pass, if need so be though he see every tittle that I have writ but not unless there be cause.

Secondly, I beseech you, let none of these things trouble your nor any other godly man's spirit concerning the place or the persons and doings here, as I know persons upon reports are sometimes strangely troubled and incensed this way and that, to judging, to withdrawing affection, to change resolutions and purposes, to change their minds and take up new thoughts, possibly never to come here, etc., for it is true we have weaknesses and wants and sins committed by us, and difference arise. Who questions this? And how can it be otherwise?

[End of manuscript]

Winthrop continued to receive letters from D'Ewes; two more responses from Winthrop survive. They are full of evidence of the colony's growth and of plans for expansion to Connecticut. Other evidence is to be found in Winthrop's journal for the summer of 1635, where one reads of fourteen ships arriving "with store of passengers and cattle. They all came within six weeks." Later a bark arrived "set forth by Sir Richard Saltonstall, to go plant at Connecticut" (see Greene's report to Saltonstall, below). In both letters to D'Ewes, however, Winthrop's chief topic is the twenty pounds that D'Ewes ventured with Hammond in 1633. The next letter from Winthrop is British Museum manuscript Harley 388, folios 189-90.

18. Winthrop wrote, "A petition was preferred by many of Dorchester, etc., for releasing the sentence against Mr. Stoughton the last general court, but it was rejected, and the sentence affirmed by the country to be just." *History*, 1:190.

John Winthrop to Sir Simonds D'Ewes
July 20, 1635

Sir:

I received two letters from you, the one written long since and put back in the *Hope*. By the other I understand your good affection to our plantation, whereof you desire we should taste the fruits. Blessed be the Lord, who hath inclined your heart thus towards us for good, and blessed be you of the Lord for it. According to your direction I spake with Hamond, who told me that he bestowed part of your money in vinegar to have made sturgeon, which being put aboard the *Richard*, was forced back again, and so by stopping and putting aboard another ship suffered much loss. I spake with Mr. Trerice, the master of the same ship,[1] who affirmed that of twelve hogsheads of vinegar there was lost by leakage about three hogsheads. Old Hamond came also before the governor (Mr. Haines) and other of us and affirmed that there came no benefit of your money but loss, so that howsoever by the bond we might have compelled them to have paid the whole thirty pounds,[2] yet respecting the loss which (by God's providence) happened in the adventure, we were content to take the principal, which the old man hath undertaken to pay, which when we have received it shall be bestowed upon some public work. In the meantime the governor and assistants return you thanks by me.

For our condition here, the Lord is pleased still to continue health and peace to us, and so to increase our numbers (there have come about thirty ships this summer already) as we are put to raise new colonies about one hundred miles to the west of us upon a very fine river and a most fruitful place. Only ships cannot come near by twenty leagues. Mr. Hooker is like to go thither next year,[3] not for any difference between Mr. Cotton and him and so report, for they do hold a most sweet and brotherly communion together (though their judgments do somewhat differ about the lawfulness of the cross on the ensign),[4] but the people and cattle are so increased as the place will not suffice them. The passengers this year (through the Lord's special providence) and their cattle are come with such speed and safety as no sickness hath been among them nor are above two persons miscarried and very few cattle. I might

1. Captain Nicholas Trerice of Charlestown.
2. Presumably principal plus interest.
3. Hooker went to found what became Hartford, Connecticut.
4. See Cudworth letter, p. 142 above.

further enlarge, but indeed I am so full of business as I can scarce get leisure to scribble these few lines. I desire you to bear with me and to continue still your good will towards us and your prayers for us, and so with my love and due respect to yourself and your worthy lady I commend you to the Lord and rest at your service.

Jo: Winthrop

Boston in New Engl[an]d,
July 20, 1635
To the right worshipful Sir Simondes Dewes, knight.

The colony of Massachusetts Bay was created by men who were motivated largely but not exclusively by religion. They were puritans, and the ministers of the colony either were sympathetic to Congregationalism when they left England or accommodated themselves to the new Congregational church polity after they arrived in America. They were not devoted to religious liberty; what they wanted was to create a new commonwealth, a unified community of like-minded people. This is not to say that the colony rejected those who had not yet been called to salvation, for at first the hope and expectation of the leaders were that such people would be converted, and many were. John Cotton wrote of "sundry elder and younger persons who came over hither not out of respect to conscience or spiritual ends but of respect to friends or outward enlargement, but have here found that grace which they sought not for." From their dealings with Roger Williams, Anne Hutchinson, and later the Quakers, the Massachusetts Bay colonists became notorious for their religious intolerance. The exile of Williams has loomed especially large to the modern consciousness and conscience, since Williams was one of the first proponents of toleration. Therefore the Commonwealth of Massachusetts penitentially cancelled out— in 1936!—the colony's action against Williams of three hundred years before. Williams himself had brought attention to his experience eight years after his departure from Massachusetts as part of his campaign to discredit the English Congregationalists or Independents.

Williams used as the occasion of his attack on the Massachusetts policy the publication in 1643 of *A Letter of Mr. John Cotton to Mr. Williams*, which had been written in 1636. Williams replied with *Mr. Cottons Letter Lately Printed, Examined and Answered* (1644). In the same year he published another, more famous, attack on Cotton's position as set forth by the Boston minister about 1635. It is this letter, as published in *The Blovdy Tenent, of Persecution*, that appears below. The circumstances of its composition are somewhat obscure. In 1647 Cotton wrote, "Mr. Williams sent me about a dozen years ago (as I remember) a letter, penned (as he wrote) by a prisoner in Newgate, touching persecution for conscience' sake, and entreated my judgment of it for the satisfaction of his friend." Williams argued that not he but a Roxbury man had given the prisoner's argument to Cotton, and when the man was not satisfied with Cotton's answers, he had forwarded them to Williams.

The details of the Williams-Cotton controversy are not relevant in the present context, though it should be noted that Cotton's position is both more intellectually sophisticated and more Christian in its orientation than has been generally recognized. His advocacy of intolerance, as set forth below, was frequently echoed by other religious leaders, each of whom conceived himself a spokesman for the colony. Richard Mather argued, "We have means to preserve the churches in unity and verity. First, the Holy Scriptures, which are a perfect rule for doctrine and practice. . . . Secondly, the ministry appointed by Christ." Thomas Shepard declared, "As for New England, we never banished any for their consciences, but for sinning against conscience, after due means of conviction, or some other wickedness which they had no conscience to plead for." Nathaniel Ward devoted a large part of his *Simple Cobler of Aggawam* to an attack on religious toleration. "I dare take upon me," he wrote, "to be the herald of New England so far as to proclaim to the world in the name of our colony that all Familists, Antinomians, Anabaptists, and other enthusiasts should have free liberty to be gone as fast as they can, the sooner the better." If these men truly spoke for the colony, and Ward believed that he did, the colony's position was strongly opposed to religious toleration.

On the other hand, it is not so easy to say that the colony

practiced intolerance. Since there was no one church in Massachusetts, only individual congregations, there was no religious standard, no confession or creed to which authorities could appeal. When in 1648 the colony's religious leaders finally put together a definition of orthodoxy, the Cambridge Platform, they limited it to the topics of church government and discipline. The Platform acknowledges the soundness of the Westminister Confession, which teaches High Calvinism, but it refers to the Confession only in a general way. There were no credal tests for office or church membership in Massachusetts; church covenants contain very little theology.

What was feared was not what the individual in his heart of hearts might believe but rather what the Platform listed: "Idolatry, blasphemy, heresy, venting corrupt and pernicious opinions that destroy the foundations, open contempt of the Word preached, profanation of the Lord's Day, disturbing the peaceable administration and exercise of the worship and holy things of God, and the like." These, the Platform declared, "are to be restrained and punished by civil authority," but the "object of the power of the magistrate are [sic] not things merely inward, and so not subject to cognisance and view, as unbelief, hardness of heart, erroneous opinions not vented, but only such things as are acted by the outward man." The ministers were opposed, not surprisingly, to disturbances of religious worship. But it was not just any heresy or corrupt opinion which the ministers would eliminate; it was heresy or opinion that would destroy the foundations of their society. Roger Williams publicly denied the validity of the colony's charter and its claim to its lands; his attack was on the foundation of the colony. Anne Hutchinson taught her followers to reject the Bible as the source of truth and substitute private revelation for it. By implication this was venting an opinion destructive to the foundations, the religious foundations, of the colony.

The usefulness of Cotton's letter against departures from religious orthodoxy is thus somewhat limited. His thesis—that there is one set of truths that can be reached through examination of the Bible—was probably accepted in principle by the great majority of colonists in the 1630s. Moreover, to the Bay colonists, huddled together on the edge of a huge wilderness, the principle of toleration meant loss of a much-desired sense of community. At the same time, the colonists prized privacy highly. To recognize the legitimacy of two sets of values, individual rights as well as the concept of truth and the need for community, the colonists in principle and officially favored Cotton's position; in practice, they were a good deal more lenient. Churches defined their doctrine, if at all, by consensus. Church members charged with heresy were tried not by a court of clergymen but by their peers in congregational meeting. Church discipline was much more frequently concerned with moral laxity than heresy. The creators of the new commonwealth were devoted to distinctive principles, but they were also practical men. The basis for the text of the Cotton letter that follows is the 1644 printed version.

John Cotton to ?
c. 1635

The question which you put is, whether persecution for cause of conscience be not against the doctrine of Jesus Christ the King of Kings. Now by persecution for cause of conscience I conceive you mean either for professing some point of doctrine which you believe in conscience to be the truth or for practicing some work which in conscience you believe to be a religious duty.

Now in points of doctrine some are fundamental, without right belief whereof a man cannot be saved. Others are circumstantial or less principal, wherein men may differ in judgment without prejudice of salvation on either part. In like sort, in points of practice some concern the weightier duties of the Law as what God we worship and what kind of worship; whether such, as if it be right, fellowship with God is held; if corrupt, fellowship with him is lost. Again, in points of doctrine and worship less principal, either they are held forth in a meek and peaceable way, though the things be erroneous or unlawful, or they are held forth with such arrogance and impetuousness as tendeth and reacheth (even of itself) to the disturbance of civil peace. Finally, let me add this one distinction more. When we are persecuted for conscience' sake, it is either for conscience rightly informed or for erroneous and blind conscience.

These things premised, I would lay down mine answer to the question in certain conclusions. First, it is not lawful to perse-

cute any for conscience' sake righly informed, for in persecuting such, Christ himself is persecuted in them (Acts 9.4).
Secondly, for an erroneous and blind conscience (even in fundamental and weighty points) it is not lawful to persecute any till
after admonition once or twice, and so the Apostle directeth
(Titus 3. 10), and giveth the reason that in fundamental and
principal points of doctrine or worship, the Word of God in
such things is so clear that he cannot but be convinced in conscience of the dangerous error of his way after once or twice
admonition, wisely and faithfully dispensed. And then if anyone persist it is not out of conscience but against his conscience
as the Apostle saith, verse 11. He is subverted and sinneth, being
condemned of himself, that is, of his own conscience. So that
if such a man after such admonition shall still persist in the
error of his way and be therefore punished, he is not persecuted
for cause of conscience but for sinning against his own conscience. Thirdly, in things of lesser moment, whether points
of doctrine or worship, if a man hold them forth in a spirit of
Christian meekness and love (though with zeal and constancy)
he is not to be persecuted but tolerated till God may be pleased
to manifest his truth to him (Philippians 3. 17; Romans 14. 1,
2, 3, 4). But if a man hold forth or profess any error or false
way, with a boisterous and arrogant spirit, to the disturbance of
civil peace, he may justly be punished according to the quality
and measure of the disturbance caused by him.

Now let us consider of your reasons or objections to the
contrary. Your first head of objections is taken from the Scripture. *Objection* 1: Because Christ commandeth to let alone the
tares and wheat to grow together unto the harvest (Matthew 13.
30-38). *Answer*: Tares are not briars and thorns but partly hyp-
ocrites like unto the godly but indeed carnal, as the tares are
like to wheat but are not wheat, or partly such corrupt doc-
trines or practices as are indeed unsound but yet such as come
very near the truth (as tares do to the wheat) and so near that
good men may be taken with them, and so the persons in whom
they grow cannot be rooted out, but good will be rooted out
with them. And in such a case Christ calleth for toleration, not
for penal prosecution, according to the third conclusion.

Objection 2: In Matthew 15.14 Christ commandeth his disciples to let the blind alone till they fall into the ditch. Therefore
he would have their punishment deferred till their final de-

Sir Henry Vane the Younger

struction. *Answer.* He there speaketh not to public officers, whether in church or commonweal, but to his private disciples concerning the Pharisees, over whom they had had no power. And the command he giveth to let them alone is spoken in regard of troubling themselves or regarding the offence, which they took as the wholesome doctrine of the gospel, as who should say, "Though they be offended at this saying of mine, yet do not you fear their fear nor be troubled at their offence, which they take at my doctrine, not out of sound judgment but out of their blindness." But this maketh nothing to the cause in hand.

Objection. In Luke 9. 54,55 Christ reproveth his disciples, who would have had fire come down from heaven to consume the Samaritans, who refused to receive him. *Objection.* And Paul teacheth Timothy not to strive but to be gentle towards all men, suffering evil patiently. *Answer.* Both these are directions to ministers of the gospel how to deal (not with obstinate offenders in the church that sin against conscience but) either with men without, as the Samaritans were and many unconverted Christians in Crete, whom Titus (as an evangelist) was to seek to convert, or at best with some Jews or Gentiles in the church, who though carnal yet were not convinced of the error of their way. And 'tis true, it became not the spirit of the gospel to convert aliens to the faith of Christ (such as the Samaritans were) by fire and brimstone, nor to deal harshly in public ministry or private conference with all such contrary-minded men as either had not yet entered into church fellowship or if they had yet did hitherto sin of ignorance, not against conscience. But neither of both these texts do hinder the ministers of the gospel to proceed in a church way against church members when they become scandalous offenders either in life or doctrine, much less do they speak at all to civil magistrates.

Objection 5. From the predictions of the prophets, who foretold that carnal weapons should cease in the days of the gospel (Isaiah 2.4 and 11.9; Micah 4.3, 4). And the Apostle professeth, "The weapons of our warfare are not carnal" (II Corinthians 10.4). And Christ is so far from persecuting those that would not be of his religion that he chargeth them when they are persecuted themselves, they should pray, and when they are cursed they should bless. The reason whereof seemeth to be that they who are now persecutors and wicked persons may become true disciples and converts.

Answer. Those predictions in the prophets do only show, first, with what kind of weapons he will subdue the nations to the obedience of the faith of the gospel, not by fire and sword and weapons of war but by the power of his Word and Spirit, which no man doubteth of.

Secondly, those predictions of the prophets show what the meek and peaceable temper will be of all the true converts to Christianity, not lions or leopards, etc., not cruel oppressors, nor malignant opposers, or biters of one another, but doth not forbid them to drive ravenous wolves from the sheepfold and to restrain them from devouring the sheep of Christ. And when Paul saith, The weapons of our warfare are not carnal but spiritual, he denieth not civil weapons of justice to the civil magistrate, Romans 13, but only to church officers. And yet the weapons of such officers he acknowledgeth to be such as though they be spiritual yet are ready to take vengeance of all disobedience, II Corinthians 10. 6, which hath reference (amongst other ordinances) to the censure of the church against scandalous offenders.

[Thirdly,] when Christ commandeth his disciples to bless them that curse them and persecute them, he giveth not therein a rule to public officers, whether in church or commonweal, to suffer notorious sinners, either in life or doctrine, to pass away with a blessing, but to private Christians to suffer persecution patiently, yea and to pray for their persecutors. Again, it is true, Christ would have his disciples to be far from persecuting (for that is a sinful oppression of men for righteousness' sake), but that hindereth not but that he would have them execute upon all disobedience the judgment and vengeance required in the Word, II Corinthians 10. 6, Romans 13. 4.

[Fourthly,] though it be true that wicked persons now may by the grace of God become true disciples and converts, yet we may not do evil that good may come thereof. And evil it would be to tolerate notorious evil doers, whether seducing teachers or scandalous livers. Christ had something against the angel of the church of Pergamus for tolerating them that held the doctrine of Balaam and against the church of Thiatira for tolerating Jesabel to teach and seduce (Revelation 2. 14-20).

Your second head of reasons is taken from the profession and practice of famous princes: King James, Stephen of Poland, King of Bohemia, whereunto a treble answer may briefly be returned. First, we willingly acknowledge that none is to be persecuted at all, no more than they may be oppressed for righteousness' sake. Again, we acknowledge that none is to be punished for his conscience, though misinformed, as hath been said, unless his error be fundamental or seditiously and turbulently promoted, and that after due conviction of his conscience, that it may appear he is not punished for his conscience but for sinning against his conscience. Furthermore, we acknowledge none is to be constrained to believe or profess the true religion till he be convinced in judgment of the truth of it, but yet restrained he may [be] from blaspheming the truth and from seducing any unto pernicious errors.

[Secondly] we answer, what princes profess or practice is not a rule of conscience. They many times tolerate that in point of state policy which cannot justly be tolerated in point of true Christianity. Again, princes many times tolerate offenders out of very necessity when the offenders are either too many or too mighty for them to punish, in which respect David tolerated Joab and his murders but against his will..

[Thirdly] we answer further that for those three princes named by you who tolerated religion, we can name you more and greater who have not tolerated heretics and schismatics, notwithstanding their pretence of conscience, and arrogating the crown of martyrdom to their sufferings. Constantine the Great at the request of the General Council of Nice banished Arrius with some of his fellows (Sozomen, liber 1, *Ecclesiastical History*, cap. 19, 20). The same Constantine made a severe law against the Donatists. And the like proceedings against them were used by Valentinian, Gratian, and Theodosius, as Augustine reported in Epistle 166. Only Julian the Apostate granted liberty to heretics as well as to pagans, that he might, by tolerating all weeds to grow, choke the vitals of Christianity, which was also the practice and sin of Valens the Arrian. Queen Elizabeth, as famous for her government as any of the former, it is well known what laws she made and executed against Papists. Yea and King James (one of your own witnesses), though he was slow in proceeding against Papists (as you say) for conscience' sake, yet you are not ignorant how sharply and severely he punished those whom the malignant world calleth Puritans, men of more conscience and better faith than he tolerated.[1]

I come now to your third and last argument, taken from the

1. In the early seventeenth century James I was a strong opponent of the puritans, though they had expected him to support their position.

judgment of ancient and later writers, yea even of Papists themselves, who have condemned persecution for conscience' sake. You begin with Hilary, whose testimony we might admit without any prejudice to the truth, for it is true, the Christian church doth not persecute but is persecuted. But to excommunicate a heretic is not to persecute; that is, it is not to punish an innocent but a culpable and damnable person, and that not for conscience but for persisting in error against light of conscience, whereof it hath been convinced. It is true also what he saith, that neither the apostles did nor may we propagate Christian religion by the sword, but if pagans cannot be won by the Word, they are not to be compelled by the sword. Nevertheless this hindereth not, but if they or any others should blaspheme the true God and his true religion, they ought to be severely punished, and no less do they deserve, if they seduce from the truth to damnable heresy or idolatry.

Your next writer (which is Tertullian) speaketh to the same purpose in the place alleged by you. His intent is only to restrain Scapula the Roman governor of Africa from the persecution of Christians for not offering sacrifice to their gods, and for that end fetcheth an argument from the law of natural equity not to compel any to any religion but to permit them either to believe willingly or not to believe at all, which we acknowledge and accordingly permit the Indians to continue in their unbelief. Nevertheless, it will not therefore be lawful openly to tolerate the worship of devils or idols or the seduction of any from the truth. When Tertullian saith, another man's religion neither hurtheth nor profiteth any, it must be understood of private worship and religion professed in private. Otherwise a false religion professed by the members of a church or by such as have given their names to Christ will be the ruin and desolation of the church, as appeareth by the threats of Christ to the churches of Asia (Revelation 2).

Your next author Hierom [Jerome] crosseth not the truth nor advantageth not your cause, for we grant what he saith, that heresy must be cut off with the sword of the Spirit. But this hindreth not, but that being so cut down, if the heretic still persist in his heresy, to the seduction of others, he may be cut off by the civil sword to prevent the perdition of others. And that to be Hierome's meaning appeareth by his note upon that of the Apostle ("A little leaven leaveneth the whole lump");

"Therefore," saith he, "a spark as soon as it appeareth is to be extinguished and the leaven to be removed from the rest of the dough, rotten pieces of flesh are to be cut off, and a scabbed beast is to be driven from the sheepfold, lest the whole house, mass of dough, body and stock be set on fire with the spark, be soured with the leaven, be putrified with the rotten flesh, perish by the scabbed beast."

Brentius [Johann Brenz], whom you next quote, speaketh not to your cause. We willingly grant him and you that man hath no power to make laws to bind conscience. But this hindreth not, but that men may see the laws of God observed, which do bind conscience. The like answer may be returned to Luther, whom you next allege, first, that the government of the civil magistrate extendeth no further than over the bodies and goods of their subjects, not over their souls, and therefore they may not undertake to give laws to the souls and consciences of men. Secondly, that the church of Christ doth not use the arm of secular power to compel men to the faith or profession of the truth, for this is to be done by spiritual weapons, whereby Christians are to be exhorted, not compelled. But this hindreth not that Christians sinning against light of faith and conscience may justly be censured by the church with excommunication and by the civil sword also, in case they shall corrupt others to the perdition of their souls.

As for the testimony of the popish book, we weigh it not, as knowing whatsoever they speak for toleration of religion, where themselves are under hatches, when they come to sit at stern, they judge and practice quite contrary, as both their writings and judicial proceedings have testified to the world these many years.

To shut up this argument from testimony of writers, it is well known, Augustine retracted this opinion of yours which in his younger times he had held but in after riper age reversed and refuted, as appeareth in the second book of his *Retractions*, chapter 5, and in his Epistles 48, 50. And in his first book against Parmenianus, cap. 7, he sheweth that if the Donatists were punished with death, they were justly punished; and in his eleventh tractate upon John, "They murder," saith he, "souls, and themselves are afflicted in body. They put men to everlasting death, and yet they complain when themselves are put to suffer temporal death."

Optatus in his third book justifieth Macharius, who had put some heretics to death, that he had done no more herein than what Moses, Phineas, and Elias had done before him.

Bernard in his sixty-sixth sermon in Cantica: "Out of doubt," saith he, "it is better that they should be restrained by the sword of him who beareth not the sword in vain than that they should be suffered to draw many others into their error. For he is the minister of God for wrath to every evildoer."

Calvin's judgment is well known, who procured the death of Michael Servetus for pertinacy in heresy and defended his fact by a book written of that argument.

Beza also wrote a book *de Haereticis Morte plectendis*, that heretics are to be punished with death. Aretius likewise took the like course about the death of Valentinus Gentilis and justified the magistrates' proceeding against him in a history written of that argument.

Finally you come to answer some main objections, as you call them, which yet are but one, and that one objecteth nothing against what we hold. It is (say you) no prejudice to the commonwealth if liberty of conscience were suffered to such as fear God indeed, which you prove by the examples of the Patriarchs and others. But we readily grant you, liberty of conscience is to be granted to men that fear God indeed, as knowing they will not persist in heresy or turbulent schism when they are convinced in conscience of the sinfulness thereof. But the question is whether a heretic after once or twice admonition (and so after conviction) or any other scandalous and heinous offender may be tolerated either in the church without excommunication or in the commonwealth without such punishment as may preserve others from dangerous and damnable infection.

Thus much I thought needful to be spoken for avoiding the grounds of your error. I forbear adding reasons to justify the truth because you may find that done to your hand in a treatise sent to some of the brethren late of Salem, who doubted as you do.[2]

2. Presumably Cotton's letter to Roger Williams, published in London in 1643 as *A Letter of Mr. John Cottons.*

The Lord Jesus lead you by a spirit of truth into all truth, through Jesus Christ.

From the disasters of the beginnings of the colony on-wards, most of its early history resulted from man's will and man's wilfulness. But human history includes acts of God, and in his journal for August 16, 1635, Winthrop recorded a hurricane:

The wind having blown hard at S. and S.W. a week before, about midnight it came up at N. E. and blew with such violence, with abundance of rain, that it blew down many hundreds of trees, near the towns, overthrew some houses, drave the ships from their anchors. The Great Hope, of Ipswich, being about four hundred tons, was driven on ground at Mr. Hoffe's Point, and brought back again presently by a N.W. wind, and ran on shore at Charlestown. About eight of the clock the wind came about to N.W. very strong, and, it being then about high water, by nine the tide was fallen about three feet. Then it began to flow again about one hour, and rose about two or three feet, which was conceived to be, that the sea was grown so high with the N.E. wind, that, meeting with the ebb, it forced it back again.

This hurricane caused a shipwreck (discussed by Winthrop in this same entry), and the account of it in Anthony Thacher's letter to his brother is of permanent interest. His letter was used by Increase Mather in his *Essay for the Recording of Illustrious Providences* (Boston, 1684); in a severely pruned version, it is Mather's first "illustrious providence." The text below is from an imperfect copy, British Museum manuscript Sloane 922, pages 205-18, but fuller than Mather's by some four hundred words. Most of Mather's changes are simply abridgments. He trimmed detail, telescoped, and omitted entirely one passage, a digression.

Anthony Thacher, a tailor, had arrived in Massachusetts on June 3, 1635. The brother to whom he wrote was rector of a church at Salisbury, Wiltshire. Because of his loss in the ship-wreck, the General Court of Massachusetts gave Anthony Thacher forty marks (about 27 pounds) and Thacher's Island, the island that he reached after the shipwreck. Later Thacher settled in Marshfield, then moved to Yarmouth on Cape Cod. He lived to be over eighty. Relics of his shipwreck were used in family baptisms for over two hundred years. Thacher's letter does not make a significant contribution to historical knowl-edge, but the tale it tells is worth preserving, especially in its fuller and hitherto unpublished form.

Anthony Thacher to Peter Thacher
September [?] 1635

*Some part of a Letter of Mr. Anthony Thachar Written in
New England and sent to his Brother Mr. Peter Thachar in
Old England Concerning his Great Deliverance out of the
Deeps of the Sea*

But now with the leaf I must alter my matter and subject and
turn my drowned pen with my shaking hand to write other
news and to rouse up my heavy heart and sadded spirits to in-
dite the story of such sad news as never before this happened in
New England and been lamented both in the public on the pul-
pit and concourse of the people and in private in the closet and
in the same places hath God's name been magnified for his great
mercy and wonderful deliverance of me out of the bottom of
the angry sea.

The story is thus. First there was a league of perennial friendship solemnly made between my cousin Avary[1] and myself made
in Mr. Graves his ship never to forsake each other to the death
but to be partaker each of other's misery or welfare as also of
habitation in one place. Now it pleased God immediately on our
arrival unto New England there was an offer made unto us, and
my cousin Avary was invited to Marblehed by the men of that
place to be their pastor, there being as yet no church there
planted but there a town appointed by the whole country to be
planted there, intended for the good of the whole country to
set up the trade of fishing.[2] Now because that many there (the
most being fishers) were something loose and remiss in their
carriage and behavior, my cousin was unwilling to go thither,
and so refusing it we went to Newberry to Mr. Parker and others
of his acquaintance,[3] intending there to sit down and plant, but
being solicited so often both by the men of the place and by the
magistrates, and counselled to it by Mr. Cotten and most of the
ministers in the patent, alleging what a benefit we might do
both to the people there and also unto the country and commonweal to settle there a plantation, at length we embraced it
and there consented to go. The men of Marblehed forthwith
sent a pinnace for us and our goods, and we were at Ipswich on
Tuesday the twelfth of August, 1635, embarked ourselves and
all and every one of our families with all our goods and sub-
stance for Marblehed, we being in all twenty-three souls, to wit

1. John Avery had been a
Wiltshire clergyman.
2. Marblehead was part of
the town of Salem until
1649.
3. Thomas Parker, minister
at Newbury, formerly at
Ipswich (or Agawam).

eleven in my cousin's family and seven in mine and one Master William Elliott and four mariners. Whence the next morning having recommended ourselves unto the Lord with cheerful and contented hearts we hoisted sail for Marblehed.

But the Lord suddenly turned our cheerfulness into mourning and sad lamentation. Thus on Friday the fourteenth of August 1635 in the evening about ten of the clock our sails being old and torn, we, having a fine fresh gale of wind, were split. Our sailors, because it was something dark would not put on new sails presently but determined to cast their sheet anchor and so to ride at anchor until the next morning and then to put [them] on. But before daylight it pleased God to send so mighty a storm as the like was never felt in New England since the English came there nor in the memory of any of the Indeans. It was [so] furious that our anchor came home, whereupon our mariners let slip more cable, yea, even to the utmost end thereof, and so made it fast only about the bit, whence it slipped away end for end. Then our sailors knew not what to do but were driven as pleased the storm and waves. My cousin and we, perceiving our danger, solemnly recommended ourselves to God, the Lord both of earth and seas, expecting with every wave to be swallowed up and drenched in the deeps. And as my cousin, his wife and children and maid servant, my wife and my tender babes sat comforting and cheering on the other in the Lord against ghastly death, which every moment stares us in the face and sat triumphingly on each other's forehead, we were by the violence of the waves and fury of the winds by the Lord's permission lifted up upon a rock between two high rocks yet all was but one rock but ragged, with the stroke whereof the water came into the pinnace. So as we were presently up to the middle in water as wet, the waters came furiously and violently over us and against us but by reason of the rock's proportion could not lift us off but beat her all to pieces. Now look with me upon our distresses and consider of my misery, who beheld the ship broken, the water in her and violently overwhelming us, my goods and provision swimming in the seas, my friends almost drowned and mine own poor children so untimely (if I may so term it without offence) before mine eyes half drowned and ready to be swallowed up and dashed to pieces against the rocks by the merciless waves and myself ready to accompany them.

But I must go on to an end of this woeful relation. In the

same room with us sat he that went master of the pinnace, not knowing what to do. Our foremast was cut down, our mainmast broken in three pieces, the forepart of our pinnace beaten away, our goods swimming about the seas, my children bewailing me as not pitying themselves, and myself bemoaning them, poor souls whom I had occasioned to such an end in their tender years whenas they could scarce be sensible of death. And so likewise my cousin, his wife and his children and both of us bewailing each other in Our Lord and only Savior Jesus Christ, in whom only we had comfort and cheerfulness, insomuch that from the greatest to the least of us there was not one screech or outcry made, but all as silent sheep were contentedly resolved to die together lovingly as since our acquaintance we had lived together friendly.

Now as I was sitting in the cabinroom door, lo, one of the sailors by a wave being washed out of the pinnace was gotten in again, and coming into the cabinroom over my back, cried out, "oh, we are all cast away. Lord, have mercy on us. I have been washed overboard into the sea and am gotten in again." His speeches made me look forth, and looking toward the sea and seeing how we were, I turned myself toward my cousin and the rest and these words, "Oh, cousin, it hath pleased God here to cast us between two rocks, and the shore not far off from us, for I saw the top of trees when I looked forth." Whereupon the said master of the pinnace, looking up at the s[c]uttle hole of the half deck went out of it, but I never saw him afterward. Then he that had been in the sea went out again by me and leaped overboard toward the rock, whom afterward also I could never see.

Now none were left in the bark that I knew or saw, but my cousin and his wife and children, myself and mine and his maidservant. I put [on] my great coat, a waistcoat of cotton but had neither sleeves nor skirts, a thin pair of breeches, a pair of boots without stockings. My coat I put off me and laid it under my poor babe's feet to raise it out of the water (a poor supporter), but my cousin thought I would have fled from him and said unto me, "Oh, cousin, leave us not. Let us die together," and reached forth his hand unto me. Then I, letting go my son Peter's hand, took him by the hand and said to him, "I purpose it not whither shall I go. I am willing and ready here to die with you. And my poor children, God be merciful to us," adding these words, "The Lord is able to help and to deliver us." He replied, saying, "True, cousin, but what His pleasure is, we know not; I fear we have been too unthankful for former mercies. But He hath promised to deliver us from sin and condemnation, through the all-sufficient satisfaction of Jesus Christ. This, therefore, we may challenge of him." To which I, replying, said, "That is all the deliverance I now desire and expect," which words I had no sooner spoken but by a mighty wave I was with a piece of the bark washed out upon part of the rock, where the wave left me almost drowned. But recovering my feet, [I] saw above me on the rock my daughter Mary, to whom I was no sooner gotten but my cousin Avary and his eldest son came to us, being all four of us washed out with one and the same wave. We went all into a small hole on the top of the rock, whence we called to those in the pinnace to come unto us. Supposing we had been in more safety than they were in, my wife, seeing us there, was crept into the scuttle of the half deck to come unto us, but presently another wave dashing the pinnace all to pieces carried away my wife in the scuttle as she was with the greater part of the half deck [carried] to the shore, where she was safely cast, but her legs were something bruised, and much timber of the vessel being there also cast, she was some time before she could get away, washed with the waves. All the rest that were in the bark were drowned in the merciless seas.

We four by that wave were clean swept away from off the rock also into the sea, the Lord in one instant of time disposing of the souls of us to his good pleasure and will. His wonderful mercy to me was thus. Standing on the rock as before you heard with my eldest daughter, my cousin, and his eldest son, [I was] looking upon and talking unto them in the bark whenas we were by that cruel wave washed off the rock as before you heard. God in his mercy caused me to fall by the stroke of the wave flat on my face, for my face was toward the sea insomuch that I was sliding down the rock into the sea. The Lord directed my toes into a joint in the rock's side as also the tops of some of my fingers with my right hand by means whereof, the waves leaving me, I remained so, having only my head above the water. On my left hand I espied a board or plank of the pinnace, and as I was reaching out my left hand to lay hold on it, by another wave coming on the top of the rock I was washed away from the rock and by the violence of the waves was driven hither and thither in the sea a great while and had many dashes against the rocks. At length past hope of life and wearied both in body and spirit I even gave out to nature, and being ready to receive in the waters of death I lifted up both my heart and hands to the God of heaven (for, note, I had my senses remaining and perfect with me all the time I was under and in the water), who at that instant lifted my head clean above the top of waters that so I might breathe without hindrance by the waters. I stood bolt upright as if I stood upon my feet but I felt no bottom nor had any footing for to stand upon but the waters. While I was thus above the waters I saw a piece of the mast as I supposed about three foot long which I labored to catch into my arms, but suddenly I was overwhelmed with water and driven to and fro again and at last I felt the ground with my right foot. Immediately I was violently thrown groveling on my face. When presently I recovered my feet [I] was in the water up to my breast and through God's great mercy had my face to the shore and not to the sea. I made haste to get out but was thrown down on my hands with the waves and so with safety crept forth to the dry shore, where, blessing God, I turned about to look for my children and friends but saw neither them nor any part of the pinnace where I left them as I supposed, but I saw my wife about a butt-length from me, getting herself forth from amongst the timber of the broken bark, but before I could get unto her she was gotten to the shore. When we were come each to other we went up into the land and sat us down under a cedar tree, which the winds had thrown down, where we sat about an hour, even dead with cold, for I was glad to put off my breeches, they being rent all to pieces in the rocks.

But now the storm was broken up and the wind was calm, but the sea remained rough and fearful to us. My legs was much bruised and so was my heart, and other hurt had I none, neither had I taken in much water. But my heart would not suffer me to sit still any longer, but I would go to see if any more was gotten to the land in safety, especially hoping to have met with some of mine own poor children, but I could find none, neither dead nor yet living. You condole with me my further miseries, who now began to consider of my losses. Now [I] called to my remembrance the time and manner how and when I last saw and left my children and friends. One was severed from me sitting on the rock at my feet, the other three in the pinnace, my little babe (ah, poor Peter) sitting in his sister Edith's arms, who to the utmost of her power sheltered him out of the waters, my poor William standing close unto her, all three of them looking ruefully on me on the rock, their very countenance calling unto me to help them, whom I could not go unto, neither could they come unto me, neither could the merciless waves afford me space or time to use any means at all, either to help them or myself.

Oh I yet see their cheeks, poor, silent lambs, pleading pity and help at my hands. Then on the other side to consider the loss of my dear friends with the spoil and loss of all our goods and provisions, myself cast upon an unknown land in a wilderness, I know not where, and how to get there we did not know. Then it came into my mind how I had occasioned the death of my children, who had occasioned them out of their native land, who might have left them there, yea and might have sent some of them back again and cost me nothing. These and many such thoughts do press down my heavy heart very much, but I leave this till I see your face, before which time I fear I shall never attain comfort. Now having no friend to whom I can freely impart myself, Mr. Cotten is now my chiefest friend to whom I have free welcome and access, as also Mr. Mavericke, Mr. Warde, Mr. Ward, Mr. Hocker, Mr. Weles, Mr. Warhad, and Mr. Parker also, Mr. Noyes, who use me friendly.[4] This is God's goodness to me, as also to set the eyes of all the country on me, especially of the magistrates who much favor and comfort me.

But I let this pass and will proceed on in the relation of God's goodness unto me. While I was in that desolate island on which I was cast, I and my wife were almost naked, both of us, and wet and cold even unto death. When going down to the shore as before I said I found cast on the shore a snapsack in which I had a steel and a flint and a powder horn. Going further I found a drowned goat. Then I found a hat and my son Will's coat, both which I put on. My wife found one of her own petticoats which she put on. I found also two cheeses and some butter driven ashore. Thus the Lord sent us some clothes to put on and food to sustain our new lives which he had given lately unto us, and means also to make fire, for in my horn I had some gunpowder, which to my own and other men's admiration was dry. So, taking a piece of my wife's neckcloth, which I dried in the sun, I struck fire and so dried and warmed our wet bodies, and

4. These men were all ministers; most of them are referred to in other places. "Mr. Warhad" is presumably John Warham. James Noyes was minister at Newbury, with Parker.

then skinned the goat, and having found a small brass pot we boiled some of it. Our drink was brackish water. Bread we had none. There we remained until the Monday following, where about three o'clock in the afternoon in a boat that came that way, we went off that desolate island, which I named after my own name, "Thacher's Woe," and the rock I named "Avary his Fall," to the end their fall and loss and mine own might be had in perpetual remembrance.[5] In the island lieth buried the body of my cousin's eldest daughter, whom I found dead on the shore. On the Tuesday following in the afternoon we arrived at Marble head, where I am now remaining in health and good respect though very poor, and thus you have heard such relation as never before happened in New England, and as much bewailed as it was strange. What I shall do or what course I shall take I know not. The Lord in his mercy direct me that I may so lead the new life which he hath given me as may be most to his own glory.

Praise God and pray to God for me.

Visiting in Massachusetts Bay at the time of the hurricane was Edward Trelawny, the brother of Robert Trelawny, a successful English merchant who in 1631 had obtained a grant of land in Maine, including Richmond Island and Cape Elizabeth, near the present Portland. He established a trading company with a resident manager. Edward Trelawny, then in his twenties, seems to have acted on his behalf during the visit documented below; his stop in Boston was part of his business trip. The sympathy that he shows for the puritanism of the Bay colonists and his admiration for their achievements must have offended his brother, for Robert Trelawny, later a member of Parliament, died in prison seemingly because of his devotion to the traditions of the Church of England and the Crown during the political supremacy of the puritans. Only three letters from Edward Trelawny survive; two are from Boston. They are portions of the Trelawny Papers that found their way from England back to Maine in the nineteenth century. The original letters are in the collection of the Maine Historical Society, Portland.

5. Thacher's Island, as it is now called, is two miles east of Cape Ann. The rock is still called Avery's Fall.

Most ever respected brother:

After the presentment of my ever due respects, you may
please to take notice how my last unto you was per way of
Darthmouth, therein advertising you of all our proceeding here,
and divers other occurrents needful (in my apprehension) for
future benefit, as the sending over some experienced men in
the making and ordering of clapboard and pipe staves,[1] the
which if you have no occasion to make use of yourself, yet no
fear of venting of them at good rates to the straitesmen.[2] They
sell here clapboard for 28 pounds sterling per U[3] and great in-
quisition made after them, and if other men (as I well perceive)
with weak means made such advantage to themselves, why
should not we, who can compass it more easier and readier
every manner of way, you may please to take it into your consideration. Also a skillful man in the manuring of hops would
also be very beneficial. I requested you to send over some saf-
fron roots of the best, and apple and pear and plum pips and
stones, or any other things that you may conceive may conduce
to the furtherance and future benefit of the plantation, for I
would let no probable thing slip, but without the trial, which is
the true settling and furthering of a plantation to future posterity. I likewise advised you of William Ganyes' ability in Virginia
for satisfaction of the bond he so long owed me, and thereupon
desired you to send George Mennefie the copy of the Bond,
with George Littletonn's certificate touching the same, under
a notary's hand, that it may be the more authentic with them
there when it comes to pleading.

Touching the manner of our proceedings here, I praise the
Lord we go on contentedly but should do more comfortably if
we enjoyed those sweet means which draws a blessing on all
things, even those holy ordinances and heavenly manna of our
souls, which in other parts of this land flows abundantly, even
to the great rejoicing and comforting of the people of God,[4] for
certainly if ever were a happy people these are they, for otherwise God would not so go along with them and make things so
prosperous unto them as he doth, that you would admire to see

1. These were exported,
first to England, later to
the Caribbean. Clapboard
was used in making barrel
staves.
2. English merchants trading with the Mediterra-
nean.
3. The meaning of the sym-
bol is, presumably, five
thousand weight or count.
I am indebted for this interpretation and other
assistance with this letter
to Professor Robert
McCusker of the University
of Maryland.
4. Robert Trelawny soon
sent the Reverend Richard
Gibson to the Maine settlement.

how all things have succeeded in so short a time as it hath and daily doth. Let all idle reports touching the conversation of God's people here be utterly abolished and find no credence with any who wish well unto Sion, for I assure you, they deserve it not; if I may speak my conscience that tells me they are a people truly fearing God and follow the paths that lead to Jerusalem, for they manifest the same apparently in the whole course of their conversation. For my part I have just cause even to bless the Lord for so high a favor in bringing me hither and shall account it the greatest happiness that ever befell me, and though I must confess, at your first motioning of it, it was somewhat averse and distasteful to my untamed and unbridled nature, yet since the (heavenly) conversations and sweet life of the people here hath so far wrought upon and vindicated my conscience that I would not (I profess seriously from my very soul) be in my former base, abominable, odious condition, no, not for the whole riches of the world. Oh dear brother, I now find what it is to be a Christian, a most difficult hard thing it is to bring that heart into frame and subjection that hath formerly even drunk in iniquity like water and run the race of all licentiousness, even with greediness. A crucified Christian, what a most honorable title is it. And yet after many a temptation, many a hard conflict and buffeting with Sathan, many a heavy sigh, deep groan, salt and sorrowful tear, I thank God through Jesus Christ our Lord, who hath brought me out of darkness into His glorious light. Oh Newe England, Newe England, how much am I bound to the Lord for granting me so great mercy as to tread on thy grounds and to enjoy and partake of these many sweet examples and holy practices as thou hast afforded me. Oh that Old England could but speak in thy language; then would not the holy and heavenly and sacred name of the great and glorious God of heaven and earth be so irreverently tossed and tumbled, so profanely torn in pieces in men's mouths; then would not thy streets be everywhere so garnished (nay, rather disfigured) with so many beastly, barbarous, belching drunkards as now they are; then would not there be so many abominations and wickedness committed in the hearth and houses of thy people, as to this day is seen, but thou shouldst then be blest and beloved of the Lord as New England is. And what is the reason of all this? Surely one is (as I conceive) that as God's people are come into a new country, where they freely enjoy the liberty of his holy ordinance without any trouble or molestation at all, either of bishop, archbishop, or any other inferior carping minister or gaping officer, so they come unto the land and to the Lord with new hearts and new lives, and enter into a new covenant, so to continue even to their ends. And who would not be among such a people and in such a land.

The Lord surely intends a blessing on this land in blessing it as he doth, in stirring up the hearts even of the noble ones, as also others of good quality, to come into these parts, for no other end nor by respect but merely for the pure worship of God, and I trust will prove good instruments of good to God's church and children here. Of late is arrived the son and heir of the controller of the king's house, a very solid, able, discreet, pious gentleman.[5] I hope you will not draw me from hence but rather further me (as formerly you have ever done) in the establishing and settling me in a course that may tend to my future good, that I may not be a spectator only, but also an actor, which I leave to your consideration.

To give you now a taste of other passages, you may please to be advertised how that at present our boats have reasonable good fishing. (I beseech the Lord to continue it to His only glory.) A late and sudden, violent, and most fierce storm wrought many evil and woeful effects, generally the land over, to the loss of many vessels and men's lives; that of any great note was of the *Angel Gabriell* of Bristoll, who was cast away as she rid at anchor at Pemaquidd;[6] others quite lost in other places in the land, no place free. We also tasted of it, though not in that measure with others, yet to the loss of one of our boats, which proved some hindrance unto us. In my last I advised you of the French's rooting out of the English at Penobscot,[7] since which the Inglish (being not willing to put up so great a wrong) have armed forth hence a ship of four hundred tons and of good defense, again to displant them, with other exploit they have performed since their departure we as yet hear not of.[8] Here hath been a design begun and undertaken by the English on the Isle of Sabell for sea horse, on which they have done good and are returned with very great voyages.[9] I have not else to enlarge; therefore with my kind salutations to my good sisters, my much reverenced friend Mr. Bedford, Cousin

5. Sir Henry Vane had arrived on October 6, 1635, just a few days before Trelawny wrote.
6. This is the hurricane described above in Anthony Thacher's letter. Pemaquid, on the Maine coast, was settled in 1625.
7. The French occupied the Penobscot area for nineteen years after this victory.
8. Captain Girling and the Great Hope were unsuccessful. See Winthrop, *History*, 1: 193.
9. Winthrop describes the search for walrus tusks on this island east of Nova Scotia in his *History*, 1: 193.

Moorehouse, with all yours, to Israel's gracious guidance I recommend you and your affairs, remaining

> Your observant brother in all respect,
> Edward Trelawny

Boston in Messachuset Baye,
10 8ber, 1635.

I shall stand in great need of necessaries for my particular use, of which have formerly advised you of, and shall desire you to be mindful of in sending me, together with a Bible.

To his much respected kind brother Mr. Robert Trelawny, Merchant, deliver in Plymouth
[Endorsed] New Ingland, My brother Edward Trelawny, Received the 15th of January

Although it has been contended that sentiment played no part in the settlement of Massachusetts, religion or the desire for worldly wealth being the only real motivations, nevertheless blood relationships and marriage ties obviously were very important. Whole families were identified with the Massachusetts Bay venture. John Winthrop's many ties help to illustrate this generalization. Winthrop's sister Lucy was married to Emmanuel Downing. By an earlier marriage Downing had three children, who came to America before he did: James, who came in 1630, and Susan and Mary, who came in 1633. Mary is referred to repeatedly as "Cousin Mary" in the letters of John Winthrop's oldest son John, whose first marriage was to his father's sister's daughter. The *Winthrop Papers* are full of references to cousins. Mary Downing lived in Massachusetts, presumably with the Winthrops, for several years before her marriage in 1638; her brother and sister were probably also members of the Winthrop household. The one surviving letter from Mary to her father gives some sense of the social pressures of the new puritan commonwealth. Mary Downing's original letter is Massachusetts Historical Society manuscript W. 4. 30.

Worthy sir, dear Father,

The continual experience that I enjoy of your tender love and
care to a child, though I confess an undeserving one, (yet) your
love emboldens me to present my humble duty and respect I
owe and shall render with my might and power to yourself so
long as it pleaseth the Lord to continue my life. I have found so
much your love and see that neither time nor distance of place
doth diminish or blast the same, which I confess and desire to
acknowledge as a great mercy and the chief comfort for a temporal, that I have to solace myself withal. Father, I trust in Him
who hath the hearts and the disposing of them in His hand that
I have not provoked you to harbor so ill an opinion of me as my
mother's letters do signify and give me to understand, the ill
opinion and hard persuasion which she bears of me, that is to
say, that I should abuse your goodness and be prodigal of your
purse, neglectful of my brother's bands [collars] and of my
slatterishness and laziness. For my brother's bands I will not
excuse myself, but I think not worthy so sharp a reproof. For
the rest I must needs excuse and clear myself if I may be believed. I do not know myself guilty of any of them. For mine
own part I do not desire to be mine own judge but am willing
to be judged by them with whom I live and sees my course,
whether I be addicted to such things or no.

For my habit, it is mean, for the most as many servants, and
if I had not had money which I had for some things here, I
might have wanted many necessaries which I could not have
been without, except I should have made you a score here,
which I was not willing to do. I writ to my mother for lace not
out of any prodigal or proud mind but only for some cross-
clothes [headbands], which is the most allowable and commendable dressing here. She would have me wear dressings
which I did so long as they would suffer me, whilst the elders
with others entreated me to leave them off, for they gave great
offence, and, seeing it hath pleased the Lord to bring me
hither amongst His people, I would not willingly do anything

amongst them that should be displeasing unto them. But for mine own part, since my sending for things gives such offence, I will be more sparing in that kind hereafter, but leave it to the Lord to deal with me according to His mercy, earnestly desiring Him to give me an heart to be content with my portion, knowing that nothing can befall me but that that He hath appointed. I may take that verse in the 106th Psalm [correctly, 107th], seventeenth verse, "Fools, because of their transgressions and their iniquities, are afflicted." So I think that just it is, whatsoever affliction shall come unto me.

Dear Father, I am far distant from you and know not how long it will please the Lord to continue it so, but howsoever, I desire to rest satisfied with His will and do earnestly desire to submit myself in all duty and obedience as belongeth unto a child to yourself and my mother, as if I were with you. Father, I perceive by your letters that you would very willingly to have me change my condition, which I must confess I might do, nay, with divers, if the Lord pleased to move my heart to accept any of them, but I desire to wait upon Him that can change my heart at His will. Thus with my humble duty to yourself and my mother, craving pardon of you both and of her if I have given her any offence, and so desiring your prayers to Him who is able to give wisdom and direction to me in all things, I rest.

> Your obedient daughter till death,
> Mary Downinge

Boston: 27th of November, 1635

An unusually curious and obscure letter has survived from the Reverend George Burdett, who sought to explain his situation to Archbishop William Laud. Burdett, who had been minister at Yarmouth, Norfolk, crossed the Atlantic in 1634 to reach the new puritan commonwealth. He lived at Salem, where he joined the church and for a year or more served as preacher. Although he was an able scholar, he found himself unsympathetic with the strict discipline of the Bay churches. So he moved northward to Piscataqua (first settled in 1623, now Portsmouth, New Hampshire), where he acted for a time as governor. He seems to have acted as a spy (perhaps a self-appointed one) for Laud, to whom he continued to write. Later, after a stay in Maine, the strange rover returned to England. Perhaps the pretentiousness of Burdett's letter has prevented publication hitherto. The original letter is in the Public Record Office, London, numbered C. O. 1/8, folio 227.

George Burdett to Archbishop William Laud
December 1635

My lord:

Actions ambiguous, capable of cross limitations, do rarely meet with inclination to the milder part. My voluntary exile is exposed to censure, levity, or dissimulation, or, which is worse, is charged upon me, but the truth is, my practice was regular, and therein obedience ecclesiatical very real. If some transient defects, impeccability is not expected. Man is vertible [changeable] and vocations of amulous [?] adversaries herein culpable. My judgment in the five articles[1] was moderate, declarations correspondent, the knot of the controversy declined. [Notwithstanding] whatever malice did inform or perjury confirm to the contrary. Herein I appeal to Him that judgeth justly. This I thought to impart to rectify your grace's judgment of me and my ways (if possibly) and stop the mouth of calumnia for my secession. The ground was impetuous and malicious prosecution, importable expense; the end, tranquility in distance, which could I yet enjoy in my native country, it would exceedingly rejoice me. Not that any present incompetency urgeth, for all the topics of motive arguments lend their aid to persuade content in temporality but some moral heterodoxies, etc. I humbly pray read and accept these lines from him who much desires a favorable line from your grace, and still remains

> Your grace's in all humble observance,
> Geo: Burdett

Salem in New-England
December. 1635.
To the most reverend father in God, the Lord Archbishop of Canterbury his Grace, Primate and metropolitan of all England, etc., at his Grace's palace at Lambeth, humbly present these.
[Endorsed] Received February 22, 1635 [/6].
From M. Burdett, out of Newe England.

1. Presumably the Five Articles of Calvinism, which, by the rule of Church of England authorities, were not to be discussed.

Whether because it offered men a new and better society or because it provided economic opportunities, Massachusetts continued to attract colonists. The inevitable result was expansion. Concord, founded in 1635, was the colony's first inland town. To the west, as Winthrop noted in his 1635 letter to D'Ewes, there was unusually fertile land, with access to the ocean by means of the Connecticut River. The Plymouth colonists had made efforts to establish a trading base on the river, and the Dutch from New York had also taken an interest in the area. A few Massachusetts men, led by the old planter John Oldham, explored the area as early as 1633, and in the winter of 1634-35 they built dwellings at what is now Wethersfield, just south of the Plymouth and Dutch trading posts at and above what is now Hartford.

In 1634, the men of Newtown, later Cambridge, under Thomas Hooker's leadership requested permission of the General Court to move to Connecticut. Hooker charged that the Massachusetts towns had been built too close together. Watertown was only a mile and a half, and Charlestown less than two miles, from Newtown. He noted also that the attractive Connecticut lands might well be unavailable to them later. Though opinion was divided, the Court did not grant the permission, since the charter did not authorize settlement in the Connecticut River area and since the loss of numbers would weaken the Bay Colony.

In 1635 Sir Richard Saltonstall, who had earlier spent a year in Massachusetts, sent a group of men from England to stake a claim to land on the Connecticut River that he believed had been granted to him. His men, under Francis Stiles, a master carpenter, went first to the Bay Colony to pick up a pilot for the voyage up the river. While they were there, a group of Massachusetts men heard of their plans and rushed to Connecticut to claim the land. This group, under Roger Ludlow, had been living in Dorchester. They used the same name, Dorchester, for their new settlement; later it was called Windsor. When Stiles arrived, they prevented him from taking possession of the land that Saltonstall had instructed him to claim, even part that they themselves had not settled. Reporting this misadventure to Saltonstall was Bartholomew Greene, who had come to Massachusetts in 1633 and seems to have been Saltonstall's agent. Greene planned to move to Connecticut himself, but he died while still in Massachusetts. Saltonstall's efforts came to little, though his expenses had been, by his account, nearly fifteen hundred pounds. In 1636 Thomas Hooker and the Newtowners moved to Connecticut and created Hartford.

Saltonstall was one of several men who were interested in owning a private plantation. Matthew Cradock, first governor of the Massachusetts Bay Company, had planned such an enterprise as early as 1629. His private plantation at Medford never amounted to much, though its presence did much to disturb the colony, since Cradock's men were unruly. Such a private plantation seems to have been what Sir Simonds D'Ewes had in mind. The most substantial venture of this kind took place when in 1635 a group including Lord Say and Seal, Saltonstall, Lord Brooke, and Sir Arthur Haslerig authorized John Winthrop, Jr., to provide a place for "men of quality," well fortified, at the mouth of the Connecticut River. This was to be a refuge for puritan noblemen and other prosperous gentlemen if the situation in England required them to leave. Only one member of the group, George Fenwick, ever made use of the settlement, named Saybrook after two of the sponsors. Bartholomew Greene's original letter is Massachusetts Historical Society manuscript W. 4. 79.

Bartholomew Greene to Sir Richard Saltonstall
December 30, 1635

Right worshipful:

My humble service is remembered.

Having so fit a messeneger, I cannot but write a word or two. This is to certify, your worship, this messenger was at Canaticoatt and can tell you how the case stands. For my part, it is a grief to me, but the truth is, I cannot nor could not do no more in it. I did use the best counsel and did use what means I could in the business for your good, but Mr. Whitt['s] commission was to be one side of the river, Mr. Stilles' on the other, and after I had used means when Mr. Whitt and Mr. Stills went and could not get a man to go by no means, and as soon as I heard they went not forward in the business I put myself upon it again and at last got a man to go to measure it out at a dear rate, and when he came there, there was not ground, neither for meadow, nor arable or pasture grounds, that would give your worship content, [so] that the men darst not lay it out. They should have done your worship wrong in the same, seeing that Dorchester men had taken up the best place before, and Plimmouth men sent a letter to discharge our men for meddling with it, saying it was their right, for I conceive that Mr. Ludlow was the chief man that hindered it. He was the only man of Dorchester that set down there. I hope that this bearer, Mr. Woodcock['s] man, will certify you how it is. I have written many letter[s] for this purpose. Other things I have been large in letters. I am loath to be troublesome to your worship in the like expression. Mr. Hooker hath expressed something that way. The Lord direct you and advise you for the best and further your offerings for His glory and your good and all ours.

Thus with my service again I commit you to the only wise God and rest.

> Your poor servant to the uttermost
> of my power to command,
> Barth[olomew] Greene

From Watertone this 30th of December, 1635
To the right worshipful and his most loving Mr. Sur Richard Saltonstall, Knight, at his house in Whitt Streete, London.

[Endorsed by Sir Richard Saltonstall] Made that this letter be sent to Mr. John Winthropp, our governor, at Conectacutt with Francis Styles his relation.

1636

Edward Trelawny was still visiting and doing business in Boston as late as January 1636. His second letter, like his first, discusses both religious and commerical concerns in the Bay Colony, which had succeeded in founding a religious society on a solid economic base. The chief source of income, it had been supposed, would be furs, but earlier traders had collected most of those available, and there were few Indians to collect the remaining ones. The geography was not helpful either, since Massachusetts lacks penetrating rivers. But because of the influx of settlers, the colony was thriving. Income came from the liquidation of the English estates of the new arrivals. Thus Trelawny describes below the profits to be made from imports to Massachusetts of corn, cattle, provisions, and even fish; the only exports he mentions are wood products and furs. Trelawny's original letter is at the Maine Historical Society, Portland.

Edward Trelawny to Robert Trelawny
January 10, 1635/6

My very good brother:

I present myself and kind affections unto you, and you may please to take notice how my last was per way of Bristoll, under cover of Mr. William Camo, advising you how necessary it was in petitioning the lords for some seasonable course to be taken with the French here. Otherwise there will be but small hopes in continuing our plantations so near them who daily draw towards us, whose neighborhood (I much fear) will prove very prejudicial unto us. I now again request you to be mindful of it, for either we must better fortify, or else expose ourselves to the loss of all, which may be prevented by a speedy preparation against all assaults. I also intimated unto you what a profitable way it would be to send over three or four men experienced in the making of clapboard and pipe staves together with a man or two about manuring of hops, things conducing to our advantage many ways. But above all I earnestly requested you for a religious, able minister, for it's a most pitiful to behold what a most heathen life we live. It's without God in the world. To feed the body and starve the soul is above all things most unwarrantable and detestable, and that for which the Lord hath threatened the pouring down of his judgments upon us. He hath already given us no small taste of his displeasure by losses since the plantation hath been settled. The next, I fear, will be greater, if not prevented. Surely something God sees amiss in us that he goes not along with us in prospering our designs, and I am persuaded that in living without the means[1] is not the least. God grant we may lay it thoroughly to heart. For my part, my conscience tells me I dare not live without it. What a most heavenly and comfortable sight is it to see with what power and purity the ordinances are administered, so that no one place in the world comes near it; I mean in the Baye, where there is such a holy walking, such a sweet communion and fellowship on all sides, that I am persuaded (unless a man were past all grace) it would convince the veriest reprobate alive. Oh that Old England were Newe; then would the Lord certainly be better pleased with it. But I have written you largely touching the particular in all my former, and therefore cease to mention it at present, though I could largely discourse of it. Only this one word: I shall request you to retain respectful thoughts of the place, and do it all the good you can, for the Lord hath a precious care of his holy ones, and your reward shall be with him. I must needs acknowledge the Lord's unspeakable free mercy and goodness (I speak with comfort to my poor soul) in casting me upon this place, where I have received more benefit than in all my lifetime before; I desire you to be sensible of it. God grant I may express my thankfulness to him by a holy and blameless walking in fear and reverence before him, not returning with the dog to his vomit, nor with the sow to her wallowing in the mire.

The country at present is sick in a general want of provisions, by reason of the multiplicity of people that came this year and relying wholly on it.[2] I trust the Lord will provide for them. I could wish you to send the *Hunter* or some other ship, with all sorts of provisions and cattle, and it will come (with God's blessing) well to pass, if seasonable. Our hogs prove not so well this year as last by many degrees, in respect (as I conceive) the plantation is overstocked. We have made since the fishermen's depar-

1. The means of grace; in this context, preaching.
2. Another reason was that corn crops had been damaged by the 1635 hurricane. See Hubbard, *General History*, 1:162.

ture some eighteen ℧ fish. If I can obtain a price reasonable I will here sell it, in respect you write it will not keep so well for a market. We have also saved about forty hogsheads of corn, which would sell at good rates, but that I fear we shall want before a supply come, which you intend not till towards March.

I have, together with Mr. Babb of London, per whom this goes, contracted for a ship's lading of clapboard, which are to be delivered on the first of June. We have thoughts of a hopeful and beneficial design for a voyage with a ship into Ireland, to come hither with provisions and cattle, where they are cheap, and so to take in the clapboard, either for the Islands,[3] Spain, or England, which Mr. Hill will advise you, for that must there be determined on. And what the one-fourth or one-eighth will amount unto, pray give order unto Mr. Hill to satisfy unto Mr. Babb, who (if he chance to stop in Plymouth) I pray you entertain him, as a friend that hath deserved much from me. The design cannot but prove most advantageous (with God's blessing). Therefore pray speed it onward, for therein consists the chief profit. I have not else at present to enlarge, only my kind salutations to my good sisters, brother Martine, Mr. Beddford, with the rest of our nearest and dearest friends. I recommend you to the keeper of all men and remain as ever,

> Your unfained loving brother,
> Edward Trelawny

Boston, 10th January 1635 [6]

Since the finishing of this letter, Mr. Babb and myself have bargained for some commodities to the value of 132 pounds, and [I] have given him a bill on you for 115 pounds at twenty days' sight, which pray see satisfied at the time, out of the 95 pounds formerly sent you per bill of exchange on Mr. Matthewe Craddocke,[4] merchant, of London. I sent it you per the *James* of London, about a month since, hoping it's ere this come safe into your hands. This bill will be 20 pounds above that, which you may please and I much desire you to disburse for me. I had but two bills given me; the second I would now have sent but that I keep it by me for my satisfaction until I hear of its acceptance. The bargain was good, which made me the more willinger to adventure on it; I cannot get less than 50 pounds profit. I shall not have them long on my hands, but shall be

3. The West Indies.
4. On Cradock, see above, p. 183.

able to return you, per the next month, maybe within these twenty days, a bill of beaver to the value of 140 pounds sterling, in which I will not, God willing, fail. Therefore you may absolutely expect it. I pray do me this favor, as you may have done many others, and I will study to deserve it.

Your respective brother,
Edward Trelawny

To my endeared loving brother, Mr. Robert Trelawny, merchant, deliver. In Plymouth

Apparently quite apart from their thoughts about establishing private plantations, some English noblemen toyed with the idea of becoming part of the Massachusetts Bay Colony. Thomas Hutchinson goes so far as to say that some of the leaders of the opposition in England "are said to have been prevented [from emigrating to New England] by express order of the King, as Mr. Pym, Mr. Hampden, Sir Arthur Haslerigg, Oliver Cromwell, &c." Hutchinson notes that the colony's leaders had deliberately chosen fewer assistants than the charter authorized in order to admit "any gentleman of distinction without leaving out any of the former assistants." Other puritan leaders, including Lord Say and Seal and Lord Brooke, did venture in 1636 to set forth the conditions under which they might come to the Bay Colony. They were eager to establish, in advance, substantial political power for themselves. Specifically they wished to create a kind of house of lords, with veto power, for themselves and their heirs. John Cotton answered the ten demands after consulting with several colonial leaders. He wrote that assistants or magistrates were elected from the ranks of gentlemen, and those had substantial power. But it was not enough for a man to have noble blood. Political leaders had to have merit, and, more particularly, they had to be church members: ". . . none are so fit to be trusted with the liberties of the commonwealth as church members. For the liberties of the freemen of this commonwealth are such as require men of faithfull integrity to God and the state to preserve the same."

In addition to providing quasi-official answers to the demands, Cotton wrote a letter over his own name to Lord Say. A personal letter, not an official statement, it provides an important description of the colony's political philosophy. In his writings and sermons Cotton strongly supported the authority of the magistrates and by implication opposed democratic tendencies. Here addressing a nobleman who was interested in having aristocratic privilege, Cotton sought to play down those aspects of the Massachusetts government that might be considered democratic in order to indicate both his own position and his sympathy for Say's position.

Cotton also described the unique relationship between church and state in Massachusetts. On the subject of this crucial aspect of the new commonwealth recent scholarship has cleared up some of the many misunderstandings created by nineteenth-century historians, even able ones such as Brooks and Charles Francis Adams. A few legal ties, but only a few, existed between church and state: the General Court's permission was required to begin a new church, attendance at church services was enforced by civil authority, and most important, the franchise was restricted to church members. (Some church members were reluctant to assume freemen's responsibilities.) At the time that this connection was established, it probably was intended merely to keep political power from heretics and the immoral. Later, as churches gradually restricted membership to those who could demonstrate saving faith, the franchise was correspondingly restricted. Even then, however, men who were excommunicated were not deprived of political office. In many ways the separation of church and state was much clearer in Massachusetts Bay than it was in England: there were no church courts and no clergy in the legislature or in other public offices. Though they were paid and housed from public funds, the ministers could serve only as advisors to the government, and their advice was not always followed even when sought. The basis for the text that follows is Thomas Hutchinson's version, published in his *History of the Colony and Province of Massachusetts-Bay* (Boston, 1764), volume 1, pages 496-501.

John Cotton to Lord Say and Seal
1636

Right honorable:

What your lordship writeth of Dr. Twisse his works *de scientia mediâ* and of the Sabbath, it did refresh me to read that his labors of such arguments were like to come to light,[1] and it would refresh me much more to see them here, though (for my own particular) till I get some release from some constant labors here, (which the church is desirous to procure), I can get little or no opportunity to read anything or attend to anything but the daily occurrences which press in upon me continually, much beyond my strength either of body or mind.

Your lordship's advertisement touching the civil state of this colony, as they do breathe forth your singular wisdom and faithfulness and tender care of the peace, so we have no reason to misinterpret or undervalue your lordship's either directions or intentions therein. I know no man under heaven (I speak in God's fear without flattery) whose counsel I should rather depend upon for the wise administration of a civil state according to God than upon your lordship, and such confidence have I (not in you) but in the Lord's presence in Christ with you, that I should never fear to betrust a greater commonwealth than this (as much as in us lieth) under such a *perpetua dictaturâ* as your lordship should prescribe. For I nothing doubt but that either your lordship would prescribe all things according to the rule or be willing to examine again and again all things according to it. I am very apt to believe what Mr. Perkins hath in one of his prefatory pages to his *Golden Chaine*, that the Word and Scriptures of God do contain a short *upoluposis*, or platform, not only of theology but also of other sacred sciences (as he calleth them), attendants and handmaids thereunto, which he maketh ethics, economics, politics, church government, prophesy, academy.[2] It is very suitable to God's all-sufficient wisdom and to the fullness and perfection of Holy Scriptures not only to prescribe perfect rules for the right ordering of a private man's soul to everlasting blessedness with Himself, but also for the right ordering of a man's family, yea, of the commonwealth too, so far as both of them are subordinate to spiritual ends, and yet avoid both the church's usurpation upon civil jurisdiction, *in*

1. William Twisse (1578-1646), a Calvinist theologian, was the author of *Dissertation de Scientia Media* (Arnheim, 1639), and *Of the Morality of the Fourth Commandment* (London, 1641).
2. William Perkins (1558-1602), a highly influential puritan preacher and teacher at Cambridge, wrote *A Golden Chaine* (London, 1591), a summary of Calvinist theology. It went through many editions. Cotton refers to a table that immediately precedes chapter one. There economics is defined as "a doctrine of governing a family well," prophecy is "the doctrine of preaching well," and academy is "the doctrine of governing schools well, especially those of the prophets."

ordine ad spiritualia [for spiritual ends], and the common-wealth's invasion upon ecclesiastical administrations, *in ordine* to civil peace and conformity to the civil state. God's institutions (such as the government of church and of commonwealth be) may be close and compact and coordinate one to another, and yet not confounded. God hath so framed the state of church government and ordinances that they may be compatible to any commonwealth, though never so much disordered in his frame. But yet when a commonwealth hath liberty to mold his own frame (*scripturae plenitudinem adoro* [I speak of the fullness of the Scripture]), I conceive the Scripture hath given full direction for the right ordering of the same, and that in such sort as may best maintain the *euexia* [vigor] of the church. Mr. Hooker doth often quote a saying out of Mr. Cartwright[3] (though I have not read it in him) that no man fashioneth his house to his hangings but his hangings to his house. It is better that the commonwealth be fashioned to the setting forth of God's house, which is His church, than to accommodate the church frame to the civil state. Democracy I do not conceive that ever God did ordain as a fit government either for church or commonwealth. If the people be governors, who shall be governed? As for monarchy and aristocracy, they are both of them clearly approved and directed in Scripture, yet so as referreth the sovereignty to Himself, and setteth up theocracy in both, as the best form of government in the commonwealth as well as in the church.[4]

The law which your Lordship instanceth in [that none shall be chosen to magistracy among us but a church member][5] was made and enacted before I came into the country, but I have hitherto wanted sufficient light to plead against it. First, the rule that directeth the choice of supreme governors is of like equity and weight in all magistrates, that one of their brethren (not a stranger) should be set over them (Deuteronomy 17.15), and Jethro's counsel to Moses was approved of God, that the judges and officers to be set over the people should be men fearing God (Exodus 18.21), and Solomon maketh it the joy of a commonwealth when the righteous are in authority and their mourning when the wicked rule (Proverbs 29. 21 [i.e., 29.2]; Job 34. 30). Your Lordship's fear that this will bring in papal excommunication is just and pious, but let your Lordship be pleased again to consider whether the consequence be necessary.

3. He refers to Thomas Hooker and to Thomas Cartwright (1535-1603), the earliest puritan to develop a systematic position.

4. As Cotton makes clear below, he means rule by God's law, not by God's ministers.

5. The bracketed passage appears thus in the source for subsequent printings, the letter as published by Thomas Hutchinson.

Turpius ejicitur quam non admittitur [more fitting to be ejected than not admitted]; non-membership may be a just cause of non-admission to the place of magistracy, but yet ejection out of his membership will not be a just cause of ejecting him out of his magistracy. A godly woman, being to make choice of an husband, may justly refuse a man that is either cast out of church fellowship or is not yet received into it, but yet when she is once given to him, she may not reject him then for such defect. Mr. Humphry was chosen for an assistant (as I hear) before the colony came over hither, and, though he be not as yet joined into church fellowship (by reason of the unsettledness of the congregation where he liveth), yet the commonwealth do still continue his magistracy to him, as knowing he waiteth for opportunity of enjoying church fellowship shortly.

When your Lordship doubteth that this course will draw all things under the determination of the church, *in ordine ad spiritualia* (seeing the church is to determine who shall be members, and none but a member may have to do in the government of a commonwealth), be pleased (I pray you) to conceive that magistrates are neither chosen to office in the church nor do govern by directions from the church, but by civil laws, and those enacted in general courts and executed in courts of justice by the governors and assistants, in all which the church (as the church) hath nothing to do, only it prepareth fit instruments both to rule and to choose rulers, which is no ambition in the church nor dishonor to the commonwealth. The Apostle, on the contrary, thought it a great dishonor and reproach to the church of Christ if it were not able to yield able judges to hear and determine all causes amongst their brethren (I Corinthians 6.1-5), which place alone seemeth to me fully to decide this question, for it plainly holdeth forth this argument: it is a shame to the church to want able judges of civil matters (as verse 5) and an audacious act in any church member voluntarily to go for judgment otherwhere than before the saints (as verse 1). Then it will be no arrogance nor folly in church members, nor prejudice to the commonwealth if voluntarily they never choose any civil judges but from amongst the saints, such as church members are called to be. But the former is clear, and how then can the latter be avoided? If this therefore be (as your Lordship rightly conceiveth one of the main objection if not the only one) which hindereth this commonwealth from the entertainment of the propositions of those worthy gentlemen, we entreat them in the name of the Lord Jesus, to consider in meekness of wisdom: it is not any conceit or will of ours but the holy counsel and will of the Lord Jesus (whom they seek to serve as well as we) that overruleth us in this case, and we trust will overrule them also, that the Lord only may be exalted amongst all his servants. What pity and grief were it that the observance of the will of Christ should hinder good things from us!

But your lordship doubteth that if such a rule were necessary, then the church estate and the best ordered commonwealth in the world were not compatible. But let not your lordship so conceive. For the church submitteth itself to all the laws and ordinances of men, in what commonwealth soever they come to dwell. But it is one thing to submit unto what they have no calling to reform, another thing voluntarily to ordain a form of government which to the best discerning of many of us (for I speak not of myself) is expressly contrary to rule. Nor need your lordship fear (which yet I speak with submission to your lordship's better judgment) that this course will lay such a foundation as nothing but a mere democracy can be built upon it. Bodine confesseth that though it be *status popularis*, where a people choose their own governors, yet the government is not a democracy if it be administered, not by the people, but by the governors, whether one (for then it is a monarchy, though elective) or by many (for then, as you know, it is aristocracy).[6] In which respect it is that church government is justly denied (even by Mr. Robinson) to be democratical, though the people choose their own officers and rulers.[7]

Nor need we fear that this course will in time cast the commonwealth into distractions and popular confusions. For (under correction) these three things do not undermine but do mutually and strongly maintain one another (even those three which we principally aim at): authority in magistrates, liberty in people, purity in the church. Purity preserved in the church will preserve well-ordered liberty in the people, and both of them establish well-balanced authority in the magistrates. God is the author of all these three, and neither is himself the God of confusion nor are his ways the ways of confusion, but of peace.

What our brethren (magistrates or ministers, or leading freeholders) will answer to the rest of the propositions, I shall better understand before the gentleman's return from Connecticutt,

6. See Jean Bodin, *The Six Bookes of a Commonweale* (London, 1606), p. 250.

7. John Robinson, spokesman for separatist Congregationalism, might have been thought to be democratic if any Congregationalist was.

who brought them over. Meanwhile two of the principal of them them the General Court hath already condescended unto. First, in establishing a standing council, who, during their lives, should assist the governor in managing the chiefest affairs of this little state. They have chosen, for the present, only two (Mr. Winthrope and Mr. Dudley), not willing to choose more till they see what further better choice the Lord will send over to them, that so they may keep an open door for such desirable gentlemen as your Lordship mentioneth.[8] Second, they have granted the governor and assistants a negative voice and reserved to the freemen the like liberty also. Touching other things, I hope to give your lordship further account when the gentleman returneth.

He being now returned, I have delivered to him an answer to the rest of your demands, according to the minds of such leading men amongst us as I thought meet to consult withal, concealing your name from any except two or three, who alike do concur in a joint desire of yielding to any such propositions as your lordship demandeth, so far as with allowance from the Word they may, beyond which I know your lordship would not require anything.

Now the Lord Jesus Christ (the prince of peace) keep and bless your lordship and dispose of all your times and talents to his best advantage, and let the covenant of his grace and peace rest upon your honorable family and posterity throughout all generations.

Thus humbly craving pardon for my boldness and length, I take leave and rest.

Your honor's to serve in Christ Jesus,
J[ohn] C[otton]

8. The standing council, created by the General Court in March 1636, was later much limited in its jurisdiction. See *Massachusetts Records*, 1:264, and Ellen E. Brennan, "The Massachusetts Council of the Magistrates," *New England Quarterly* 4 (1931): 54-93.

Other writers were not so diplomatic as Cotton nor so reticent as Winthrop, and the novel practices of the Massachusetts Bay churches became known in England. This fact is clear from a long letter of advice and warning that Winthrop received from England probably in the spring to 1637. The letter, unsigned to protect the author's identity, discusses "sundry letters from some with you unto others with us (and I fear there have been very many such sent over to us into diverse parts of our land), wherein there are many weak and dangerous passages, which if they should come to the eyes or ears of any one of many thousands of your adversaries, it would afford them matter enough to attempt your undoing what in them did lie." The letter writer congratulates Winthrop, on the other hand, for his "disclaiming of Mr. Williams' opinion and your dealing with him so as we hear you did." Winthrop's actions, he writes, "took off much prejudice from you with us, and hath stopped the mouths of some."

It was Williams's identification with separatism that made him offensive to many. Williams had arrived in Massachusetts in February 1631. Since John Wilson, minister of the Boston church, was returning to England for a time, Williams was asked to serve as minister. He refused on the grounds that the Boston church had not separated itself from the Church of England, which he considered corrupt and not a true church. Winthrop sought to convince him that reformation was possible without separation. When the church at Salem later expressed an interest in Williams, Winthrop had to explain that his separatism disqualified him for a pastoral position. In his journal Winthrop noted that Williams also believed that "the magistrate might not punish the breach of the Sabbath, nor any other offence, as it was a breach of the first table" of the Ten Commandments. In other words, Williams did not believe that religious matters were the concern of secular authorities. Williams withdrew to Plymouth.

There he remained until 1633, when he returned to Salem, where Skelton was ill and soon to die. For a time Williams, who was liked even by his opponents, served the church in an unofficial capacity, but finally he was given an official position. Williams taught a number of extreme positions at Salem: that the king of England had no authority to grant the land occupied by the colony, for example, and that the king was guilty of blasphemy for using the word *Christendom*. When he was challenged by Winthrop, Williams backed down; but soon he was taking the same position again. This time John Cotton, then minister of the Boston church, persuaded Williams to stop. But finally Williams's separatism required him to teach that the regenerate and the unregenerate ought to be distinctly separated in religious matters, and should not worship together, even at a blessing after a meal. Moreover, when the clergy asked the magistrates to remove Williams from his office because of his opinions, Williams declared that the Salem church should withdraw from the other Massachusetts churches since they had demonstrated by their appeal to civil authority that they were impure. Thereupon the General Court met and ordered Williams to leave the colony within six weeks. Williams continued his teachings despite the decision, and when in January 1636 the magistrates decided to send him to England on the next ship, Williams escaped through the cold of winter to Rhode Island.

All this information may prove useful in understanding the letter that John Cotton wrote, probably in 1636, to a questioner in England. Cotton, conservative by nature, admitted that the practices of the Massachusetts Bay churches might seem questionable to those unfamiliar with them. But he sought to deny that they were as new and radical as some of their opponents argued.

The manuscript of this letter has not survived; the text below is based on a printed version of 1641 entitled *A Coppy of a Letter of Mr. Cotton of Boston, in New England, sent in answer of certaine Objections made against their Discipline and Orders there, directed to a Friend.* Cotton and Thomas Hooker had come to Massachusetts together in 1633 and brought special dignity to the Massachusetts Bay Colony, for both were well-known puritan clergymen in England. When Hooker left Massachusetts for Connecticut in 1636 he lost some of his influence in the Bay Colony. Cotton was at the center of Massachusetts in Boston till his death in 1652.

John Cotton to ?
1636

There have been things (as it seemeth) reported unto you: first, that we receive none into our church fellowship until they first disclaim their churches in England as no churches but as limbs of the devil. Now I answer, God forbid. God forbid. It is true, one Sheba of Bickry blew a trumpet of such a seditious separation. I mean one Mr. Williams, late teacher of Salem, but himself and others that followed stiffly in that way who were all excommunicated out of the church and banished out of the commonwealth, for men in that way and of such a spirit are wont not only to renounce the churches of England but ours

also, because we held communion with them in England in the
things which are of God. See, therefore, how unjustly we are
slandered for renouncing communion with you, as is mentioned,
and for it they themselves are punished in our commonwealth,
censured in our churches, for such antichristian exorbitures [de-
partures from customary courses]. By this you may see the objection clearly answered.

The second calumny is that our members must profess their
repentance for all former communion with the churches among
you. Now for the answer. We profess no such things but only in
general so far as we have polluted ourselves with any corruptions or inventions of men or defiled God's ordinances with any
corruption of their own, whereby you may gather answer from
the second calumny.

The third calumny is that we enter into covenant, solemnly
never to have communion with the present churches of England,
whereas in truth we never have such words or meaning in any
part of our covenant but that we profess to walk in all the ordinances of the Lord, according to his will revealed in His Word.

Of the fourth report you mention there is some ground for it,
our practice. Power indeed is given among us to the people to
choose their ministers, so likewise to receive any member unto
the church fellowship and to join in the excommunication of
such as grow scandalous, which yet is very rare. Among us
through the goodness of God scarce two or three have been excommunicated out of our churches, which is more for rejecting
communion with the churches than for any other crime. It is
true also that we allow any members of the church to complain
of an offence given him by any brother if a private way of admonition according to the rule have not reformed him (Matthew 18. 17), but that hath fallen out very seldom since I came
hither, for aught I have heard either in our own or other
churches. They much wrong both you and us who told you
that Master Wilson was suspended from his ministry for his journey into England or for any communion he had with the
churches there, nor to my remembrance did any of the brethren
question him about it till of himself he began to give some account of his journey to the church, and then indeed two or
three grave and godly men desired him to clear a passage or
two: first, how he could leave the whole congregation above
twelve months together without their consent, and how he

1. Very similar sentiments and language appear in *The Humble Request of His Majestie's loyall Subjects, the Governour and the Company late gone for New-England: To the rest of their Brethren, in and of the Church of England, For the obtaining of their Prayers* . . . (London, 1630), by Winthrop, Dudley, Johnson, and their fellows. Here the puritan leaders declare that they are among those who "esteem it our honor to call the Church of England, from whence we rise, our dear mother, and cannot part from our native country, where she especially resideth, without much sadness of heart and many tears in our eyes, ever acknowledging that such hope and part as we have obtained in the common salvation, we have received it in her bosom and sucked it from her breasts."
2. The sense seems to be that though the ministers and elders meet together to to plan the business of the church meeting, actual decisions are made only in congregational meetings.
3. Prophesying here means lay preaching.

could leave his wife (as I remember) without her consent; to both which he gave a satisfactory answer and was not at all suspended by the church, but of himself he forebare one day or at the least half a day till he had declared both the particulars. That which you add of grace and gifts of Christ or of his presence in the ministry of his servants among you, we willingly and thankfully acknowledge and do profess that the hope which most of us have obtained of the common salvation we received from the preaching of God's faithful ministers among you, we cannot, we dare not deny to "bless the womb which bear us and the paps which gave us suck," and long may these lights shine among you, with all peace, purity, and power, Amen.[1]

What you speak of separatists and Brownists we generally here do consent with you that the bitterness of separation whereby men do not only cut themselves from the inventions of men but also from the ordinances of God and fellowship of his servants, for who so have done, they never were blessed with peace. As for those scruples you pray me to weigh without prejudice, we here do consent with you therein, only there is a passage or two which I crave leave to explain myself in first, that you say our pastor Master Wilson affirms among you that we did not follow Calvin's platform as an episcopal. He saith he doth not remember any such word to have fallen from him. Only thus much he confesseth, as we do all here, that we do not transact all things so reservedly in a consistory, but though we [who] be prebestary [presbytery?] do prepare all things for the church, yet we transact no public act but in their presence and with their consents unless any of their brethren can give a reason from the scripture to the contrary or some better intelligence of his own, which latter sometimes falls out.[2] Secondly, what you speak of prophesying, I need not say much of it. It is very warily used here unless it be in absence and weakness of ministers, and for any abuse herein allow it not but dislike it as you do.[3]

Now you have showed so much for to inquire the truth of these matters, I pray you inform others also what answer you have received, which will be a further testimony of your love. Pray for us as we do for you. So taking leave I rest

Your unworthy, weak brother in Christ,
John Cotton

The last episode in the relationship of the Hammonds, Winthrop, and Sir Simonds D'Ewes is revealed by a letter from Winthrop in June of 1636. One can only be curious about the possible irony of Winthrop's first words to the stuffy antiquarian. The original letter is British Museum manuscript Harley 388, folio 191.

John Winthrop to Sir Simonds D'Ewes
June 24, 1636

Sir:

The benefit which we have received from that which you were pleased in your kindness to bestow upon our plantation calls upon me to give you accompt thereof and to acquaint you further with our estate here. As soon as I understood your mind in it, I acquainted the governor and the rest of the assistants with it, and calling Hamonde before us, and finding by such evidence as he produced that part of the 30 pounds he received of you miscarried by the way, and that his estate was not able to answer what might be required of him, we thought fit to accept of 20 pounds, whereof he hath paid 10 pounds, but the other 10 pounds is now desperate, for young Wm. Hammonde going with all that his father and he could make and borrow to trade in Virginia for corn, the vessel was cast away upon Longe Iland and seven persons drowned. Hamonde escaped on shore but was killed by the Indians and one other with him, whereby the old man's estate is wholly overthrown. It hath been observed that God hath always crossed us in our trade with Virginia. Divers of our people went thither about half a year since but have not been yet heard of. There was a very great mortality last winter: about sixty masters of ships and other officers died there, but our people (I praise God) have their health well here.
Sir Hen[ry] Vane his son and heir is our governor this year, a godly gentleman and of excellent parts.[1] Here have been already eleven English ships and four dutch. Most of them were but five weeks in their passage. My time is short and I have many letters

1. Henry Vane the Younger arrived in Massachusetts in 1635. He was only twenty-three when elected governor.

to write, so as I cannot enlarge. My love and due respect to
yourself and lady remembered I rest.

> At your service,
> Jo: Winthrop

Boston, N[ew] E[ngland], June 2[4?], 1636
To the right worshipful Sir Simonds Dewes, Knight, at Stowe
Langthon in Suff[olk], to be left with Mr. Gurdon at Assington
in Suff[olk]

On August 17, 1635, the founder of New England's illustrious Mather family arrived in Boston, having survived a
near shipwreck on the Isle of Shoals as a result of the hurricane
described by Thacher. A minister with sixteen years of experience, Richard Mather agreed in the following spring to serve a
group in Dorchester just organizing a church. He soon found,
with some embarrassment, that the men of Dorchester had mis-
judged their readiness to establish a church that would meet the
high standards of the new Bay Congregationalism; a delay and
additional preparation were required. But Mather was already
so persuaded of the rightness of the New England Way that he
was ready to defend it—a defense he undertook less than a year
after his arrival in the new commonwealth in reply to critical
letters he had received from William Rathband and another minister. (It must have astonished many English clergymen to see
their friends change their outlook on religious matters upon
crossing the Atlantic.) Mather later incorporated his letter de-
fending the New England Way into a work he prepared for publication, "A Plea for the churches of Christ in New England."
Though it was never published, the complete work is extant in
manuscript at the Massachusetts Historical Society, and is the
basis of the text below. Remarkably, Mather transcribed in his
manuscript comments about the situation of the colonists
quite remote from matters of church polity. For him, what
was attractive about New England was its religious practices—
nothing else.

The gracious love of God the Father in and through
His Christ be more and more shed abroad into your hearts
by the Holy Ghost.
Reverend and beloved in Christ Jesus:

I have received from each of you a letter by H. W., for which I
am much your debtor. Yet straits of time and your intimacy
each with other and my uncertainty whether you, Mr. R[ath-
band], be in Lancashire or no make me again to join you both
in one letter, certifying you hereby and entreating your help to
praise the Lord for it, that I and mine are all of us in good and
perfect health of body and comfort and contentment of mind,
wanting nothing but hearts to be thankful for and to walk
worthy of the Lord's abundant goodness to us both for soul
and body.

The thing that you call for, for a set platform of doctrine and
discipline, I have seriously acquainted all the elders withal before Mr. H. his going hence, and all of them thank you for your
care of us and like well of the motion and intend with all convenient speed to do their endeavor that something may be done
that way. And oh that you were here (if God so pleased) that
you might be informed by seeing with your own eyes the ways
wherein we walk and lending your helping hand to do what is
needful to be done. For the mean time, take this taste and relation how things are.

A law is made in the General Court that no church shall be
here set up without the knowledge of the magistrates and the
neighbor churches, that it may be known who and what they
are that call themselves a church and that they be not Papists,
Arminians, Anabaptists, Familists, or the like. For the magistrates think it needful to know whom they protect and whom
the commonwealth harbors, and the churches think it needful
to know whom to give the right hand of fellowship unto that
they may do it in faith and not at random or blindfolded. And
when a church is erected it is done in public view and presence
of all that please to be present from any place under the patent.

And the manner of proceeding is this. A day of solemn humiliation is kept by them that intend to join together in a church
body, and in the latter end of the day each of them (their number is about eight or nine or thereabout) do make public profession of their faith, having done it privately before amongst
themselves and having approved themselves unto one another's
consciences in the sight of the Lord. In this confession they
declare their knowledge in the grounds and principles of religion
and likewise the working of God upon their own souls in their
conversion to Christ Jesus. As for renouncing of England, there
is no such thing used, much less required in their confessions,
but the good knowledge of the Lord and faith unfeigned in
Christ Jesus is all that is required and is required in all that erect
any church here. Now when their confessions are all made and
approved, the company do unite and combine themselves together to the Lord Jesus and one to another by a solemn covenant, practicing herein nothing else but that which Dr. Ames
teacheth in his *Medulla* in the chapter "de ecclesia instituta."[1]
The covenant is set down in writing and openly read and heard
of all men present, and though the covenant of one church do
vary from the covenant of another church, for form of words,
each one expressing their own covenant in those words which
God helps them to conceive and express it in, yet for the sub-
stance of the matter they all agree and the points of it generally
are such duties to God and one another as concern the nature
of a church and their edification in the Lord. When these things
are done, the churches present do by their elders or deputies
declare their approbation of them and acknowledging of them
to be a church of Christ, and accordingly give them the right
hand of fellowship.

Now this company thus combined and united into a church
body are acknowledged to have power to choose officers to
themselves, and so they do, and admit members as any shall desire to join unto them and to exercise all the Lord's ordinances
as He hath appointed. Members are admitted as the church state
was first erected, viz., by solemn confession publicly before the
whole church and by joining with the church in the covenant,
in which the church was joined at her first gathering together.
And no man is refused or rejected from memberly communion
if he desire it unless he be found unworthy and that charity can
see no ground to believe the party to be a member of Christ, and

1. Book 1, chapter 8.

all such are kept out though they offer themselves to be taken in. And hence it is that many are in the country and not members of any church because indeed their ignorance, their profaneness, their carnalness, etc., being seen by their lives, and testified by them that know them, doth show them to be unworthy and keeps them out, and these (some of them in passion and revenge) report evil of the churches and talk their pleasure.

The officers whom they choose are the same that are in the most reformed churches, viz., pastors, teachers, elders, and deacons, though divers churches there are which are not completely furnished with all these officers because they want fit men thereunto. Now all these officers are chosen by the joint and free votes of the church, being gathered publicly together to solemn seeking of God by prayer and in the election of elders (under which are comprehended pastors, teachers, and ruling elders), there is fasting added also. And when they are chosen, they are likewise solemnly ordained, in which ordination imposition of hands is used. This imposition of hands in ordaining of officers is performed by elders, except at the first when the church hath no elders, but the elders themselves are to be chosen and ordained, and then some prime men in the name of the church are nominated and deputed to impose hands in such ordination as the children of Israel did by their hands upon the Levites, Numbers 8:10, which could not be otherwise but by some in name and stead of the children of Israel, because all the Israelites could not impose hands. The deacons do receive the contributions of people every Lord's Day, and out of the church treasure in their hands they serve tables; I mean they provide bread and wine, etc., for the Lord's Supper, they distribute to the necessities of the poor, and in some places (I cannot tell whether in all) they afford maintenance to the elders or ministers. The elders that labor in the Word and doctrine do likewise dispense the seals of the covenant, baptism and the Lord's Supper, and this they do only to members and their children and to such as are known to be members of some other reformed church and not to be under any censure.

The government of the church is conceived to be as Mr. Parker and Dr. Ames teach (for the powers of it), originally in the church, and (for the actual exercise of it) in the elders and presbytery, the church giving power to her elders in their election and ordination, which she could not give if it were not in herself before, because none can give what itself hath not, and exercising her powers and those acts by her elders, which *ipsa per se obiri satis commode requit* [she by herself cannot properly perform]. In a word, that very same is here holden and used which Mr. Parker teacheth, *polit. eccles.*, Book 3, section 7, and chapter 12, page 26 and page 77, 78.[2]

Prophesying, that is, the public speaking of God's word to the edification of the church, by them that have gifts and abilities thereunto, though they be not church officers, is held generally by the most to be lawful in some cases, as in the minister's absence, sickness, etc., but not of any such necessity that it must be used even in the minister's presence, and therefore when ministers are not wanting, such prophesying is not used. But besides the pains which the ministers take on the Sabbaths, they do also keep divers weekly lectures, as at Boston, Newtowne, Roxebury, and at Dorchester. Boston is kept by Mr. Cotton; Newtowne by Mr. Shepard since Mr. Hooker's departure to Conectacut, Roxbury by Mr. Weld and Mr. Eliot, and ___ [Dorchester] is yet put on me only. Besides the ministers do also often meet in private to confer of any question that may arise and to give one another their best advice.

Synods, that is public meetings of all the elders to confer and consider of any business or question publicly, I have known none but one, nor occasion of any more since my coming hither, and at that meeting the elders did not exercise any act of power or authority but only disputed and argued the case pro and con, and agreed upon one uniform judgment and advice, and so gave it up to the church whose the case was and whom the business concerned, leaving that church still to her liberty to do in her own matter as God should direct them, though they gladly and freely embraced and followed the advice and judgment which was given by the assembly or synod.[3]

I am weary of relating, and should I be much larger, I doubt I could not speak to all the particulars that you may think on, and indeed how should I, unless I knew your thoughts? But my unfeigned love unto you both and desire to give you what information I can hath moved me to mention these particulars and will move me still hereafter to acquaint you (as God shall give opportunity, and yourselves express the particulars wherein) with anything that we here practice, and likewise to tell you our grounds for anything amongst us which you may question

2. Robert Parker, *De Politica ecclesiastica Christi* (Frankfort, 1616). Parker, who died in 1617, was like his associate William Ames a proto-congregationalist.

3. This incident, involving the Charlestown church and its pastor, Thomas James, is discussed by Winthrop in his *History*, 1:217.

the warrantableness of. But till I know your minds, I know not
what points this way to speak unto.

For danger by Indians amongst us, by Turks, or any enemies
without us, we see not any, we fear not any, but trust in the
Lord, whose promise is that upon all the glory shall be a defense and that His salvation shall be for walls and bulwarks to
Sion and that He Himself will be the glory in the midst of her,
and a wall of fire round about her. Nevertheless we desire not to
tempt God by security and neglect of any means which He puts
into our hands for our own safeguard, and therefore we train up
our people in feats of arms and maintain many captains, lieuten-
ants, and sergeants of bands, whose office is in every town to
train soldiers and to instruct them in military discipline. Besides,
we have a fort and a castle with many pieces of ordnance
mounted, and soldiers lying there continually in garrison, and
no ship can come into the bay but must veyle [vail? (pay respect)] to the castle. But except the Lord keep the city, etc.,
Psalm 127:1. No, it is the Lord only on whom we desire to rely,
as our castle, our fort, our high tower, our deliverer forever.
Even He is our God forever and ever, and we hope He will be
our guide even to the death.

The land looks not pleasant to the eye in many places, being
a rude and unsubdued wilderness yet with labor yields sufficient
sustenance for men of moderate minds. The dearth and hard-
ship which some sustained the last winter was not through
barrenness of the ground but by means of the many thousands
that came in with slender provision after that foul weather near
harvest had hurt the corn on the ground. This year there is more
corn planted that looketh fair on the ground and promiseth by
God's blessing a plentiful harvest, and the passengers come over
are yet under the number of a thousand, and they are all come
as plentifully furnished with provision as we could desire, besides five or six ships that have come hither being wholly laden
with provisions and nothing else, so that I hope we shall have
sufficient and plenty, if God bless our provisions and our store.

I hear that Mr. Gee, Mr. Ridgeley, Mr. Nichols, and divers others of the Lord's messengers are gone to rest with the Lord. I
desire to condole with God's people who suffer the loss of their
teachers by the cruel hands of wicked men and the holy and
just hand of God. The Lord make a gracious supply as pleaseth
Him best, and prosper the labors of you both, and of everyone

John Cotton

And oh that you were here (if god so pleased) that you
might bee informed by seeing with your owne eyes those
wayes wherein wee walke, and lending your helping hand
to do what is needfull to bee done. for the meane time,
take this tast and relation how things are. A Law is
made in the Generall Court that no church shalbee hereof
sett up without ye knowledge of ye magistrates, and the
neighbour Churches, that it may bee knowen who & what
they are that call ymselves a church, and that they bee
not Papists, Arminians, Anabaptists, familists or ye like.
For the magistrates thinke it needfull to know whom yey protect, and whom ye Comonwealth harbors; and ye churches
thinke it needfull to know whom to give ye right hand of
fellowship unto, that they may do it in faith and not at ran-
dome or blindfolded. And when a church is erected it is
done in publike view & presence of all that please to bee
present from any place under the patent. And ye manner
of proceeding, is this. A day of solemne humiliation is
kept by them that intend to joyne together in a church-body,
and in the latter end of the day each of ym (their numbre
is about 8 or 9 or thereabout) do make publike profession
of their faith, having done it privately before amongst
themselves, and having approved ymselves unto one and
thers consciences in ye sight of ye Lord. In this confession

From Richard Mather's "Plea for the churches of Christ in New England,"
the basis for his June 25, 1636, letter to William Rathband and Mr. T.

that helpeth with us and laboreth. So with my dear love in Christ and my wife's remembered to you both and your wives, to Mr. Bo., Mr. N., Mr. Ball, Mr. T.S., and all other my Christian friends and acquaintance in your parts, I commend you and all them to the Lord, resting

Your ever-loving brother in the Lord,
R[ichard] M[ather]

June 25, 1636

The desire of the Bay Colony to become a new Canaan was threatened in 1636 and 1637 by insecurity and disunity. Early in 1636 Roger Williams and some of his followers departed for Rhode Island. Thomas Hooker and a substantial body of colonists moved to Connecticut. A group under John Davenport arrived in Boston but were not certain where to settle; later they founded New Haven. The magistrates were disagreeing with each other, and the deputies were seeking greater power. The Indians were threatening, and finally in 1637 the Pequot War broke out. Even the colony's charter was in doubt. (The troubles over the charter are discussed below.) The French were still making the Bay colonists uncomfortable, and in England the colony was being condemned for both its religious position and the uncertainty of its right to the territory it occupied. Many of these concerns are reflected in a portion of a letter preserved in a copy at the Public Record Office, London, numbered C. O. 1/9, folio 46. It is labelled "October 3, 1636. A passage in a letter to Mr. Controller, about the estate of New England. Dated July 28, 1636." The *Calender of State Papers* tentatively identifies the sender as Henry Vane, Jr.; the recipient was Sir Henry Vane. The younger Vane was governor from May 1636 to May 1637; he returned to England soon after he left office and later became a leading figure in the Commonwealth government of England.

The present face of things here is very tumultuous. The French continually encroach, and, by vending of pieces and powder strengthen the natives for civil wars and gain all the trade. The natives themselves are very treacherous, cruel, and cunning, and let slip no advantages of killing and pilfering if they may do it and not be discovered. The common report is also that the patent is damned, in which regard much unsettlement is like to grow amongst ourselves and great discouragement to the whole plantation, for those that are truly sincere and are come out to advance the kingdom of the Lord Jesus must either suffer in the cause or else labor for such retreat as God shall direct them to, in either of which cases I do not doubt but within two years this plantation, which is now flourishing, would become desolate, and either possessed again with Indians or emptied by pestilence. For it is not trade that God will set up in these parts but the profession of His truth, and therefore if God's ends be not followed, men's ends will never be blessed nor attained.

1637

In a time of great uncertainty, the colonists especially valued
community and unity. Since the leaders of the colony as well as
many of their followers had (in the words of the letter above)
"come out to advance the kingdom of the Lord Jesus," any
threat to that advancement was conceived of as fundamental.
At Boston there was brewing what residents of other towns
thought to be just such a threat. The source of religious disunity
was a woman. In 1634 Anne Hutchinson arrived in Boston with
her husband and children, and two years later came her brother-
in-law, the Reverend John Wheelwright. Both became members
of the Boston church. Something of a charismatic personality,
Mrs. Hutchinson was soon attracting a following; many members of the Boston church came to her house to discuss religious
ideas and experiences. Some people seem to have been drawn
to her because she offered a less moralistic form of religion than
the clergy did. Inspired by the pietistic teachings of John Cotton
and Wheelwright, both of whom she had heard preach in England, she was soon a divisive force: she distinguished sharply
between the "legal" preaching of the great bulk of the Bay
Colony's ministers, including Boston's own John Wilson, who
tended to emphasize works, and the preaching of Cotton and
Wheelwright, who emphasized the importance of faith.

Boston began to be considered by people in the outlying
towns as a center of heresy at a time when unity was much
needed. The leader of the Hutchinson faction was now Henry
Vane, the very young governor during the year 1636-37; he and
his party were opposed by a group lead by John Winthrop.
Unity came at a high price. Wheelwright was tried for sedition,
convicted and banished; Vane returned to England; a synod of
ministers condemned the "Antinomian" errors; Anne Hutchinson was excommunicated and banished. Some forty Boston
families, including many wealthy and important ones, felt obliged to leave the colony. John Cotton himself was sufficiently
embarrassed by the affair that he too contemplated leaving for
New Haven. These events were the most traumatic in the colony's early years, so important that they constitute a turning
point in its history.

Efforts to resolve the crisis began in the summer of 1637, when ministers conferred with John Cotton to reach some kind of consensus, or at least agreement on the area of disagreement. Finally the ministers found that they had to proceed more formally, and they called a synod, to which the laity, including the Hutchinsonians, were invited. The first meeting was held on August 30, with twenty-five ministers in attendance. Peter Bulkeley of Concord and Thomas Hooker of Hartford were chosen moderators. After much debate and weeks of discussion in an atmosphere well described in the letter below, the synod identified eighty-two doctrinal errors, for example that "The church in admitting members is not to look to holiness of life, or testimony of the same." The synod also condemned two practices of the Antinomians: questioning their ministers, and holding private religious meetings apart from the church.

Four effects of the controversy can be detected. First, the ministers now sought to halt the democratic tendency of Congregationalism and to increase their own authority in their churches in order to prevent future disorders. Second, religious enthusiasm was severely dampened. "Heart-religion," identified now with the Hutchinsonians, became a thing of the past in New England until the time of the Great Awakening. Third, the churches settled into a pattern of formalism and soon developed a kind of tribalism: they were concerned with only their own members and members' offspring, not the unconverted. Fourth, orthodoxy having been more precisely defined, the colony became more intolerant of religious aberrations. The text of the following letter, or rather portion of a letter, is based on the version in Thomas Hutchinson's *History of Massachusetts Bay*, volume 1, pages 68-69.

? to ?
Summer 1637

The synod being met, much time is spent in ventilation and emptying of private passions. At length, divers truths are concluded upon, as the nature of grace and faith, the necessity of repentance and good works, the perfection of the scriptures, and like truths of common allay were assented unto by common suffrage. But when they came to the nature of the covenant, the qualifications preceding it, the use of it, the seal of the Spirit, the Helenaes[1] for which they strive, there they were as different as ever, resolved in nothing but this, that no one would be resolved by another, but therein was the wisdom and excellent spirit of the governor [Winthrop] seen, silencing passionate and impertinent speeches as another Constantine, desiring the divine oracles might be heard speak and express their own meaning, adjourning the assembly when he saw heat and passion, so that, through the blessing of God, the assembly is dissolved, and jarring and dissonant opinions, if not reconciled, yet are covered; and they who came together with minds exasperated by this means depart in peace, and promise, by a mutual covenant, that no difference in opinion shall alienate their affections any more but that they will refer doubts to be resolved by the great God, at that great day when we shall appear at His tribunal.

How the 1630 colonists expected to establish a viable economy is not clear. They do not seem to have assumed that fish and furs would be very important, though these, especially the latter, had been emphasized by such promoters as Captain John Smith. Richard Saltonstall in 1632 suggested the export of natural resources. During the first decade, food shortages and the seeming richness of much of the land made nearly all of the Massachusetts Bay colonists, even the Bostonians, into farmers. (The Bostonians were allotted agricultural land off their narrow peninsula.) Vegetables, grains, and later fruit trees and vineyards were planted. Most early reports reflect the great success that flowed from the farmers' efforts, and this success and the remarkable creation of a new and godly commonwealth with pure churches caused most of the colonists to overlook whatever shortcomings Massachusetts might have. Of course it was not an agriculturalist's paradise. A few accounts of disappointment survive, two in letters that Thomas Hutchinson collected in his *History*. Both are anonymous. The first was written within the first decade; the text is from Hutchinson, volume 1, pages 482-83.

1. Presumably a reference to Helen of Troy.

? to ?
Early 1637

The soil, it is, for the nature of it, mixed; the upland rather
participates of sand than clay, yet our rye likes it not, an argument it is both cold and barren. Yet I find some of it manured
to yield some increase but not to answer expectation. The lowlands are, for the most part, covered with underwoods. The soil,
which is a mixture of clay and sand, seems to have been fattened
by the continual fall of leaves from the trees growing thereon.
This soil is like your woodland in England, best at first, yet afterwards grows more barren. This raised the report of so rich a
soil, but we that came after found, by dear experience, that
affection, not judgment, was the author of it, for, after five or
six years, it grows barren beyond belief, and whereas after the
land in England proves fertile for grass, this yields none at all,
but like the land about Dunstable,[1] puts on the face of winter in
the time of summer. I do believe that if we had marl, lime, or
other manure, this barrenness might in part be cured, but as yet
we are destitute of these supplies. The natural coldness confutes
the opinion of those who did conceive it to be originally fertile,
and experience confirms this to be true, for beans, millet, and
fitches and roots, which delight in a cold soil, prosper here alike.
For the present, we make a shift to live, but hereafter, when our
numbers increase and the fertility of the soil doth decrease, if
God discover not means to enrich the land, what shall become
of us I will not determine, but it is probable we must either dis-
band ourselves, like beasts straitened in their pasture, and so be
liable to destruction from the natives (I mean the Pequods[2]) or
else, continuing together, be made the subject of some fearful
famine and the misery that accompanieth it. Hay we have here
of the lowlands, such as it is, which in my opinion is inferior
in goodness to our reed and sedge in England, for it is so devoid
of nutritive virtue that our beasts grow lousy with feeding upon
it and are much out of heart and liking. Besides, it breeds among
them sundry diseases which we know not how to cure. Some
have learned to make better provision by burning the grass when
it is near ripe and so suffering a new crop to spring out of the
the ashes of the old. This they cut down before it be half ripe
and make it into hay, but this proves like your aftermath in

1. An agricultural town in
Bedfordshire.
2. These Indians were all
but eliminated later in
1637.

Old England, not fit to labor with, yielding a faint nourishment,
which brings our cattle so low and many times to diseases of
which they hardly ever recover.

The second letter in Hutchinson's *History*, written "a few years
later," suggests that the early glowing reports were written "in
strawberry time." The author complains that "The air of the
country is sharp, the rocks many, the trees innumerable, the
grass little, the winter cold, the summer hot, the gnats in summer biting, the wolves at midnight howling." Her only kind
words refer to New England's religious virtues: "Look upon it,
as it hath the means of grace, and, if you please, you may call it
a Canaan." More satirical comments can be found in a poem
that circulated in England, "The Summons to New England,"
which includes this stanza:

There twice a year all sorts of grain
Doth down from heaven like hailstones rain;
You never need to sow or plough,
There's plenty of all things enough:
Wine sweet and wholesome drops from trees,
As clear as crystal, without lees;
Yea, and a Church unspotted, pure,
From dregs of Papistry secure.

In England John Cotton had consulted with John Dod,
the wise old man of puritanism, as to whether he should
go to America, and Dod had encouraged him to go. It must
therefore have been painful to Cotton to find Dod among the
thirteen puritan clergymen who signed a letter written in 1637
to their "brethren in New England." In it the writers charged
the New Englanders with having "embraced new opinions."
The thirteen describe newly developed congregational principles
such as these: "that the children of godly and approved Christians are not to be baptized until their parents be set members
of some particular congregation" and that a "minister can perform no ministerial act in any other congregation" than his
own. The letter writers severely chide the New Englanders:

"Yourselves have judged that to be error, which now you take to be truth." Worst of all, the New Englanders have caused many to suppose that "nonconformists in practice are Separatists in heart." The New Englanders are asked to defend themselves; if they fail to do so adequately, they can expect to be admonished.

Cotton replied with some difficulty; the extant draft of his letter (in the Department of Rare Books and Manuscripts, Boston Public Library) begins with a false start. Cotton did not supply at this time the defense that had been requested, but a reply was forthcoming. The original request, the official reply made by John Davenport, and a rejoinder were all published in London in 1643 as *A Letter of Many Ministers in Old England, Requesting The judgment of their Reverend Brethren in New England concerning Nine Positions Written Anno Dom. 1637. Together with their Answers thereunto returned. Anno 1639. And the Reply made unto the said Answer, and sent over unto them. Anno 1640.*

John Cotton to John Dodd
December 19, 1637

To the Reverend Mr. John Dod. Grace and peace be multiplied to you in Jesus Christ.
Reverend and dear sir:

In your letter received the last summer

The elders of the churches in this country received a letter from you and sundry other of our reverend and godly brethren, the ministers of divers churches in our native country, all of them being very well known to divers of us and esteemed in the vineyard at home very highly in love for their works' sake and for this labor of love unto ourselves. It seemeth you have heard that our practice here doth somewhat differ from yours there in the administration of God's ordinances in the church and do therefore in your letter require of us the grounds of our difference from you, that if they be found to bear weight in the balance of the sanctuary, you may give us the right hand of fellowship therein, but if they be found too light, you may then endeavor (in a brotherly way) to discover the errors of our course to us. As they do thankfully accept your brotherly love, so they our brethren here have taken your motion into serious

consideration, and beholding the face of Christ in it, holding
forth and breathing a spirit of holy wisdom and Christian love,
and faithful and watchful care of the establishment of the kingdom of the Lord Jesus in truth and peace. And they have desired me to certify unto yourself and do desire you to convey
to the rest of our reverend brethren with you that it is their
purpose (by the help of Christ) to give you a plain and just
account of our proceedings here according to all the demands
you require of us. Wherein we have been letted for a season by
some late ___[?] we have been called unto for the compassing
of some controversies amongst ourselves,[1] which being now
brought by the hand of the Lord to some issue, it is our next
care and endeavor (by the Lord's help) to dispatch a speedy
answer unto you by the next trusty and convenient passenger.
Meanwhile let us still and ever enjoy the help and comfort of
your brotherly love and fervent prayers and faithful advertisements, as occasion shall require. Our native country and the ordinances of God therein, and our holy brethren we have left not
in affection but in place, but our native corruptions and selves
we still carry about with us, and Satan bestireth himself as
mightily, and as busily here, as amongst you, if not more, as
having great wrath against the simplicity of the name and kingdom of the Lord Jesus, and pouring dishonors thereupon by the
infirmities of God's servants when he cannot pour but his rage
by the wickedness of the enemies. But the Lord tread down
Satan under his and our feet shortly. Strive with him in prayer
for that end as (by God's grace) we do for you.

We do all heartily salute you in the Lord with the rest of our
reverend and beloved brethren, by name Mr. Cleaver,
Mr. Bourne, Mr. Winston, Mr. Ball, and the rest. My wife is still
mindful and sensible of your gracious counsel when you kindly
brought us onward of our way, and the Lord warmed our hearts
with your heavenly conference. We both of us commend our
hearty thanks and love to you and your wife, with your son
Timothy. The Lord Jesus still give you to abound in holy fruit-
fulness to him and to his people, till you have finished your
course in his peace.

In him I rest, desirous of your continual prayers.

    Your very loving friend and brother in our Lord Jesus
    J[ohn] C[otton]

Boston this 19th of 10th[2]

1. The Antinomian contro-
versy.
2. December was the tenth
month, since the new year
did not begin till late
March.

One thing let me entreat further of you. I hear there is a written book goeth up and down in England under my name as my catechism.[3] I did indeed go over the principles of religion in way of catechism here according to the five heads expressed in Hebrews 6. And therewith I handled also the principles of church-government. But what notes [have] been taken of it from my mouth, I know not. Sure I am I never perused any copy to be sent for England. And therefore if you hear of such a writing, I pray you, do me this Christian favor, to bear witness for me, I do not own it, as having never seen it, although [it] may be. Sundry things in it were delivered by me, which I do acknowledge.

To my reverend and dear friend and brother in Christ Mr. John Dod.

3. Probably the work eventually published as part of *A Treatise* (n. p., 1713).

1638

Massachusetts Bay protected its sovereignty by wearing the face of humility and subservience in its dealings with English officialdom, as the next letter demonstrates. I have been unable to identify the recipient or the person being discussed. The version below is based on a draft in Winthrop's hand in the early court records on file in the clerk's office of the Supreme Judicial Court for the county of Suffolk (Massachusetts).

John Winthrop to Lord ____
April 6, 1638

Right Honorable:

Your letters on behalf of Jo: Th: I have received and communicated with those of our council, and we do with all thankfulness acknowledge your wisdom and integrity, that you are pleased to call for no other at our hands than right and justice shall require, which though (we trust) we shall always have respect unto, yet our care and endeavor herein shall be the more quickened upon your lordship's gentle reminding us of that which duty binds us to in this behalf, and more (I perceive) your lordship expects not from us in this case, which makes us the more forward to tender ourselves to your command in whatsoever we may be serviceable to your lordship. So I humbly take leave and shall ever desire to be your lordship's servant.

> J[ohn] W[inthrop]

B[oston] in N: E:
April 6, 1638

Throughout the 1630s the legal status of the Massachusetts Bay charter was uncertain. As has already been noted, Sir Ferdinando Gorges viewed the Bay colonists, creators of the new commonwealth, as interlopers on his territory.

In 1632 he reactivated the Council for New England. At first his plan was to obtain a new charter that would enable him to exercise authority over the whole of New England. He had as allies such men as Thomas Morton and Christopher Gardiner, both of whom had been banished from Massachusetts Bay. They were encouraged by the actions in 1634 of the Privy Council to make migration difficult. The whole story of what might happen to the colony must have been made known to its leaders when John Humphry, who had been questioned by English governmental officials, arrived in Boston in 1634. Soon the colonists took steps to defend themselves from invasion. The situation became even more threatening when the newly created Commission for Regulating Plantations called in the colony's charter. When it was found that the charter was not in England, the Massachusetts Bay Company was charged with having exceeded its authority in fourteen particulars and in 1635 a writ of *quo warranto* (by what warrant) was issued, a legal move preliminary to revoking its charter. In so many words the colony was told to defend itself. Among the charges was that its legal practice violated the laws and customs of England.

Members of the company who were in England disclaimed the charter, and when Winthrop and the other American members of the company did not appear, in 1637 they were outlawed and the charter was considered cancelled. Gorges and his associates had in the meanwhile been given the task of delivering the writ containing the charges. For that purpose they prepared a "great ship." But it never sailed, for it was damaged in launching. All that could be done was for the commissioners on April 4, 1638, to send to Winthrop a strong letter in which they "strictly require and enjoin" him or whoever has custody of the charter to return it, adding that, "in case of any further neglect or contempt," they "will move his Majesty to reassume into his hands the whole plantation." In Massachusetts the General Court took up the matter. Winthrop reports in his journal that there "it was agreed that, whereas a very strict order was sent from the lord commissioners for plantations for the sending home our patent, under pretence that judgment had passed against it upon a *quo warranto*, a letter should be written by the governor, in the name of the court, to excuse our not sending of it." Winthrop's letter, an eminently sensible one, makes no effort to defend the departures from English ways that Massachusetts Bay had developed. Perhaps the governor knew that the commissioners could only threaten. Although some further steps were taken to force a new charter on the colony and to limit its independence severely, affairs at home soon discouraged the English government from any drastic action. Massachusetts Bay retained its charter in fact if not in law until 1684. Winthrop's original letter seems not to be extant; an official copy is in the Massachusetts Archives, volume 361, page 1.

John Winthrop to the Lord Commissioners for Foreign Plantations
September 6, 1638

To the right honorable the Lord Commissioners for Foreign Plantations: The humble petition of the inhabitants of the Massachusets in New-England of the General Court there assembled the sixth day of September in the fourteenth year of the reign of our sovereign lord King Charles.

Whereas it hath pleased your lordships, by order of the fourth of April last, to require our patent to be sent to you, we do hereby humbly and sincerely profess that we are ready to yield all due obedience to our sovereign lord the king's majesty and to your lordships under him and in this mind we left our native country and according thereunto hath been our practice ever since, so as we are much grieved that your lordships should call in our patent, there being no cause known to us nor any delinquency or fault of ours expressed in the order sent to us for that purpose, our government being according to his majesty's grant, and we not answerable for any defects in other plantations, et cetera.

This is that which his majesty's subjects here do believe and profess, and thereupon we are all humble suitors to his lordships that you will be pleased to take into further consideration our condition and to afford us the liberty of subjects, that we may know what is laid to our charge and have leave and time to answer for ourselves before we be condemned as a people unworthy of his majesty's favor or protection. As for the *quo warranto* mentioned in the said order, we do assure your lordships we were never called to answer to it, and if we had, we doubt not but we have a sufficient plea to put in.

It is not unknown to your lordships that we came into these

remote parts with his majesty's license and encouragement under his great seal of England, and in the confidence we had of that assurance, we have transported our families and estates, and here we have built and planted, to the great enlargement and securing of his majesty's dominions in these parts, so as if our patent should now be taken from us, we shall be looked on as renigadoes and outlaws and shall be enforced either to remove to some other place or to return into our native country again, either of which will put us to unsupportable extremities, and these evils (among others) will necessarily follow. (1) Many thousand souls will be exposed to ruin, being laid open to the injuries of all men. (2) If we be forced to desert this place, the rest of the plantations (being too weak to subsist alone) will, for the most part dissolve and go with us, and then will this whole country fall into the hands of the French or Dutch, who would speedily embrace such an opportunity. (3) If we should lose all our labor and costs and be deprived of those liberties which his majesty hath granted to us, and nothing laid to our charge nor any failing to be found in us in point of allegiance (which all our countrymen do take notice of and will justify our faithfulness in this behalf), it will discourage all men hereafter from the like undertakings upon confidence of his majesty's royal grant. Lastly, if our patent be taken from us (whereby we suppose we may claim interest in his majesty's favor and protection), the common people here will conceive that his majesty hath cast them off and that, thereby, they are freed from their allegiance and subjection and thereupon will be ready to confederate themselves under a new government for their necessary safety and subsistence, which will be a dangerous example to other plantations and perilous to ourselves of incurring his majesty's displeasure, which we would by all means avoid.

Upon these considerations we are bold to renew our humble supplication to your lordships that we may be suffered to live here in this wilderness and that this poor plantation, which hath found more favor from God than many others, may not find less favor from your lordships; that our liberties should be restrained when others are enlarged; that the door should be kept shut unto us while it stands open to all other plantations; that men of ability should be debarred from us while they give encouragement to other colonies.

We dare not question your lordships' proceedings: we only desire to open our griefs where the remedy is to be expected. If in anything we have offended his majesty and your lordships, we humbly prostrate ourselves at the footstool of supreme authority. Let us be made the object of his majesty's clemency and not cut off in our first appeal from all hope of favor.

Thus with our earnest prayers to the King of Kings for long life and prosperity to his sacred majesty and his royal family and for all honor and welfare to your lordships, we humbly take leave.[1]

Throughout the 1630s new towns were created in Massachusetts both by newcomers and by colonists dissatisfied with their current locations. One of the town-founders was Edmund Browne, who came to Massachusetts in 1637 on the same ship with Thomas Lechford and Emmanuel Downing. Born in 1606, Browne had been graduated from Cambridge in 1624 and had served as a minister in Sudbury, Suffolk. He was well-to-do and a person of considerable accomplishments, including playing the bass viol. Soon after he arrived in Massachusetts he wrote, as presumably he had promised to do, to Sir Simonds D'Ewes, who still contemplated coming to America. Browne's letter and the very full report that accompanied it show how quickly Massachusetts was becoming settled and civilized. It was only later that Browne became familiar with the frontier. He had met a group living at Watertown, and with them and others he petitioned the General Court for a town grant south of Concord. The grant was awarded on the day before he wrote his letter; perhaps because of Browne, the new town was named Sudbury. There Browne became minister, and there he stayed, despite political squabbles in which he played a central role, until his death about 1678.

In his 1638 letter Browne gives his impressions of the transatlantic voyage and the new land, as others did earlier. He describes in detail Mary Dyer's misshapen foetus, as did Winthrop later in his *Short Story*, 1644, sent to tell old England how Antinomians were treated in New England. The unpleasant details were much discussed because they seemed to Winthrop,

1. The Massachusetts Archive copy, used here, is endorsed, "This is a true copy compared with the original on file as I testify. Edward Rawson." Rawson was secretary of the colony beginning in 1650.

and perhaps to Browne, to demonstrate how evil were the Antinomian opinions. Browne has unfortunately much less to say about the beginning of the new college, about which few details are available. In addition, he tells D'Ewes more than Eliot and Winthrop had chosen to report concerning the New England Way; he says something about the two crucial matters of church membership and baptism. He also discusses at some length the Antinomian crisis, which was doubtless the most traumatic event in early Massachusetts history. Browne's original letter is British Museum manuscript Harley 388, folio 19.

Edmund Browne to Sir Simonds D'Ewes
September 7, 1638

Right Noble Sir:

After Providence with a most merciful hand carried me over the seas, with as upon or under an extended wing, and crowned my desires with an enjoyment of what I long desired to see, I presently considered your loving request to present unto you a description of our New E[ng]l[a]n[d] estate. Therefore, as a testimony of my real honoring of your worth, and as a significant character of my grateful reflex, I have addressed a miscellaneous display, to attend your gracing of it with a favorable surveying of it. Had I enjoyed time of inditing more refinedly, I should have presented it in a more polished form, though I hate flattery and would rather both speak and do *sancte* than *cincte* [?].

I hope your worship will not be displeased if by the way it calleth in at Broomely to wait upon your brother Sir Thomas, my endeared master,[1] and his lady, to whom I am much obliged.

Concerning your letter sent to Mr. Hooker, I have not yet spoke to him, being an hundred miles distant from me,[2] but for your satisfaction I shall, if it please God, send unto you our churches' apology, either this year or the next, to be agreed upon by all our elders and other divines, and to be dispersed for the satisfying of all questionists out of desire of the truth.[3]

And lastly, concerning a plantation for your worship, I have travelled about to see the country, and I have seen good places. The best for soil is one Merrimacke, within seven miles of Ipswich and adjoining to Newberry, yet for temper the southern

1. Sir Thomas Bowes's wife was Sir Simonds D'Ewes's sister.
2. Thomas Hooker was at Hartford.
3. Perhaps Richard Mather's semi-official *Church-Government and Church-Covenant Discussed* (London, 1643), written in 1639.

side is more excellent. We have grants of six hundred acres to some gentlemen. There be many lords that have plantations here, but if a gentleman intendeth not to come himself or to send some honest friend, nor be careful in his electing of godly and able men in agriculture, he will be a loser by it. Therefore in such a case it is best to venture a sum of moneys to be turned into cattle at the assignment and approbation of the governor, Mr. Winthrope, a godly and wise gentleman, with whom I had some discourse about your worship and [he] desireth to tender his respect unto you. There is much to be gotten here that way according to the custom of the plantation, if the Lord bless the increase. If therefore your worship by a plantation should not make provision of refuge for harsh times, if they should happen at England, my advice is that you would venture something by degrees to be employed in the breeding of cattle, as 20 pounds, 40 pounds, or 60 pounds, or more as it shall please you, and I will become undertaker for the improvement of it in breeding cattle, and so when of a little stock shall be raised then to enter upon some lot to break up ground, which will then yield forty shillings per annum by the acre, if good. If you shall please to adventure such a sum, I intend to send for my father over the next year if we live, but if you shall venture this year then that he would come over this year, and so both myself and he shall be obliged unto you (for by that means he shall have something to employ him in). I thank the Lord I have convenient maintenance at 20 pounds per annum and much land, but now in case that I should change my condition, I would be glad to have a stock for a lot, as the rest of the elders have, but I am not able to stock it, whereas if yourself now would adventure but the tithe of what you intended, it will conduce much for my benefit, the Lord blessing it. I have appointed one to wait on you for an answer.

There came over one knight, and a lady widow,[4] besides personages of worth, and the plantations are much peopled and enlarged this year. Thus with my service to yourself and ingenious lady, and my prayers for either of your enlargements, I rest, remaining

> Your worship to command
> in all Christian service
> Edmund Browne

Boston: September 7th

4. Lord Ley, nineteen-year-old son of the Earl of Marlborough, visited Boston briefly; Lady Deborah Moody, another daughter of the Earl of Lincoln, settled at Salem but later left the colony for Long Island.

My office is yet to preach to some four or five great families, but I know not whether I shall settle here, if it prove not a church, I suppose I shall not.

When God, by an overruling hand, denied me liberty, which I expected in the ship called the *Nicholas of London*, the Lord presented it me in another ship called the *Thomas and Frances*, wherein I found some company of worth, as one Mr. Downing, who married the governor's sister,[5] to whom I was much obliged for her matron and mother-like care over me in supplying my wants out of her treasury of provision. I was joined in the mess with them, had an often refreshing with fresh meat and bottle beer, et cetera.

I was a little sick but had my health in a competent manner. The time of our floating on the sea was some eight weeks from the Downs, and yet we had but two large winds to purpose, *sct.* [*scilicet*, namely], in carrying us out from the Downs, and in bringing us in to the land upon our discovery of it, *viz.*, Cape Cod, lying south from the Bay. We were often put into some fear of pirates or men-of-war, but our God preserved us. When we had been three weeks at sea the contagious pox struck in amongst us, yet ordered by the Lord's power, as if it had not been infectious. I suppose some thirty had it, yet directly I think but one or two died. It was confined within one division in our ship, *sct.*, middle deck, the gunroom being free unless some two or three children which had them sparingly, and all other room, although there was converse with them, were free and enjoying health. The next day of our arrival I was invited to the governor's to dinner, where we had an old England table furnished for our entertainment to my admire. In the afternoon I heard Mr. Cotton, viewing their comely order and faith, blessed be the Lord for them. The plantation I found to exceed her sisters, though her ancestors in time, as Virginia, Bermudas, and which not of their time, in convenient buildings, settled courts,[6] and adjacent towns. Of the Lord yet be its protector and enlarger, to the praise of his name and silencing bitter spirits with the news of her glory.

Now concerning the plantation, this I affirm. The soil I judge to be lusty and fat in many places, light and hot, in some places sandy-bottomed and in some loamy, reasonably good for all

5. Emmanuel Downing, mentioned frequently above.
6. Four inferior courts of the first instance were established in 1636, at Ipswich, Salem, Newtown, and Boston.

sorts of grain without manuring, but exceeding good with manure, some for wheat, some for rye, etc. I saw much good corn of all sorts this year. The ground grazeth not so well as O[ld] E[ngland], for we have not brought it into a way of bearing English grass, though in some places our E[nglish] clover is found, yet it feedeth cattle very well. I have seen oxen here that were worth some 14 pounds an ox in O[ld] E[ngland], and good beef, notwithstanding their labor. We plow and cart with them. Some farms have two yoke of them. In many towns there be two hundred head of cattle, yet because of freshcomers do hold the price of 20 pounds a cow or ox, and mares be of the same. The land is rocky in many places, yet that ground beareth good Indian corn, which grain is in many places manured with fish. The corn yieldeth great increase, and doth compare if not excel your O[ld] E[nglish] wheat in puddings and in being used as boiled wheat. The land is grovey and hilly in many places; the air clear and dry; the sun is seldom enerved [weakened] by any cloudy interposition.

The fruits of the earth naturally growing are abundance of strawberries, raspberries, gooseberries red and green, most large grapes yet not so delicious as old E[nglish] grapes for not pruned nor dressed, and abundance of plum trees, all sorts of garden fruits, as roots and herbs. We have three kinds of melons that be most delectable, the one called an apple squash, so called from its size and pleasantness being boiled and so prepared; a musk melon which is here so ripened with the sun as both in smell and taste it may compare with goodly pears; also a watermelon not inferior to the best, both of these last are eaten raw. Apple trees, pear trees, and plum trees grow and bear notably here, being planted.

Here is great store of fish which the sea furnisheth us with, as abundance of sturgeon, some salmons, hollyboat, cod, bass, a fish that in his head excelleth the salmon's jowl, mackerel all the summer and catched with hooks and excelleth our O[ld] E[nglish] mackerel by far in fatness. There is some time a one thousand pound [of] bass caught in a draught at a time. Here be abundance of oysters very large and fat, great lobsters, with other shell fish, much fresh water fish, though differing much from the kinds in England in regard of shape, yet not inferior to any in goodness.

Here is a large kind of deer whose flesh is sold for two pence a pound in the winter. Here be wild rabbits and hares that have been caught, and many of our tame rabbits breed excellently here. Mutton and pork are usually eaten here. Here be hum birds feathered in colors and not bigger than a dor [beetle], a strange wonder. Here be many upland fowl, eagles and hawks, turkeys very large, many pigeons, abundance of black birds, etc., fair partridges in coveys and many quails; abundance likewise of sea fowls, as swan, goose, duck, teal, etc., of which abundance is taken. We had in Mr. Thomas' family thirty to pluck in an evening the last year.

Our summer for a month exceedeth in heat our O[ld] E[nglish] summers and our winters be colder, as I am informed by reason of a northeast wind. To conclude this relation, if the Lord put us some way of trading we shall be happy in outward enjoyments, and I do conclude that here is that which will bring in benefit, for its subsistence and enrichment. I suppose we shall have a trade in fishing the next year, as being for the present the most secure way to fall upon.

Here be yearly many new plantations set upon in both the patents [7] to the great comfort of our spirits. Our greatest enemies are our wolves, but yet [they] flee man, and the musceta, being our English gnat, is exiled out of places inhabited. The Indians are wholly subjected, and we more secure from land enemies and annoyances by thieves than in O[ld] England. I tell you no untruth: our outward door hath stood by a quarter of a year unlocked, and men ride and travel abroad ten or twenty miles without sword or offensive staff, for both wolves and Indians are afraid of us. (The Lord be praised.) There be very few Indians.

Now concerning our church way and order, both in its gathering together, electing of members, presbytery, careful admittance, confederate walking, and exact ejecting out by church censure, I judge apostolical. Our members either transient or manent (by a stricter tie) perform no more or are not required to do anything (as I have received by information) than what the Scripture requireth or may be performed by any true professor, whereby the church is preserved pure from sin, unless it erreth from this rule. We have not (praised be God) such mixed assemblies as elsewhere (which was sometime my burden.) [8] Now whereas it was reported that many godly men, judged so in England, are without any particular church, the reason is

7. That is, in Massachusetts Bay and Plymouth.
8. Church membership was limited to "visible saints": those who gave evidence of being saved.

because for some reason of not being settled they do not
seek it, or else have so tainted their life that their condition
is questionable.

And concerning the not promiscuous baptizing of infants, I
judge the order apostolical, for first the child of unbelievers is unclean and unholy, the meaning of which text I would know.[9] Now
suppose the parents of a child new-born should be excommunicated upon a scandalous course, I conceive during that time as
they are in their persons not to partake of the sacrament, so not
their child till they shall return by repentance, and to be so ejected
or not admitted conditioneth men alike. Second, no pastor nor
teacher hath any call to baptize so, for they be only pastors and
teachers of those that have elected them. I mean those in the body
(then or after admitted), I say the pastor being not ordained in
general for other places or to live and die a pastor in case he resign-
eth up his place. So then, if the child hath no right nor pastor to
call to baptize without his charge, as he nor the church hath aught
to judge them that be without, why do we so blame this order and
idolize the ordinances? But because of haste, if any shall desire
my farther reasons, I shall, if the Lord please, unpart my mind
more fully, and I think you will see the elders' answer to it, for it
is to be sent into England, and I shall if God please direct it to my
friends, viz., your worship, etc.

Lastly, concerning the controversies, they are thus far composed: that of them which are resident in the Bay only
Mr. Cotton affirmeth that primitive evidence is from the im-
mediate witness of the Spirit; now other elders would have the
Lord left free which way to work. He [Cotton] is with us at
Boston, and all the opinionists that remain so are removed either with Mr. Wheelwright to the eastward or with Mrs. Hutchinson unto the south part. Thus God hath given a two-fold
peace unto the churches here. His name be praised.[10]

Mr. Wheelwright was exiled upon conceit that he intended
hostile sedition in a sermon of his, concluding all his brethren
presbyters and their people not tenentized with him to be under
a covenant of works. Mrs. Hutchinson was and is a woman who
led aside silly men and women into strange conclusions. I have
here presented some of them unto you: that union with Christ
is not by faith, (2) that faith is a law, Romans 3. 27, and therefore killeth, (3) that there is an engraftment into Christ and not
by faith, and that a soul may be in Christ and yet Christ not in

9. See 1 Corinthians 7:14.
10. Wheelwright settled in
the Piscataqua area to the
north; Anne Hutchinson
settled in Rhode Island
but later moved to Long
Island, where she was
killed by Indians.

11. Anne Hutchinson seems to have had a hyda-tiform mole. See Emery Battis, *Saints and Sectaries: Anne Hutchinson and the Antinomian Controversy* (Chapel Hill, N.C., 1962), pp. 247-48.

12. Browne's report was used by Samuel Eliot Morison to date the opening of the college, still unnamed until the following March, when, from the benefaction of John Harvard, it was named for him. An existing house had been altered to serve as the college building. Newtown was renamed Cambridge on May 2, 1638. This passage also dates the year of the letter, for the press was set up in January, 1638/9. Morison, *The Founding of Harvard College* (Cambridge, Mass., 1935) pp. 199-209; *Massachusetts Records*, 1:228.

13. See above, note 4. I have not succeeded in identifying the knight.

it, (4) that there are no graces in the soul but the presence of Christ acting, the soul being wholly passive, with a many other strange contradictory conclusions, boasting much of her revelations and scripture-like certainty of them. But as the Lord hath scattered these conceited persons, so hath he followed them strangely, and that in two monstrous births that one Mrs. Dyers and Mrs. Hutchinson had. The former whilst she lived in Boston, who with her husband, being young and lusty and active in holding forth Mrs. Hutchinson's conceits or some of them, was delivered of a large woman child in time two months before her compt. It was stillborn, yet alive two hours before birth. It was on this form: it had no back part of the head, the face stood low upon the breast, it had no forehead but four horns in the room, two being an inch long and hard, and two less. It had apish ears placed upon the shoulders; the eyes and mouth were strangely butting out, the nose crooked upward, the back and breast were pricky like a thornback. The sex-distinguishing parts were placed on the backside beneath the backbone, and the hips were alike placed. Likewise in the back were two holes and two pieces of flesh appearing out of them. Upon the toes of each foot were three claws like to a young fowl. The women called to the travail were taken with great vomiting (although fasting) before the very act of bringing forth, and were sent for home with all speed because (then and not before or since) their children were taken with convulsions, by which means only two being left and one asleep besides midwife Hawkis (of the same stamp with her) when she was delivered, at which time there was a great stink and the bed shaked. It was concealed by a confederacy, but revealed strangely and confessed, and for the truth's sake was digged up and found so, and applied conjecturally to their opinions. Also since their removal up to the island Mrs. Hutchinson is brought to bed of a monstrous shape but in what form it is not yet known as the governor told me, but reported to be many false conceptions in a lump.[11]

We have a Cambridge here, a college erecting, youth lectured, a library, and I suppose there will be a press this winter.[12] There was with us the last year a lord and this year came to live with us a knight and a lady widow, besides others persons of worth.[13]

Another report on the development of Harvard College is included in a letter written by John Wiswall to George Rigby, a clerk of the peace in Lancashire. Wiswall's letter provides a suitable close to this collection, for it indicates how fully established the new commonwealth was just ten years after Higginson wrote his first letter: a building for the new college being constructed; many shops in the colony's central town, Boston; a well-regulated harbor; a total of eighteen towns settled. While the unity of the commonwealth had been damaged by the Antinomian controversy, that wound had healed well enough so that the scars were scarcely visible. Hard times were to come temporarily with the cessation of migration. But the Massachusetts Bay Colony would flourish because of the achievements of its first ten years: a new form of church government, town-meeting government, representative commonwealth government through its General Court, a unique legal system—all working cooperatively. In a time of bloody wars and revolutions, Massachusetts enjoyed peace because she was a covenanted community. These achievements could not be seen by John Wiswall's eye, for he lacked the necessary historical perspective. But it is worth noting that the new arrival was to make his mark in both the new church and the new commonwealth. An ironmonger, Wiswall settled first in Dorchester, where he became a deputy, and later moved to Boston, where he became ruling elder of its church. Wiswall's original letter is in the collection of Lord Kenyon, at Gredington, Whitchurch, Shropshire.

John Wiswall to George Rigby
September 27, 1638

Being mindful of your worship's kindness and readiness at all times to do me good and rescue me out of the hands of immeriting and afflicting [?] men, according to the place and power God had set you in, I could not excuse myself of great ingratitude if I should not show my thankfulness some way, and not knowing how more acceptably to do it, I have adventured to present a few rude lines unto your worship's view, certifying your worship of our prosperous, pleasant, and speedy journey unto New England in seven weeks and odd days. Twenty-three ships more besides us, I think, have come but none so speedy. We were the first of all in Nantasket. It is a place where ships ofttimes anchor before they go down into Boston or Charlestown River. In the way there is a pretty castle and fort to which the ships lower their topgallant before they pass into Boston, and divers there shoot two or three cannons, and then the fort will welcome and salute them with one.

For the land, it is a fine land, good for corn, especially Indian, which is a very precious grain for divers uses besides bread, good for pasture, and good hay land, plenty of wood. It is a pleasant country to look upon. Truly, sir, I like it very well, and so I think any godly man God calls over will, when he sees Moyses and Aaron, I mean magistrate and minister, in church and commonweal to walk hand in hand, discountenancing and punishing sin in whomsoever, and standing for the praise of them that do well. Our sovereign lord and king is King Charles, whose crown and honor is daily prayed for in all the churches. Under him we have a governor, deputy, and council, and men called assistants, in power much like your justices. Constables we have in every town. Men we call committees we send from every town to the General Court. Plantations there are divers, and they succeed and prosper well. Boston is a pretty town. In it there are fine houses and some six or seven shops finely furnished with all commodities. There is a pretty key [quay] and a crane, as at Bristol, to lade and unlade goods. There is a warehouse wherein strangers' and passengers' goods may be put. Newtowne now is called Cambridge. There is a university house reared, I hear, and a pretty library begun. There is also Roxbury, Dorchester, Salem, and divers towns. There are at Conectichute, there are some pretty plantations. But to wind up all in one word, things prosper well, and men of pretty parts God sends over, both for church and commonweal.

The Indians are a pretty active, ingenious people in kind, yet loving to us, and but weak neither in comparison—I mean in their general for personal strength. I think it not inferior to us, if not exceed[ing]. They are active to "cram" as they speak, that is, kill deer, fish, fowl, beaver, and divers wild beasts in the woods. Our plantations are not annoyed with any. Some wolves now, at this time of the year, come down after deer and do some hurt to calves, goats, and swine, etc., but it is but little.

But time bids to an end and so cease further to trouble your worship with these rude lines, and so with my humble service and duty to your worship and your kind bedfellow, wishing both your worships' welfare as so your sweet babes, with my love to all your friends, I rest and end.

> Yours to command,
> John Wiswall

Dorchester in New England

I have for my own share a pretty house and outhouses with fifty-two acres of my own land, besides half a good house, to which pertains forty-seven, my share being then twenty-three and a half.

To his worshipful and much respected kind friend
Master George Rigby . . . of Peele, give these. Old England.
[Endorsed] John Wiswall's letter to me, received
22 January 1638/9.

The early years of America's first three permanent English colonies are properly celebrated in the annals of history because they are America's beginnings. They were also celebrated, properly, by contemporary chroniclers. The struggles to survive at Jamestown are reported by Captain John Smith in the first American "book," the letter Smith wrote in 1608. *A True Relation of Virginia* is an informal account, seemingly dashed off as the ship that was to carry it to England readied for return. It is best read in the Hakluyt Society edition of *The Jamestown Voyages* (1969), edited by Philip L. Barbour. The more elaborate report of 1612, *A Map of Virginia*, and the full-dress version of 1624, *A Generall Historie of Virginia*, both have more literary grace, but since they were written in England several years later, they lack the immediacy of the earlier letter. The *Map* is in *The Jamestown Voyages*, and Philip Barbour is undertaking an edition of the *Generall Historie*. Meanwhile, one must use the Edward Arber edition (1910, reprinted 1966).

The beginnings of Plymouth are memorialized in *Mourt's Relation* (1622), by William Bradford and Edward Winslow. A journal of the events of the colony's first year, it is full of incident, directly reported. Henry M. Dexter's valuable edition (1865) was reprinted in 1969. Winslow also reported on the second and third year in *Good Newes from New England* (1624), a less vital account. The most accessible edition is Edward Arber's in *The Story of the Pilgrim Fathers* (1897). Quite different is what is probably the greatest book of seventeenth-century America, Bradford's *Of Plimouth Plantation*. The first edition did not appear till 1856, though it was known to other seventeenth-century historians, such as Nathaniel Morton, who used it in compiling *New Englands Memoriall* (1637, facsimile reprint, 1937). Bradford's virtues as a historian are his ability to communicate the piety that motivated the Plymouth venture, his sense of meaning in history, and his personality. The work was written over many years, and the events that Bradford describes had taken place several years before he was writing. His work thus does not attempt to capture the experience of the colonists. *Of Plimouth Plantation* is best read in the elaborately annotated and illustrated edition of Worthington C. Ford (1912, reprinted 1968), or the much more spare and "modern" edition of Samuel Eliot Morison (1953). The two facsimile editions of the manuscript (1896, 1898) are also highly recommended; Bradford's hand was clear.

The beginnings of the Massachusetts Bay Colony are celebrated far more fully than those of Jamestown and Plymouth, a hardly surprising fact, since the undertaking of the 1630s was on a much larger scale and since the Bay colonists were on the whole well educated. Once again it is possible to choose between chronicles written with some sense of proportion and perspective, or letters, reports, and journals prepared on the spot. The first work that might be called history is Edward Johnson's ecstatic account written in the year 1651, *A History of New England* (1653), better known by its running title, *The Wonder-working Providence of Sion's Saviour in America*. Johnson had lived in Massachusetts during some of its earliest years, and his account is full of information and some misinformation. On his material Johnson superimposed a kind of epic pattern, and though the heroic manner is sometimes effective, it is usually tiresomely verbose. An appreciation of what Johnson was doing can be gained from Sacvan Bercovitch's essay, "The Historiography of Johnson's *Wonder-working Providence*," in the Essex Institute's *Historical Collections* for 1969. The most satisfactory edition is an unsympathetic one prepared by J. Franklin Jameson (1910, reprinted 1959).

Johnson's *History* contrasts sharply with the *General History of New England* composed by William Hubbard, an Ipswich minister, in the 1670s (but not published till 1815). Hubbard is much less moralistic than Johnson and his prose is more straightforward. Though the work is derivative (Hubbard had access to Winthrop's journal, among other materials), it is much underrated. Despite an annoying lack of structure, it provides much valuable information on the early years. The more satisfactory of the two editions of the work is that by W. H. Harris (1848), but this edition lacks the preface and portions of the beginning and ending. Supplemental sheets correcting this lack were published in 1878, and some copies have the whole bound together, as was intended. The completed edition was reprinted in 1972. Another work by Hubbard is more highly regarded: *The Present*

State of New-England. Being a Narrative of the Troubles with the Indians in New England, From the first Planting thereof to the present time (1677); it is available in a facsimile reprint with a useful introduction by Cecelia Tichi (1972) and in a good edition prepared by Samuel G. Drake, retitled *The History of the Indian Wars* (1865, reprinted 1968).

Two smaller works of interest are Samuel Maverick's *Briefe Discription of New England* and Joshua Scottow's *Narrative of the Planting of the Massachusetts Colony*. Maverick's description was written in 1660 but not published till 1885. It reflects his knowledge of earlier days in Massachusetts, even before 1629, for Maverick was in the Boston area long before Winthrop. Scottow's narrative, first published in 1694 when he was in his seventies, recalls the early days rather vaguely. A reprint is in the *Collections* of the Massachusetts Historical Society (1858).

Three valuable early books on Massachusetts are the accounts of William Wood, Thomas Morton, and Thomas Lechford. Wood's charming description of *New Englands Prospect* (1634) tells much about geography, weather, natural history, and "the several plantations," with almost half the book describing the Indians. Wood had lived for three years in the area that is now Lynn. A modern but unannotated edition was prepared by Charles Deane and reprinted in 1967. Wood's book is often witty, but Morton's *New English Canaan* (1637) can be described as satiric, for in addition to its attractive descriptions of landscapes and Indians, it provides an amused look at pilgrim and puritan life styles. Morton saw little of the Bay colonists, though it was John Endecott of Salem who felled the famous Maypole of Merry Mount set up by Morton's followers. (Morton obviously scorned Endecott, whom he called "the great swelling fellow of Littleworth.") Charles Francis Adams prepared a full-dress edition (1883, reprinted 1966). Another outsider's view is Lechford's *Plain-Dealing; or Newes From New England* (1642). Lechford was a lawyer and no puritan; his account of the colony was intended to show Englishmen what might happen if they eliminated episcopacy. But the book is surprisingly objective if unsympathetic. *Plain Dealing* is best read in J. Hammond Trumbull's heavily annotated edition (1867, reprinted 1970).

John Josselyn kept a journal of his visit to New England in 1638, and though slight, it provides a few vivid pictures, such as one of Samuel Maverick's black slave, who protested to Josselyn that "she had been a queen in her own country." *An Account of Two Voyages* (the second was in 1663) was first published in 1674, and in 1865 it was handsomely reprinted.

Three autobiographies offer some scenes of early Massachusetts. Thomas Shepard includes a dozen pages on the years 1635 to 1646; his concerns are chiefly religious. A first-rate modern edition of the autobiography, along with Shepard's journal (which is, even more than the autobiography, religious in orientation), is that of Michael McGiffert, entitled *God's Plot* (1972). More useful are Roger Clap's *Memoirs*, written in the 1670s and first published in 1731. Clap was a founder of Dorchester, and his story is particularly interesting for its account of the arrival in Massachusetts of the Dorchester men, who came separately from Winthrop's group. It is best read in Alexander Young's *Chronicles of the First Planters of the Colony of Massachusetts Bay, From 1623 to 1636* (1846, reprinted 1971). Young published many contemporary documents in an eminently readable and intelligently annotated form, including Richard Mather's journal of his 1635 voyage to America. Another autobiography is John Dane's narrative, written in 1682, telling of his experiences in Massachusetts after 1638. Its most valuable feature is that it begins in England and describes Dane's reasons for migrating. At present the only printing is in the *New England Historical and Genealogical Register* for 1854. A more readable and available edition is much needed.

The most valuable and the fullest account of the early years is John Winthrop's journal of the years 1630 to 1649. Winthrop was at the center of activities and recorded a great deal of valuable information on religion, politics, and everyday life in the colony. Many of his entries are extended, and those provide a strong sense of Winthrop's outlook. Serving often as governor and always as one of the colony's leaders, Winthrop was quite as much an insider as Lechford was an outsider. Though the journal was well known to historians, it was not published till 1790, when Noah Webster finally saw the bulk of it into print. The best edition now available, a classic, was prepared by James Savage and published in 1853 as *The History of New England*. Savage's learned but eccentric notes make this version a joy to read. A more solidly useful edition is in the offing.

Complementing the journal, but less useful to anyone without fairly sophisticated knowledge of Winthrop and his times, are the *Winthrop Papers*, still in process of publication by the Massachusetts Historical Society. Five volumes, covering the years 1498 to 1649, have appeared since 1929. Mostly letters received by Winthrop and members of his family but including many of Winthrop's own writings, the collection is a mixture of trivia and essential documents.

Readers who find Winthrop's journal appealing might look into the first volume of the *Records of the Governor and Company of Massachusetts Bay*, edited by Nathaniel B. Shurtleff (1853-55, reprinted 1967). The daily life of the colonists is revealed on every page of the records of the colony's governing body. Less interesting are the *Records of the Court of Assistants of the Colony of Massachusetts*, edited by John Noble and John F. Cronin. The first part of volume 2 (1904) covers the early years.

Another volume of documents associated with Winthrop is *A Short Story of the Rise, reign, and ruine of the Antinomians, Familists & Libertines that infected the Churches of New-England* (1644). The six documents on the Hutchinsonians, four written by Winthrop, include a report of Mrs. Hutchinson's examination in court. The *Short Story* and other contemporary documents on the Hutchinson affair are in David D. Hall's excellent *Antinomian Controversy, 1636-1638: A Documentary History* (1968).

Not to be neglected is Thomas Hutchinson's *History of the Colony and Province of Massachusetts Bay*. Though an eighteenth-century work, it includes extracts from many contemporary documents. The best edition is Lawrence Shaw Mayo's (1936). Hutchinson also collected other documents, many of which are highly illuminating, in *The Hutchinson Papers*, originally entitled *A Collection of Original Papers Relative to the History of the Colony of Massachusetts Bay*. The best edition is that of the Prince Society (1865, reprinted 1967). A modern collection of value and interest is Alden Vaughan's *Puritan Tradition in America, 1620-1730* (1972). And one should not ignore Cotton Mather's massive *Magnalia Christi Americana* (1702), an epic-tribute to the founders of Massachusetts. Mather filtered everything through his eccentric consciousness and wrote in an ornate baroque style, but he gives much information about the first generation. A new edition (1975-) edited by Kenneth Murdock makes the *Magnalia* more accessible.

One significant event only touched on in the letters of this collection is the Pequot War of 1637. The most interesting account is John Mason's *Brief History of the Pequot War*, written in the 1650s and first published in 1677 by Increase Mather in his *Relation of the Troubles that have Hapned in New England.* Mason was commander of the Connecticut forces gathered to put down the Pequot Indians, who were troublesome to other Indian tribes as well as to the colonists. The Pequots were almost exterminated. Two accounts written earlier are those of John Underhill, leader of a group of Massachusetts soldiers, who wrote *Newes from America or A Late and Experimentall Discoverie of New England* (1638), and Philip Vincent, an English clergyman who somehow put together an account based on reports of eyewitnesses, which was published as *A True Relation of the Late Batell Fought in New England Between the English and the Salvages* (1637). Finally, there is an account by Lion Gardiner, also a military leader in the war. His version, first published as an appendix to Samuel Penhallow's *History of the Wars of New England* (1726), is called *Relation of the Pequot Warres.* All four of these accounts, none very long, were brought together by Charles Orr in a convenient collection, *History of the Pequot War* (1897); it deserves to be reprinted.

The early accomplishments of the Massachusetts Bay colony were celebrated in a famous promotion pamphlet, *New Englands First Fruits* (1643). Compiled by Henry Dunster (president of Harvard), Thomas Welde (the colony's agent in London), and others, the work makes much of the efforts to Christianize the Indians, describes Harvard College's academic program (it includes a list of theses), and commends the colony for its progress and prosperity by answering a series of charges made against its weather, its lack of currency, and other alleged shortcomings. An edition is included in Samuel Eliot Morison's *Founding of Harvard College* (1935).

Poetic responses to early New England should not be overlooked. Thomas Tillam composed an effective poem, "Upon the first sight of New England, June 29, 1638," which is included in Harrison T. Meserole's *Seventeenth-Century American*

Poetry (1968). Poetry makes up the bulk of a work now attributed to the historian-poet Edward Johnson, *Good Newes from New England, with an Exact Relation of the First Planting of that Countrey* (1648). This brief survey closes with a passage from Johnson's poem "On the arrival of our English Nation at the Mattachusets Bay"—not very good poetry but a striking picture.

> ... to land this people came,
> 'Mongst trees and men that naked been, whom labor did not tame.
> Small entrance did they make therein, for why diseases stay,
> Their long unwonted legs to walk, in wilderness the way.
> In booths and huts lamenting lie, both men and women eke,
> Some breathing out their latest breath, and others faintly speak,
> Unto their friends for succor soon that strength they might recover,
> Which once attain'd, they search the land, tracing the country over.

NOTES

Each note is correlated to the text by page number and the first and last words of the paragraph to which the note refers.

[p. xiii. Some . . . it. . . ."] Joshua Scottow, *A Narrative of The Planting of the Massachusetts Colony* (Boston, 1694), in Massachusetts Historical Society *Collections*, 4th ser. 4 (1858): 292-93; Carl Bridenbaugh, *Vexed and Troubled Englishmen, 1590-1642* (New York, 1968), pp. 467-73.

[p. xiii. Though . . . admiration.] William Hubbard, *A General History of New England,* written about 1680 (Boston, 1848), pp. 247-48. For a discussion of the late seventeenth-century "Invention of New England," see Robert Middlekauf, *The Mathers: Three Generations of Puritan Intellectuals, 1596-1728* (New York, 1971), pp. 96-112, and Perry Miller, *Errand into the Wilderness* (Cambridge, Mass., 1956), pp. 1-15.

[p. xvi. What . . . Colony.] Allyn B. Forbes et al., ed., *Winthrop Papers,* 5 vols. to date (Boston, 1929-), 2: 156, 3: 397-98.

[p. xvii. This . . . 1630/1).] Omitted from this collection are the letters of the Reverend Ralph Smith written from Boston in 1636 and 1638 but addressed to Holland. These add little on Massachusetts Bay Colony affairs. See the versions in D. Plooij, *The Pilgrim Fathers from a Dutch Point of View* (New York, 1932), pp. 112-14.

[p. 1. As . . . year.] John White, *The Planters Plea* (London, 1630), p. 74 (this anonymous work is generally recognized as White's); Hubbard, *General History,* pp. 106-8; Frances Rose-Troup, *The Massachusetts Bay Company and Its Predecessors* (New York, 1930), pp. 16-38, and *John White* (New York, 1930), pp. 57-121; Samuel Eliot Morison, *Builders of the Bay Colony* (Boston, 1964), pp. 21-50; George D. Phippen, "The 'Old Planters' of Salem," Essex Institute *Historical Collections* 1 (1859): 97-110, 145-53, 185-99, 4 (1862): 127-29; Clifford Shipton, *Roger Conant* (Cambridge, Mass., 1944), pp. 60-87; Lawrence Shaw Mayo, *John Endecott* (Cambridge, Mass., 1936), pp. 6-20.

[p. 1. A . . . puritanism.] Charles Francis Adams, "The Old Planters," Massachusetts Historical Society *Proceedings* 16 (1878): 194-206, and "The Settlement of Boston Bay," in *Three Episodes in Massachusetts History,* 2 vols. (reprint ed., New York, 1965), 1: 1-360; Mellen Chamberlain, *A Documentary History of Chelsea,* 2 vols. (Boston, 1908), 1: 6-19; Charles Knowles Bolton, *The Real Founders of New England* (Boston, 1929), passim. Christopher Gardiner arrived in early 1630 and established a residence on the shore of the Neponset River, in what is now Quincy. This was before Winthrop arrived. See Louis D. Scisco, "Sir Christopher Gardyner," *Publications* of the Colonial Society of Massachusetts 38 (1944-51), : 3-15.

[p. 2. There . . . laws.] Nathaniel B. Shurtleff, ed., *The Records of the Governor and Company of the Massachusetts Bay in New England* 5 vols. in 6 (Boston, 1853-54), 1: 10-12 (hereafter cited as *Massachusetts Records*); Charles M. Andrews, *The Colonial Period in American History*, 4 vols. (New Haven, 1934-38), 1: 344-65; Rose-Troup, *Massachusetts Bay*, pp. 59-63; Morison, *Builders*, pp. 33-34; Bridenbaugh, *Englishmen*, pp. 437-38; Robert Earle Moody, "A Re-Examination of the Massachusetts Bay Company's Charter of 1629," Massachusetts Historical Society *Proceedings* 69 (1956): 58-60.

[p. 2. By . . . Smith.] Christopher Hill, *Society and Puritanism in Pre-Revolutionary England* (London, 1964); Allen French, *Charles I and the Puritan Upheaval* (London, 1955); Bridenbaugh, *Englishmen*, pp. 434-40; Everett H. Emerson, *English Puritanism from John Hooper to John Milton* (Durham, N.C., 1968), pp. 38-41.

[p. 3. The . . . responsibilities.] Larzer Ziff, *Puritanism in America: New Culture in a New World* (New York, 1973), pp. 3-31; William Haller, *The Rise of Puritanism* (New York, 1938), pp. 49-82; T.H. Breen and Stephen Foster, "Moving to the New World: The Character of Early Massachusetts Migration," *William and Mary Quarterly*, 3rd ser. 30 (1973): 189-222.

[p. 4. Within . . . puritan.] Thomas Hooker, in British Museum Additional Manuscripts 6394 (Boswell Papers, vol. 1), fol. 146; quotation from Hooker by Raymond P. Stearns, *Congregationalism in the Dutch Netherlands* (Chicago, 1940), p. 109; Perry Miller, *Orthodoxy in Massachusetts* (New York, 1970), p. 109; Champlin Burrage, *The Early English Dissenters in the Light of Research, 1550-1641*, 2 vols. (Cambridge, Eng., 1912), 1: 357-64; Middlekauf, *The Mathers*, pp. 42-44; William Ames, *The Marrow of Theology*, ed. John D. Eusden (Boston, 1968), p. 5; George H. Williams, "The Pilgrimage of Thomas Hooker (1586-1647)," *Bulletin of the Congregational Library* 19 (October 1967): 11; Geoffrey Nuttall, *Visible Saints: The Congregational Way, 1640-1660* (Oxford, 1957), pp. 1-42.

[p. 4. Although . . . purity.] Bridenbaugh, *Englishmen*, pp. 355-433; B. E. Supple, *Commercial Crisis and Change in England, 1600-1642* (Cambridge, Eng., 1959), pp. 102-12.

[p. 4. It . . . be.] The sermon, "Christian Charitie. A Modell Hereof," is published in *Winthrop Papers*, 2: 282-95. Its importance is suggested by the January 1635 request made of John Winthrop the younger by the Reverend Henry Jacie, a puritan clergyman who thought he might go to America. He sought six vital documents: a copy of the map (probably Winthrop's map of 1633-34), the charter, the "Model of Charity," the oath, "Mr. Higgison's letter," and *The Humble Request of His Majesty's Loyal Subjects* (1630). See *Winthrop Papers*, 3: 188-89.

Although the historical importance of the Massachusetts Bay Colony's innovations was recognized at least as early as De Tocqueville, I have seen only one study that recognizes adequately what happened in the early days of the colony. Despite some misunderstandings, it is a fundamental study: Arthur H. Buffington, "The Massachusetts Experiment of 1630," *Publi-*

cations of the Colonial Society of Massachusetts 32 (1933-37): 308-20.
Another study showing the innovative nature of the colony, Thomas
Jefferson Wertenbaker's *Puritan Oligarchy* (New York, 1947), follows
the common practice of generalizing about the first sixty years; it mini-
mizes the changes that took place in those years.

[p. 5. Winthrop . . . direction.] *Massachusetts Records*, 1: 386; *Winthrop
Papers*, 4: 170. The above discussion owes much to Edmund S. Morgan,
The Puritan Dilemma: The Story of John Winthrop (New York, 1958),
pp. 84-100. Winthrop spelled out the covenant theory in "A Defense of
an Order." There he argued that the basis of a commonwealth such as
Massachusetts Bay was "the consent of a certain company, to cohabit to-
gether, under one government for their mutual safety and welfare."
Winthrop Papers, 3: 423. See also George L. Haskins, "Representative
Government in Early New England," in *Liber Memorialis Sir Maurice
Powicke* (Louvain and Paris, 1965), pp. 85-98; B. Katherine Brown,
"Letter to the Editor," *William and Mary Quarterly*, 3rd ser. 25 (1968):
339; and Michael Kammen, *Deputyes and Libertyes: The Origins of Rep-
resentative Government in Colonial America* (New York, 1969), pp. 20-24.

[p. 6. Though . . . government.] The oath is taken from *The Oath of a
Freeman, with a Historical Study* by Lawrence C. Wroth (New York,
1939). Wroth treats the oath as a token of the colony's sense of independence; it was the first work printed by the Massachusetts press. This
oath and the inhabitant's also appear in *Massachusetts Records*, 1: 354.

[p. 7. If . . . utopian.] Sumner Chilton Powell, *Puritan Village: The For-
mation of a Puritan Town* (Middletown, Conn., 1963) p. 179. On Dedham,
see Kenneth A. Lockridge, *A New England Town: The First Hundred
Years* (New York, 1970).

[p. 7. The . . . meetings.] *Fourth Report of the Record Commissioners of
the City of Boston* (Boston, 1883), p. 3; Anne Bush MacLear, *Early New
England Towns: A Comparative Study of Their Development* (New York,
1908), pp. 107-8; Darrett B. Rutman, *Winthrop's Boston: Portrait of a
Puritan Town, 1630-1649* (Chapel Hill, N.C., 1965), pp. 65-67, 161-63;
Charles Francis Adams, "The Genesis of the Massachusetts Town, and the
Development of Town-meeting Government," Massachusetts Historical
Society *Proceedings* 27 (1891-92): 174-211.

[p. 7. The . . . was.] Boston-Charlestown Covenant in Williston Walker,
The Creeds and Platforms of Congregationalism (New York, 1893), p. 131;
John Cotton, *The True Constitution Of a particular visible Church, proved
by Scripture* (London, 1642, but written by 1636), p. 10; David D. Hall,
ed., "John Cotton's Letter to Samuel Skelton," *William and Mary Quar-
terly*, 3rd ser. 22 (1965): 482. Cotton changed his mind after he came to
America. See Edmund S. Morgan, *Visible Saints: The History of a Puritan
Idea* (New York, 1963), pp. 85-87, 95-98; and Everett H. Emerson, *John
Cotton* (New York, 1965), pp. 54-59. On the relationship of Congregationalism to town-meeting government, see the suggestive remarks in
Rutman, *Winthrop's Boston*, pp. 59-67.

[p. 8. Closely . . . law.] Winthrop, *The History of New England*, ed. James Savage, 2 vols. (Boston, 1853), 1: 389; George L. Haskins, *Law and Authority in Early Massachusetts* (New York, 1960), pp. 141-221; Christopher Hill, *God's Englishman: Oliver Cromwell and the English Revolution* (London, 1970), pp. 140-41. Punishments for breaking the law were often less severe than the law authorized. See Jules Zanger, "Crime and Punishment in Early Massachusetts," *William and Mary Quarterly*, 3rd ser. 22 (1965): 471-77.

[p. 8. If . . . households.] Darrett B. Rutman, *American Puritanism: Faith and Practice* (Philadelphia, 1970), passim. Philip J. Greven argues that the town of Andover was "a replica of an English village." See "Old Patterns in the New World: The Distribution of Land in Seventeenth-Century Andover," Essex Institute *Historical Collections* 101 (1965): 147-48. See also F. Grave Morris, "Some Aspects of the Rural Settlement of New England in Colonial Times," in *London Essays in Geography*, ed. L. D. Stamp (London, 1951), pp. 219-27. Particularly conservative was Hingham, whose settlers came in a body from Hingham, Norfolk. Its church followed presbyterian, not congregational ideals (church officials made the vital decisions without consulting the church members), and the town had a strong hierarchical system. See John J. Waters, "Hingham, Massachusetts: An East Anglian Oligarchy in the New World," *Journal of Social History* 1 (1967-68): 351-70. Early Massachusetts towns were really townships containing a village or perhaps several villages. See Edna Schofield, "The Origin of Settlement Patterns in Rural New England," *Geographical Review* 28 (1938): 652-63. On the clergy, see David D. Hall, *The Faithful Shepherd: A History of the New England Ministry in the Seventeenth Century* (Chapel Hill, N.C., 1972). On the family, see Philip J. Greven, "Family Structure in Seventeenth-Century Andover," *William and Mary Quarterly*, 3rd ser. 23 (1966): 234-56; and Edmund S. Morgan, *The Puritan Family* (rev. ed., New York, 1966).

[p. 9. Change . . . rapid.] Rutman, *Winthrop's Boston*, pp. 261-75; Donald W. Koch, "Income Distribution and Political Structure in Seventeenth-Century Salem, Massachusetts," Essex Institute *Historical Collections* 105 (1969): 50-69; Morgan, *Visible Saints*, passim; Bernard Bailyn, *The New England Merchants of the Seventeenth Century* (Cambridge, 1955), pp. 102-12, passim. Hill, *Society and Puritanism*, pp. 124-44. A consideration for men of wealth in the late 1620s was the political situation. With Charles I ruling without benefit of Parliament, some men were unwilling to accept the king's demand for a loan and were imprisoned. The puritan Earl of Lincoln was a particularly active resister, so that in the county of Lincoln only three persons subscribed. He was imprisoned. See Elizabeth Wade White, *Anne Bradstreet: "The Tenth Muse"* (New York, 1971), pp. 79-89. Another resister who was imprisoned was William Coddington, who became a leading Boston merchant (and later governor of Rhode Island). See Emily C. Williams, *William Coddington of Rhode Island* (Newport, R.I., 1941), p. 5. A recent study showing how difficult it is to distinguish economic from religious motivations for migration to

New England is the above-mentioned one by T. H. Breen and Stephen Foster, "Moving to the New World."

[p. 11. The . . . Naumkeag.] *Massachusetts Records*, 1: 386, 394; Alexander Young, ed., *Chronicles of the First Planters of the Colony of Massachusetts Bay* (Boston, 1846), pp. 142, 160, 209-11, 317; *Dictionary of National Biography* (hereafter *DNB*), s.v. "Higginson, Francis"; E. C. Felton, "Samuel Skelton," *New England Genealogical and Historical Register* 52 (1898): 347-57, 53 (1899): 64-71; Miller, *Orthodoxy*, pp. 128-31.

[p. 24. By . . . Boston.] *Winthrop Papers*, 2: 156.

[p. 27. In . . . voted.] "Governor Bradford's Letter Book," Massachusetts Historical Society *Collections*, 1st ser. 3 (1810): 67-68; Young, *Chronicles of Massachusetts*, pp. 241-42.

[p. 28. The . . . transform.)] Walker, *Creeds and Platforms*, pp. 93-115, with the Salem covenant on page 116; Cotton Mather, *Magnalia Christi Americana*, 2 vols. (Hartford, 1853), 1: 362; Keith L. Sprunger, "William Ames and the Settlement of Massachusetts Bay," *New England Quarterly* 39 (1966): 66-79, and *The Learned Doctor William Ames* (Urbana, Ill., 1972). John Humphry, writing to John Winthrop on December 12, 1630, observed, "I have sent you Dr. Ames' *Cases of Conscience* newly come forth, wherein you will find many things of especial use and singularly helpful for present direction and satisfaction . . ." (*Winthrop Papers*, 2: 332). The tradition to which the leading Bay ministers belonged was strongly opposed to separatism. See Burrage, *Early English Dissenters*, 1: 264.

The best brief treatment of this complicated issue is David Hall's in his *Faithful Shepherd*, pp. 78-86. Hall concludes that "the situation of the immigrants was still fluid when they reached New England," and "many preachers in the [puritan] brotherhood for the first time in their lives were taking seriously in the 1630s problems of ecclesiology" (p. 85).

[p. 28. The . . . arrived.] Hall, ed., "John Cotton's Letter to Samuel Skelton," pp. 478-85; Miller, *Orthodoxy in Massachusetts* (introduction by David Hall); Larzer Ziff, "The Salem Puritans in the 'Free Aire of a New World,' " *Huntington Library Quarterly* 20 (1957): 373-84; Morgan, *Visible Saints*, pp. 80-88; Rutman, *Winthrop's Boston*, pp. 283-85.

[p. 38. Included . . . 1630).] Young's *Chronicles of Massachusetts* prints Graves's contract, pp. 65-69. Also see Young, pp. 152-53; "The Early Records of Charlestown," in Young, *Chronicles of Massachusetts*, pp. 374-76; Richard Frothingham, *The History of Charlestown* (Boston, 1845), pp. 20-21; James E. Thorold Rogers, *Six Centuries of Work and Wages* (London, 1906), pp. 293-94.

[p. 41. Having . . . ours. . . ."] *Winthrop Papers*, 2: 91-92; Morgan, *Puritan Dilemma*, pp. 3-25. Winthrop's autobiography, written in 1636, demonstrates his puritan orientation. It appears in *Winthrop Papers*, 3: 338-44.

[p. 41. Gradually . . . *where*.] *Winthrop Papers*, 2: 133-34, 151-52;

Massachusetts Records, 1: 49-51. Probably it was illegal for what was chartered as a trading company to become a colony governed overseas from England. See Charles M. Andrews, "Historic Doubts Regarding Early Massachusetts History," *Publications* of the Colonial Society of Massachusetts 28 (1930-33): 280-99; William G. Robbins, "The Massachusetts Bay Company: An Analysis of Motives," *The Historian* 32 (1969): 83-98.

[p. 42. In . . . below.] Charles E. Banks, *The Winthrop Fleet* (Boston, 1930).

[p. 42. Winthrop . . . plantation.] *Winthrop Papers,* 2: 114-15.

[p. 42. Winthrop's . . . Winthrop.] *Winthrop Papers,* 2: 301.

[p. 43. John . . . meetinghouse.] "Charlestown Records," in Young, *Chronicles of Massachusetts,* pp. 375-78. The appealing correspondence of John and Margaret Winthrop was published as *Some Old Puritan Love Letters,* ed. Joseph Hopkins Twichell (New York, 1894).

[p. 44. Winthrop's . . . her.] Lawrence Shaw Mayo, *The Winthrop Family in America* (Boston, 1948), passim.

[p. 48. The . . . 45.] Robert C. Black, III, *The Younger John Winthrop* (New York, 1966), passim.

[p. 52. Winthrop . . . 46.] Massachusetts Historical Society *Proceedings* 5 (1860-62): 131; Massachusetts Historical Society *Collections,* 3rd ser. 8 (1843): 322-23; Walker, *Creeds and Platforms,* pp. 105, 108.

[p. 53. On . . . Dorchester.] *Massachusetts Records,* 1: 73-74.

[p. 54. Perhaps . . . 47.] *Massachusetts Records,* 1: 75.

[p. 59. On . . . status.] *Massachusetts Records,* 1: 12, 79-80, 366; Morgan, *Puritan Dilemma,* pp. 90-91.

[p. 59. Winthrop's . . . 49.] "Charlestown Records," in Young, *Chronicles of Massachusetts,* pp. 380-81; Michael J. Canavan, "Mr. Blackstone's 'Excellent Spring,' " Colonial Society of Massachusetts *Proceedings* 11 (1906-7): 295-328, and "Isaac Johnson, Esquire, The Founder of Boston," Colonial Society of Massachusetts *Proceedings* 27 (1927-30): 272-85; Rutman, *Winthrop's Boston,* pp. 27-29. Blackstone is celebrated in Conrad Aiken's poem "The Kid."

[p. 63. Five . . . 84.] "Charlestown Records," in Young, *Chronicles of Massachusetts,* pp. 384-85; *Winthrop Papers,* 3: 17.

[p. 66. Much . . . 1634.)] Charles Deane, ed., *The Life of Mr. Thomas Dudley* (Cambridge, 1870), presumably by Cotton Mather; White, *Anne Bradstreet,* pp. 56-57; Augustine Jones, *The Life and Work of Thomas Dudley* (Boston, 1899); Irvonwy Morgan, *Prince Charles's Puritan Chaplain* (London, 1957), pp. 28-29; Winthrop, *History,* 1: 40 n; Young, *Chronicles of Massachusetts,* pp. 303-4; Banks, *Winthrop Fleet.* The fullest discussions I have found of the Earl of Lincoln's connections with the Massachusetts Bay Company are Mather's *Dudley;* White's *Bradstreet,* pp. 50-61, 71 ff.; and Arthur M. Cook, *Lincolnshire Links with the U.S.A.* (Lincoln, Eng., 1956), pp. 34-43.

[p. 83. Another . . . 245.] Banks, *Winthrop Fleet*, p. 80; *Winthrop Papers*, 2: 69 n; *New England Historical and Genealogical Register* 91 (1937): 68-71; Charles H. Pope, *The Founders of Massachusetts* (Boston, 1900), p. 305.

[p. 85. Four . . . 50.] *Winthrop Papers*, 3: 27-28, 33; Winthrop, *History*, 1: 60-61, 76-80; Mayo, *Winthrop Family*, p. 21.

[p. 87. Another . . . 51.] *Winthrop Papers*, 2: 324; Robert C. Winthrop, ed., *Life and Letters of John Winthrop* (Boston, 1867), 2: 78.

[p. 89. The . . . manuscript.] *Winthrop Papers*, 3: 15.

[p. 91. After . . . crop."] *Massachusetts Records*, 1: 86, 88; Winthrop, *History*, 1: 62-83.

[p. 91. The . . . Derbyshire.] *Dictionary of American Biography* (hereafter *DAB*), s.v. "Saltonstall, Richard"; Massachusetts Historical Society *Proceedings*, 2nd ser. 8 (1892-94): 208-9.

[p. 93. Although . . . thereof. . . ."] Massachusetts Historical Society *Proceedings*, 2nd ser. 8 (1892-94): 383.

[p. 93. These . . . Terling.] Winthrop, *History*, 1: 98, 93; *DAB*, s.v. "Welde, Thomas"; Alice Clare Carter, *The English Reformed Church in Amsterdam in the Seventeenth Century* (Amsterdam, 1964), pp. 19, 79, 80; *Winthrop Papers*, 3: 60; Colonial Society of Massachusetts *Publications* 13 (1912): 128-32.

[p. 98. The . . . 63.] Morison, *Builders of the Bay Colony*, pp. 21-50.

[p. 103. Throughout . . . Indians.] Mather, *Magnalia*, 1: 53; Ola E. Winslow, *John Eliot* (Boston, 1968), pp. 5-26.

[p. 103. Eliot's . . . pounds.] Samuel Eliot Morison, *The Founding of Harvard College* (Cambridge, Mass., 1935), pp. 168, 233. Eliot's letter and one from William Hammond were first published by Franklin M. Wright in "A College First Proposed: Unpublished Letters of Apostle Eliot and William Hammond to Sir Simonds D'Ewes," *Harvard Library Bulletin* 8 (1954): 255-88. I am much indebted to Wright's valuable editorial commentary.

[p. 103. Eliot . . . taxes.] *Massachusetts Records*, 1: 79, 95; Haskins, "Representative Government," pp. 85-98.

[p. 104. Sir . . . hand."] J. O. Halliwell, ed., *Autobiography and Correspondence of Sir Simonds D'Ewes* 2 vols. (London, 1845), 2: 116; *DNB*, s.v. "D'Ewes, Sir Simonds"; Mary F. Keeler, *The Long Parliament, 1640-1641: A Biographical Study of its Members* (Philadelphia, 1954), pp. 156-57.

[p. 109. Eliot . . . 35.] Wright, "A College First Proposed."

[p. 112. Compared . . . 186.] See Winthrop's 1634 letter to D'Ewes. Winthrop's preoccupation with finding a middle way between excessive zeal and indifference in moral and religious matters is the theme of Morgan's *Puritan Dilemma*. See also Morgan, *Visible Saints*, pp. 114-15.

[p. 115. Winthrop . . . 421.] *DNB*, s.v. "Rich, Nathaniel"; Winthrop Papers, 2: 329; Arthur P. Newton, *Colonizing Activities of the English Puritans* (New Haven, 1914), pp. 61-62.

[p. 119. When . . . 88.] *Winthrop Papers*, 2: 293; Thomas Lechford, *Plaine Dealing*, ed. J. Hammond Trumbull (Boston, 1867), pp. 16-17 n.

[p. 120. The . . . supreme).] *Calendar of State Papers, Domestic Series, of the Reign of Charles I, 1633-1634* (London, 1863), p. 450; *Acts of the Privy Council, Colonial Series* 1 (1908): 199, 200-201; Charles Edward Banks, *The Planters of the Commonwealth* (Boston, 1930), pp. 32-40; John D. Eusden, *Puritans, Lawyers, and Politics in Early Seventeenth-Century England* (New Haven, 1958), pp. 114-19; Andrews, *Colonial Period*, 1: 400-413.

[p. 121. The . . . 14.] Banks, *Planters*, 32-40.

[p. 124. Despite . . . wife.] Black, *The Younger John Winthrop*, pp. 84-94.

[p. 124. The . . . independence.] *Massachusetts Records*, 1: 146; Winthrop, *History*, 1: 75; Worthington C. Ford, "The Ensign at Salem," Massachusetts Historical Society *Proceedings* 42 (1909): 226-80; Howard M. Chapin, *Roger Williams and the King's Colors* (Providence, R. I., 1928).

[p. 125. The . . . parish.] Cotton, *Some Treasure Fetched out of Rubbish* (London, 1660), p. 3; Larzer Ziff, *The Career of John Cotton: Puritanism and the American Experience* (Princeton, 1962), pp. 3-49.

[p. 126. At . . . *Plantation*.] Ziff, *John Cotton*, pp. 49-63; Hall, ed., "John Cotton's Letter to Samuel Skelton."

[p. 126. Soon . . . pastor.] Ziff, *John Cotton*, pp. 64-83; Pishey Thompson, *The History and Antiquities of Boston* (Boston, Lincolnshire, 1856), pp. 417-18.

[p. 126. Soon . . . is.] Emerson, *John Cotton* , pp. 54-84, 156-58; Young, *Chronicles of Massachusetts*, pp. 438-44.

[p. 131. While . . . Massachusetts.] Black, *Winthrop*, pp. 79-83; Mayo, *Endecott*, pp. 67-71; Raymond P. Stearns, *The Strenuous Puritan, Hugh Peter, 1598-1660* (Urbana, Ill., 1954), pp. 31-32, 39-40, 128.

[p. 134. The . . . 54.] Alden T. Vaughan, *New England Frontier: Puritans and Indians, 1620-1675* (Boston, 1965), pp. 55-56, 122-54.

[p. 137. A . . . University.] Adams, *DAB*, s.v. "Endecott, John"; Mayo, *Endecott*, pp. 67-70.

[p. 138. Many . . . wrote.] *Winthrop Papers*, 2: 88-89; Rose-Troup, *John White*, pp. 294-97.

[p. 138. Cudworth . . . War.] Nathaniel Shurtleff and David Pulsifer, eds., *Records of the Colony of New Plymouth*, 12 vols. (Boston, 1846-61), 1: 43; George Langdon, *Pilgrim Colony: A History of New Plymouth, 1620-1691* (New Haven, 1966), pp. 33, 39, 107-14; Samuel Deane, *History of Scituate, Massachusetts* (Boston, 1831), pp. 245-48; *New England Historical and Genealogical Register* 14 (1860): 101-4.

[p. 143. Cudworth's . . . state.] James Truslow Adams, *The Founding of New England* (Boston, 1921), pp. 121-22. Adams's reference to disenfranchisement is misleading; he should have said that eligibility for franchisement required church membership. However, some male church members did not choose to be freemen. On the discipline of the church, see Larzer Ziff, "The Social Bond of the Church Covenant," *American Quarterly* 10 (1958): 154-62. On deterrents to church membership, see Wilfred O. Cross, "The Role and Status of the Unregenerate in the Massachusetts Bay Colony, 1629-1729," (diss., Columbia University, 1957).

[p. 143. Israel . . . 52.] Rose-Troup, *John White*, pp. 297-98; Massachusetts Historical Society *Proceedings* 58 (1924-25): 446-58. The best discussion of early Massachusetts government is that of Haskins, *Law and Authority*.

[p. 153. Winthrop . . . 90.] Winthrop, *History*, 1: 192.

[p. 155. The . . . Independents.] John Cotton, *The Way of the Congregational Churches Cleared* (London, 1648), p. 102. See also Roland H. Bainton, "The Puritan Theocracy and the Cambridge Platform," in *The Cambridge Platform of 1648*, ed. Henry W. Foote (Boston, 1949), pp. 82-83. Dudley's letter shows that "profane and debauched persons" were not welcome. One such seems to have been Thomas Walford, who lived at what became Charlestown before 1629. Another, an Anglican minister unsympathetic with puritanism, came with Skelton and Higginson but was promptly shipped back to England.

[p. 156. Williams . . . Williams.] John Cotton, *The Bloudy Tenent, Washed and Made White in the Bloud of the Lambe* (London, 1647), p. 1; Roger Williams, *The Bloody Tenent Yet More Bloody* (London, 1652), p. 4.

[p. 156. The . . . toleration.] Thomas Shepard, *New Englands Lamentation for Old Englands Present Errors* (London, 1645), p. 3; Richard Mather, *Church-Government and Church-Covenant Discussed* (London, 1643), p. 62; Nathaniel Ward, *Simple Cobler of Aggawam* (London, 1647), p. 3. See also Clifford K. Shipton, "The Locus of Authority in Colonial Massachusetts," in *Selected Essays: Law and Authority in Colonial America*, ed. George A. Billias (Barre, Mass., 1965), pp. 136-48. The Cotton-Williams debate is well discussed by Sacvan Bercovitch in "Typology in Puritan New England: The Williams-Cotton Controversy Reassessed," *American Quarterly* 19 (1967): 166-91, and by Jesper Rosenmeier in "The Teacher and the Witness: John Cotton and Roger Williams," *William and Mary Quarterly*, 3rd ser. 25 (1968): 408-31.

[p. 157. What . . . colony.] Walker, *Creeds and Platforms*, pp. 236-37; Edmund S. Morgan, "The Case Against Anne Hutchinson," *New England Quarterly* 10 (1937): 635-49.

[p. 157. The . . . version.] David Flaherty, *Privacy in Colonial New England* (Charlottesville, Va., 1972); Shipton, "Locus of Authority"; Emil Oberholzer, Jr., *Delinquent Saints: Disciplinary Action in the Early Congregational Churches of Massachusetts* (New York, 1956).

[p. 167. From . . . digression.] Winthrop, *History*, 1: 195-96. A full account of the hurricane is provided in Sidney Perley, *Historic Storms of New England* (Salem, Mass., 1891), pp. 3-10.

[p. 167. Anthony . . . form.] *Massachusetts Records*, 1: 157, 191; Winthrop, *History*, 1: 196-97; James Thacher, "Biographical Sketch of the Thacher Family," *New England Magazine* 7 (1834): 8-11. Thacher's cousin, who died in the storm, is remembered in a poem by John Greenleaf Whittier, "The Swan Song of Parson Avery."

[p. 174. Visiting . . . Portland.] James Phinney Baxter, ed., *The Trelawny Papers* (Portland, Me., 1884), pp. xix-xxv and passim.

[p. 178. Although . . . 30.] Bridenbaugh, *Englishmen*, p. 463; Charles E. Park, "Friendship as a Factor in the Settlement of Massachusetts," American Antiquarian Society *Proceedings* 28 (1918): 51-62; *Winthrop Papers*, 2, 3: passim; Rutman, *American Puritanism*, passim.

[p. 180. An . . . 227.] Hubbard, *General History*, pp. 353, 354, 361; John Gorham Palfrey, *History of New England* (Boston, 1859), 1: 517-19.

[p. 182. Whether . . . Hartford.] William Bradford, *Of Plimouth Plantation*, ed. Worthington C. Ford (Boston, 1912), 2: 216-24; Andrews, *Colonial Period*, 2: 67-72.

[p. 182. In . . . Colony.] Winthrop, *History*, 1: 167-68.

[p. 182. In . . . Hartford.] *Winthrop Papers*, 3: 229-30, 217, 219; Andrews, *Colonial Period*, 2: 67-74. In March 1636 Saltonstall complained to John Winthrop, Jr., of the treatment Green had suffered. See his letter in the *New England Historical and Genealogical Register* 51 (1897): 65-67.

[p. 183. Saltonstall . . . 79.] Black, *The Younger John Winthrop*, pp. 85-87; *Massachusetts Records*, 1: 394; Andrews, *Colonial Period*, 1: 364, 407; 2; 75-76, 120-21; Newton, *Colonizing Activities of the Puritans*, pp. 172-86; *Winthrop Papers*, 3: 198-99.

[p. 185. Edward . . . Portland.] Bailyn, *New England Merchants*, pp. 16-37.

[p. 188. Apparently . . . same."] Thomas Hutchinson, *History of the Colony and Province of Massachusetts-Bay*, ed. Lawrence S. Mayo (Cambridge, Mass., 1936), 1: 39, 413; Ziff, *John Cotton*, pp. 98-105.

[p. 189. Cotton . . . 501.] Edmund S. Morgan, ed., *Puritan Political Ideas, 1558-1794* (Indianapolis, 1965), pp. xxv-xxxv; Edwin Powers, *Crime and Punishment in Early Massachusetts, 1620-1692: A Documentary History* (Boston, 1966), pp. 100-162; A. B. Seidman, "Church and State in the Early Years of the Massachusetts Bay Colony," *New England Quarterly* 18 (1945): 211-33; David Hall's chapter "Church and State" in his *Faithful Shepherd*; Darrett B. Rutman, "The Mirror of Puritan Authority," in *Selected Essays: Law and Authority*, ed. Billias, pp. 149-67; B. Katherine Brown, "A Note on the Puritan Concept of Aristocracy," *Mississippi Valley Historical Review* 41 (1954): 105-12; Richard C. Simmons, "Godliness, Property, and the Franchise in Puritan Massachusetts: An Interpretation," *Journal of American History* 55 (1968): 459-511. The first act of the Court of Assistants was to provide for the pay and housing of the ministers and such other public servants as physicians and military officers. See John Noble and John F. Cronin, eds., *Records of the Court of Assistants, 1630-1692*, 3 vols. (Boston, 1901-28), 2: part 1, p. 1.

[p. 194. Other . . . some."] *Winthrop Papers*, 3: 397, 399. In the passage quoted, "weak" presumably means demonstrating scruples; see St. Paul's comment in Romans 14:2.

[p. 195. It . . . Plymouth.] Winthrop, *History*, 1: 63; Samuel H. Brockunier, *The Irrepressible Democrat Roger Williams* (New York, 1940), pp. 41-44.

[p. 195. There . . . Island.] Morgan, *Puritan Dilemma*, pp. 115-33; Ola E. Winslow, *Master Roger Williams* (New York, 1957), pp. 107-24; Hubbard, *General History*, 1: 202-9.

[p. 196. The . . . 1652.] Emerson, *John Cotton*, passim; Haller, *Rise of Puritanism*, pp. 69-79; Emerson, *English Puritanism*, pp. 219-33.

[p. 200. On . . . else.] Mather's journal in Young, *Chronicles of Massachusetts*; Middlekauf, *The Mathers*, pp. 50-51. In the same year, 1636, Mather once again defended the New England Way in a letter to an English correspondent. Although it too is included in the manuscript "Plea," from which the letter here published is taken, it lacks the qualities of a letter: the extant portion consists of Mather's answers to a series of questions put to him. It has been published by B. Richard Burg as "A Letter of Richard Mather to a Cleric in Old England," *William and Mary Quarterly*, 3rd ser. 29 (1972): 81-98. Two 1637 letters protesting Massachusetts Bay religious innovations are in the *Winthrop Papers*, 3: 389-90 and 397-403.

[p. 206. The . . . England.] *Calendar of State Papers, Colonial Series, 1574-1660* (London, 1860), p. 239; Andrews, *Colonial Period*, 1: 476; Hutchinson, *History*, 1: 410-13.

[p. 211. Boston . . . history.] Emery J. Battis, *Saints and Sectaries: Anne Hutchinson and the Antinomian Controversy in the Massachusetts Bay Colony* (Chapel Hill, 1962), esp. pp. 248-89; David D. Hall, ed., *The Antinomian Controversy, 1636-1638: A Documentary History* (Middletown, Conn., 1968); Rutman, *Winthrop's Boston*, pp. 117-24; Morgan, *Puritan Dilemma*, pp. 134-54; Jesper Rosenmeier, "New England's Perfection: The Image of Adam and the Image of Christ in the Antinomian Controversy, 1634 to 1638," *William and Mary Quarterly*, 3rd ser. 27 (1970): 435-59 (a good study of the theological differences between the two parties). A contemporary letter quoted by Thomas Hutchinson suggests the dimensions of the conflict: "I am persuaded that he [Vane] hath kindled those sparks among us, which many ages will not be able to extinguish." *History*, 1: 58. Charles Francis Adams argued that the Antinomian controversy was the crucial event in the creation of an authoritarian society in Massachusetts. See his *Massachusetts: Its History and Its Historians* (Boston, 1893). On Cotton's interest in moving to New Haven, see his own comment in *The Bloudy Tenent Washed* (London, 1647), part 2, p. 51.

[p. 212. Efforts . . . church.] Charles Francis Adams, *Three Episodes in Massachusetts History*, 1: 468-74; Hall, *Antinomian Controversy*, pp. 9, 219-43. Hall's collection includes Winthrop's *Short Story*, which lists the errors. The Reverend John Wilson had been questioned and deliberately embarrassed by the Boston Hutchinsonians.

[p. 212. Four . . .69.] Hall, ed., *Antinomian Controversy*, pp. 9, 20; J. F. Maclear, " 'The Heart of New-England Rent': The Mystical Element in Early Puritan History," *Mississippi Valley Historical Review* 42 (1956): 621-52; Morgan, *Puritan Family*, pp. 161-86; Rutman, *Winthrop's Boston*, p. 148; Haskins, *Law and Authority*, p. 116.

[p. 213. How . . . 83.] Everett H. Emerson, *Captain John Smith* (New York, 1971), pp. 107-8; Rutman, *Winthrop's Boston*, pp. 68-75, 177-81.

[p. 215. The . . . secure.] Hutchinson, *History*, 1: 405; C. H. Firth, ed., *An American Garland* (Oxford, 1915), p. 29.

[p. 215. In . . . admonished.] *Cotton Papers*, Boston Public Library, part 2, no. 11.

[p. 216. Cotton . . . *1640*.] Cotton was only one of the New England ministers to receive the original inquiry. Davenport mentions in the work$_2$ noted "your Letters being sent to the Ministers of the Churches" —fol. A^2 recto. Cotton himself defended the rejection of written prayers from the extended criticism of one of the signers of the inquiry discussed above. See *A Modest and Cleare Answer to Mr. Balls Discourse* (London, 1642). On the whole question, see Walker, *Creeds and Platforms*, pp. 132-42, and Hutchinson, *History*, 1: 72.

[p. 219. Throughout . . . England.] *Acts of the Privy Council, Colonial Series*, 1 (1908): 183, 184-85; Andrews, *Colonial Period*, 1: 400-420; Thomas Hutchinson, *Collection of Original Papers Relative to the History of . . . Massachusetts-Bay* (Albany, 1865), 1: 114-16.

[p. 220. Members . . . 1.] Hubbard, *General History*, p. 269; Winthrop, *History*, 1: 323-24, 330; Andrews, *Colonial Period*, 1: 420-23.

[p. 223. Throughout . . . 1678.] Edward Everett Hale, Jr., ed., *Notebook Kept by Thomas Lechford* (Cambridge, Mass., 1885), pp. 44-45; Colonial Society of Massachusetts *Publications* 7 (1900-1902): 74-80; *Massachusetts Records*, 1: 238; Powell, *Puritan Village*, pp. 41-42, 116, and passim. Powell's book includes many valuable sketches of early Sudbury buildings.

[p. 223. In . . . 19.] Hubbard, *General History*, p. 247; Hall, *Antinomian Crisis*, p. 20.

[p. 231. Another . . . Shropshire.] Pope, *Founders of Massachusetts*, p. 509; Richard D. Pearce, *The Records of the First Church of Boston*, 3 vols., Colonial Society of Massachusetts *Publications* 39 (1961), 1: liv; Timothy H. Breen and Stephen Foster, "The Puritan's Greatest Achievement: A Study of Social Cohesion in Seventeenth-Century Massachusetts," *Journal of American History* 60 (1973): 5-23.

INDEX